The Augmentation of Man

The Acquiescence of Humanity

+———•••———+

The Ancients and
Professors of Higher Realms of
Understanding

Verdiance

TABLE OF CONTENTS

ACKNOWLEGEMENTS

What an exceptional journey this has been! We are eternally grateful for this opportunity to be of service to our God, the Creator, the quantum of all understanding, and the Ancients, our mentors and guides, and all the professors of the spirit realm, who have provided this information to be shared. Our lives have changed diametrically for the better with the new and profound understanding of our Creator and all of creation. The awesomeness is far beyond our wildest dreams. Our desire to repay in kind will only be achieved by sharing of the depth of knowledge that we have been taught. We are also grateful for their eternal patience with us, in recognition of the arbitrary nature of our humanness and the challenges it presents for our guides.

We want to acknowledge our dear friend, Edie, who played a huge role in recognizing the path that was opening before us. She has shared her vast spiritual knowledge, inspiring others in their paths. As she completes this life cycle, we celebrate her life and the impact that she had on others.

It is with much gratitude that our friend and student, who does not want to be acknowledged, has dedicated her time and knowledge base to edit, reedit, and edit again, adding insight and suggestions for an improved learning experience. She has been our cheerleader and given such enormous support to what we have tried to accomplish in this work. You know who you are.

To all our friends and family who have added their input on *The Augmentation of Man: A Study in Renaissance*, so that we may adapt this book to better meet the needs of the reader without altering the integrity of the original messages—thank you!

DISCLOSURE

The *Augmentation of Man* series contain lessons that have been received while Kent is in a deep trance, where he "hears" dictation in his mind and sees visions that come from other entities. Some of the material found in these lessons can be scientific and may include math, astronomy, and physics. We had no preexisting knowledge in these areas, except where related to the education associated with our occupations of fire fighter/hazardous materials investigator and registered nurse.

We also had no prior knowledge of the New Thought movement, Buddhism or Hinduism until our path opened up at the end of 2006 and we gradually began to learn about these belief systems. Therefore, we had no preconceived beliefs pertaining to the concepts and definitions previously belonging to each system's lexicon, which is brought forth in a new light in this book. In other words, we were a tabula rasa, a mind not influenced by previous impressions or experiences.

These are beginning conceptual lessons, in the eyes of the universe, of the spiritual-physical aspects of our world and beyond. In time, and with further exploration, we will be able to gain more understanding of the concepts being offered here. Human genetic upgrades will certainly help to enable a higher degree of intellectual understanding in the near future.

We do not profess to be the authors of *The Augmentation of Man* series. These are lessons given to us from our spiritual mentors. The true authors are the Ancients, professors of higher realms of understanding, and other teachers outside of our Earth realm. We have simply agreed to be the transistor and the scribe, and to publish the lessons at the request of our mentors. Their dictation is left in its original form, verbatim, at their request. With our mentor's permission, we have added our translation to simplify the lessons so that others may more easily understand them. Our understanding at this time may not have reached the ultimate level but will help give others direction to their path.

INTRODUCTION

What is it that drives us from within in our search for truth? We are following a guidance from within, chasing a deeper understanding of our world, a more meaningful life and a deeper connection to God, our Creator. There are many faithful followers who find what nourishes their soul with the traditional religious setting. But there are also a growing number of people trying to find a more meaningful spiritual connection, searching for that which has not yet manifested itself in our world, leaving a void. Change is on the horizon and a new day is dawning.

Our physical world is an experiential learning field for our spiritual journey. We are exploring and interacting with each other in the three-dimensions of space within the fourth dimension of time. It is a vibrational journey. And everything is vibration. Vibration forms the subatomic particles that make the atoms that form our physical world. Our spiritual essence has a vibration. Our thoughts are attuned to a vibration that reflects our level of understanding. Events are created from the energy we put forth, the energy having vibration. The understanding of the event carries a relative vibration. As we create events from our decisions, we turn inward in contemplation, searching for answers. We are observing other people's events as well, gathering a perspective from another angle. It is all focused on learning from an individually and collectively designed script to feed the soul a higher level of understanding. In doing so, we are raising the vibration within ourselves as we align to a more perfect truth. The matter within our field is also being raised. So, as a group, we are entangled not only in our own events but events with others; observing, reflecting, and growing in our knowingness.

We also have help from outside in the form of spiritual guides. These are mentors who observe the events and our response to them. They are able to determine our level of understanding of each event and help to further our comprehension by sending us thoughts that clarify our thinking process, delivering a more perfect truth. Have you ever noticed when something that was really puzzling suddenly becomes clear? It may not be just your thoughts that brought you to that epiphany, you may have had help.

It sounds so surreal, but why does it seem so contradictory to what is playing out on the world stage today? We live in chaotic times, where such a completely cohesive creation seems to evade us. That is because people are not listening to that inner voice. We have at our disposal a litany of entities that will teach and expand our understanding of ourselves and our interactions within our environment. But, if we are not listening, we may not find that ultimate understanding. This creates a disconnect that is reflected into our world: where we are out of balance because we don't have the completeness of the developing picture and where we often try to fill in the blanks with assumptions. It is the assumptions that are based on our perceptions that are reflected into our behaviors that cause the problems. Our survival is highly dependent upon our universal connection to bring a more complete understanding, which ultimately brings stability to a culture.

No one can deny the fact that our world is out of balance. The predictable weather has become unpredictable. Ocean levels are rising. Cancer rates have gone up, as have autism and Alzheimer's. And why are we so polarized? We cannot seem to agree on why all this is happening because everyone has their own truth, yet no one has the complete truth. The truth simply does not exist anymore and society seems to be falling apart. But, on a spiritual level, our misperceptions are being destroyed and a new truth is being born.

As we proceed through this process of awakening, reflection will deliver a deeper understanding of why we are at this place in time. What were the decisions that we have made collectively that created the world we live in currently? This reflection will enable us to make a conscious shift to a new and remarkable reality. A new world is being created for a different paradigm, unbeholden to the corruptive thoughts of the past. All that is manifesting at this time is a step in the process to bring humanity to a new and profound understanding. Not only a surreal one, but also one that knows the truth of our past. This includes the truth of who we are and where we have come from. Each event unfolding before us is meant to be examined and reflected upon—from a neutral point of view. Be the observer, the one to see all angles, the full panoramic view. Watch as though you are looking through a foggy window: you see what is going on but are not scrutinizing every detail. Watch the play unfold.

Open your mind to a more expansive understanding. Things are not as we see them. Take the perceptions of the past and toss them aside. You will not need them anymore. A transformation is coursing its way throughout creation, changing everything as we know it. It is a developing energetic and vibrational field taking place on a vast scale right under our noses and we don't even recognize it. We will not see it until everything is in place. Then, suddenly, our reality will shift.

Everything is truly related and connected, from all that we see to all that we don't. When you find the truth, it all makes sense. All the dots connect. There is no separation between spirituality and science, or math, or astronomy, or any other subject. It all falls on the same spectral line, just in a different spot. In *The Augmentation of Man* series, you will see how it all connects. God, the Creator, is the quantum of all understanding, all vibration and all energy. He, for lack of a better word, wants to share his understanding with us and has designed All That Is to support this goal. That includes the understanding of all the Universal Laws and Concepts, the laws that keep the universes in order with the conceptual understanding that explains why.

All the universe was created for our contemplation of everything that exists. It is a giant school, originally created through the release of small vibrations. The vibrations built amplitude over an enormous amount of time to the point of an energy release, creating the big bang, converting energy to mass and light. It is represented in the equation $e = mc^2$. Like mass coagulates together to form an electrical and magnetic flux into itself, compressing that mass into a sphere that becomes a planet or sun. The livable planets become learning spheres for our spiritual growth. The Creator creates and enlists others who he has created to carry out the plan for an ever-expanding universal consciousness. All structures and all higher entities in all of the universes serve this divine plan. God created it all for us to explore, learn and grow in understanding.

Our development is accomplished in steps. As we come to understand one level, we are moved to the next. It is a natural progression, first building a solid foundation by taking the time to understand the basics. Though it is tempting to want to leap forward, to do what others have achieved, it is important that we learn the basics and that we follow our own path, the one we chose and designed prior to our coming here. It is the one that the higher self, the part of our soul that determines our learning path, has designed. It is also important that we take the time to find and ponder the truth. Ineffective is one who rushes to the top, only to find their foundation is crumbling.

This is where we are today: our foundation is crumbling. Gone are the truths that once existed, replaced by a distant semblance of what was. Truth is no longer recognizable. Today's "truths" do not form a solid foundation for our understanding. This sets the stage for our constant battles between each other, creating disunity. Soon the buildings we have constructed on unstable ground will come tumbling down. Our search for answers will bring the realization of a new truth to form a sturdy base from which to build. Our arrogance will be replaced by a humbleness that, together with our new understanding, will gain us access to our higher self and the vast trove of knowledge stored in our souls. Once we realize the higher self, we can then gain entrance to the expanded network of connecting entities whose sole purpose is to teach and fulfill the directive of the Creator in the ever-expanding universal consciousness. This is where we become One. Each is a step in the process. Some people have done much work in past lives, being able to progress faster in this life. For this reason, we cannot compare where we are and what we can do with other people. Build your solid foundation first. All else will come as you are ready.

We have come to the end of a cycle, having made its completion December 21, 2012. The reversing of the field poles between planets marks the beginning of the next cycle. Cycles are tied to periods of learning and are influenced by the vibrational interplay between the ever-changing rotation of planets. Earth's cycle of perceptual learning is now drawing to a close. Perception is based on our previous experiences and not an exact truth. It results in various degrees of truth intermingled with non-truths. The events playing out today will shine the light on our misperceptions, including the way we see the material world and our place in it. This enables us to give up our past misperceptions to accept a universal truth. A new world will be built on this and a developing trust and acceptance of each other. We will come to understand that our survival as a species depends on our continuous connection to our universal brothers and sisters who will, once again, teach and guide us. This is the divine plan for creation, a network of entities that support expanding universal consciousness through the sharing of intellectual information.

There are numerous streams of energies coming to Earth now to bring about the necessary changes, in ways one could never have imagined. Earth's vibrational spectrum is rising to a new level and, with it, our learning is also changing. We are being pushed, literally, into a new era of enlightenment and renaissance. The changes not only affect Earth and her inhabitants, but all the universes. Everything is moving to a new and higher value. Everything is rebalancing. Everything is changing and moving upward in an effort to support and promote a new and higher conscious network. A human genetic upgrade is a part of this change, enabling humanity to be able to receive a communication from within and process a higher conceptual understanding. Humanity is moving into a more intellectual thought-being with an ability to communicate telepathically. A bright horizon awaits with an anticipation of a new human species that will be able to participate in the interconnection with other universal races in the sharing of knowledge. It is the dawn of a new day for mankind, who will be able to grasp a deeper understanding of God, the Creator, and All That Is.

Peace be with you on your journey to enlightenment. May all that has eluded you, now become clear. It is just the beginning!

PREFACE

We did not intentionally set out on this path. We were normal people—Kent, a firefighter, and Renee, a nurse—living a normal life. Kent was a two-time cancer survivor with an unexplained spontaneous healing the second time around, years prior to our meeting. It began with the blending of two families that would later take a 180-degree turn, leading us on a path of enlightenment beyond our wildest dreams.

It took Kent four years to accept his skill at being able to communicate with the spirit world. Event after event was predicted through our spiritual guides and fulfilled, each time pulling Kent in, only to have him jump off a week later. He was a Deputy Fire Marshal and an expert witness for the courts. He had a reputation to maintain, and an ego. It was not until he had received several confirmations from Native Americans and, finally, an Indian guru, that Renee announced, "I'm getting off this roller coaster. You either believe or quit." He finally got on board.

The Augmentation of Man series offers an exceptional understanding of the purpose of life. Our lives and our understanding have been completely transformed by the knowledge. After several years of channeled lessons, we were asked by our primary mentors, the Ancients, to put them into books to share with others. The Ancients are beings who have existed since the beginning of time. They are teachers and mentors of God, our Creator. We will have to discuss how to read their messages, as the manner in which they dictate is unlike our language and syntax, and is sometimes difficult to understand. It does not adhere to the rigid rules we put on language, rather is a fluid use of language to deliver a conceptual understanding.

The Ancients are our primary Source of information, but these lessons come from many teachers: professors of various fields of study, like any college or university, and a variety of other beings, both physical and non-physical. There are too many to list and they do not want this type of attention, so we have left names out. Occasionally, however, we will put their title, just to give the reader a better understanding of the structural network of the conscious field. The lessons are usually received while Kent is in deep trance, or what we often refer to as meditation. Meditation is not exactly the correct word. Trance is correct. But we like using the word meditation. Kent must be completely relaxed and have cleared his mind of all of his thoughts to receive the thoughts of another, higher being. The thoughts are transferred from the teacher through the use of telepathy to Kent, who "hears" dictation in his mind. He repeats what he hears or sees in visions and Renee records it on a digital recorder and writes it down. Kent is an exceptional channeler. We have not met a person yet who has the ability that he has. Not that they do not exist, they just are very few.

First, and above all else, these dictated messages, in their original form, are meant to be understood in layers. The first read will be very confusing and it will appear that the lessons make absolutely no sense. But they absolutely do. It is meant to be read repeatedly, gaining a little understanding, then a little more, and a little more. Then, all-of-a-sudden, the light bulb comes on and an epiphany descends upon you with a most profound understanding. These lessons are given intentionally this way to produce a higher level of knowledge through steps in a process. It requires our participation and study. It is a new manner of teaching and learning for humanity that relies on cause and effect. And it works.

In English, the adjective precedes the noun; in other languages it is the opposite. At first, it causes one to stumble in the thinking process because everything is worded in reverse. As you become acclimated to conjugating and speaking a new language, it becomes easier and easier for your brain to follow a new syntax, a new arrangement of words. This works in the same way. It is the way the universe communicates. In order to communicate with the universe, *we* have to adapt.

Before the computer was invented, there were no words to describe the parts it is made of or the various things that a computer does. The words had to be developed to describe the functions of all the parts and mechanisms. They had to be constructed from the root words that make up the building blocks that form our language. The lessons in *The Augmentation of Man* series work the same. There are new words constructed from the basic building blocks of Greek and Latin root words to describe new conceptual ideas.

We have gathered all of the various topics that we received over the years and separated them into each cohesive chapter. We have asked additional questions to try to fill in the gaps. Many hours have been spent trying to find the correct spelling of the root words, piecing them together and then assigning a definition. All the new words presented here have a real definition, only you may not find them in your dictionary. Again, they are constructed from our Greek and Latin root words. Other words that are used in these lessons may be in the dictionary, but the more uncommon definition may be used. We have refined the definitions to the most appropriate application and created a glossary at the end of the book to make your studies easier. It is absolutely necessary to use the glossary, unless of course, you like doing that research yourself.

Because the syntax is different from our own, we would recommend that you start by looking up the various definitions, then rewriting the sentence in an arrangement that makes sense to you. Use the margins of the book or the blank page at the end of each chapter to make your notes, but do it in pencil. We guarantee that you will come back at a later time and erase your old notes to write new and more profound ones!

People ask why we don't just translate the whole book and print it in our words. Or, why the mentors don't make it easy on us by speaking like we do. There are a number of reasons. First, English is not their primary language. They use a much more complicated universal language. Think about how we might have to translate a higher conceptual idea in another language. English lacks the correct translation for many of the conceptual ideas they are teaching. To adequately describe something that does not yet exist in our thinking, they have to create new words using our Greek and Latin root words. Some universal words are also used, and those definitions have been supplied. Most importantly, the manner in which these lessons were delivered were done in such a way as to deliver a most exceptional understanding. And for this reason, we were asked not to change the wording. We have, however, added more translations to each chapter in *The Acquiescence of Humanity* in a more expanded "our understanding." This differs from *A Study in Renaissance*, where we used a shorter synopsis. We are planning a second edition that expands our interpretations, mirroring the changes in this book. It is to make your journey to enlightenment easier in this busy, busy world. But keep in mind, it is *our* understanding, which may not be complete understanding. It is recommended you do your own homework for the most profound results. Our translations will give you the head start.

To understand the difference between our translations and the exact channeled dictation, our words are contained in the wide texts and the mentor's dictation is in narrow texts. Our questions start with a "Q" and are usually followed by the teacher's answer, unless it is a vision Kent received, which will be within wider texts. We don't use "A" for answer because many dictations do not start with a question.

New to this book, besides more of our interpretations, are more direct translations of the original dictation itself. After reading our translation, go back to the original message to cross-reference. This will enable you to more quickly learn how to decipher the language yourself. We have included some of our own limited scientific research to help connect the dots. Phrases have been added to the glossary so you can gain a more conceptual understanding than looking up the words individually. We have differentiated the physical self, uncapitalized, from Self, capitalized, a reference to the higher self. Use your discernment, though, as some lessons refer to both the physical self and the higher self within the same paragraph and it is entirely possible that we may have misrepresented which self is being used by the capitalization or lack of. We have started capitalizing Light when it is used in reference to the communicative energy that delivers a more expansive understanding. We have also capitalized Creative when referencing any energy, force, understanding, etc. coming from a Creative being, or representative of the Creator. Also new to this book, we have combined the chapter glossaries into one glossary in the back of the book.

Language was meant for the communication of ideas for greater understanding. But it has been transformed into a collection of idioms that no longer support the true intention of language. Our language is now inconsequential to expanded understanding. A true understanding is a consequence of actual learning attained. In these books, however, the language remains true to its purpose. The meanings will either be literal or metaphoric. The metaphor helps to draw a parallel to something we can see in our mind's eye.

That being said, this is not a perfect science. Sometimes new and unusual words are difficult to decipher from the dictation. Punctuation can be very difficult to figure out, as it is not provided. A period inadvertently placed in the wrong spot can change the context of the sentence. We have kept with the addition of some of our words in brackets to aid in the flow of the reading, without altering the original dictation. There can be similar words that are difficult to decide which meaning was implied, such as distallation and distillation, or magnitudinal and magnetudinal, or self and Self (as in a reference to the higher self). And, don't forget our English language, a conglomeration of several other languages, holding its own confusing and conflicting paradigm. For example, the word "another" can mean either one more of the same, *or* something different. So, you will need to make your own judgement calls. You may even decide that your translation differs from ours. That is okay. We all have had different learning experiences and different views. We haven't been on this path for very long and there certainly will be people who have a more extensive knowledge base to draw from.

But don't let that enable a closed mind. Many people, in their search for truth, have done much research. When they finally have figured it all out, they put up fences around their beliefs, never to look at a new thought again. Humans are one of the least knowledgeable beings in all the universe and truth is an ever-elusive thing to try to attain. Truth is ever-evolving and is completely dependent upon this moment in time and what data we currently have in our possession. We are only beginners in the universe, just graduating from kindergarten. Push those parameters out of your way and really start to look at all that exists around you. Unfortunately, many ancient teachings have morphed over the eras to become nonexistent truths. So, we are presenting new information to this period in time, that was originally aligned to a more perfect truth, but the meaning has changed over the years. This is a period of correction. Keep your mind open and use your deciphering skills to add balance in your understanding.

We have a blog on our website to help you with understanding the lessons found in *The Augmentation of Man* series. For those who like videos, visit our YouTube or vimeo channels. We are also making plans to start a podcast. All these are presented to help you on your journey to a deeper spiritual connection and a more enlightened state through various forms of social media that best suit your needs. No matter what your preferences for learning are— audio, visual or by reading—you have resources to go to, to assist you in understanding these important lessons. Check out our social media sites listed in the back of the book, on the "About the Authors" page.

Our enlightenment does not happen by osmosis. It takes work. We are often reminded, "Study. Do not do other's work to understanding. Self-proclamation is virtuous in contemplating the works of understanding." Even though we have done much to help you, the spiritual truth-finder, you will not gain the deepest level of understanding by just reading and listening to our translations, although they will certainly help get you started. To get the full effect, you must do the work yourself. Use the videos, the blog, the podcast to give you the basic understanding in English. Then start reading the lessons as they were given, using the glossary and taking the time to contemplate. Let it sink in and connect the dots. When that epiphany falls upon you and you realize that truth at such a deep level, you will rejoice. It is truly a remarkable feeling! With the new understanding, comes a vibrational attunement. You have corrected your thoughts to a more perfect truth, and, as even our thoughts have a relative vibration, you have qualified your understanding to have a vibrational correction. Your new vibration will attract new people and events into your life, transforming your paradigm!

These lessons correct past misperceptions. For this reason, they may present a different explanation than what you might have been taught. The original truths given have been transformed over time to become a partial truth. Keep an open mind. Read the lessons with the eyes of a child, with the open curiosity not yet filled with prejudice. These are certainly new conceptual ideas and you may find that, as you progress through this book and in your levels of understanding, you may experience physical changes. One of these changes may include feeling your body vibrate. Do not be alarmed, your body is merely going through vibrational attunements in relation to a correction in your understanding. You may also start waking up feeling like, instead of sleeping, you have been in a classroom all night. You will have been. It is a part of the higher learning process. Pay attention to all the minute details going on around you and watch your life transform to a serendipitous unfolding of experiences!

We want to finish by emphasizing how much your life will change for the better through this new knowledge. You will not only have a remarkable understanding of our world and your purpose, but your spiritual fulfillment will be like no other. If you want the spiritual truths, they are here. Blessed be your path to enlightenment. Enjoy the journey!

Resources are found at the back of the book in "About the Authors".

"Get in touch with your inner Self. You have to know who you are because, once you know who you are, your meditation will bring clear concepts and truth. Knowing Self can be rigorous, can be difficult, but satisfactory in the end. Do not fear who you are. Do not only accept the joys, but accept the sorrows, because it is what makes you who you are; the path you chose. Credence given to all those who understand themselves."

—An Ancient

Chapter 1

Earth is a Lab

So many people skip over the Introduction and the Preface, ready to jump right into the real substance of the book. If you are one of those people, we would have to urge you to at least read the Preface to understand how to read and interpret this book. It will absolutely not make sense to you if you do not understand the basics of why this book is presented in this unusual manner. Even if you have read the first book, *The Augmentation of Man: A Study in Renaissance*, we have made some minor changes you may want to know about. At the end of the book, on the "About the Authors" page, are listed all our social media resources to help you with interpretation of these lessons. The language is difficult, but you will be amazed by the results when you put forth the work to truly understand the lessons! If you find the language too difficult at first, skip to the areas marked **"our understanding,"** reading it first, then go back to the beginning of that section to read the original dictation. It will help you get a jump start. That being said, let's get started...

History, as we know it, is incorrect. Creation is teaming with intelligent life, of all varieties. It is a communicating creation that seeks to fulfill the Creator's directive of an ever-expanding universal consciousness: the intellectual and spiritual understanding of All That Is. In this chapter, the mentors explain that humanity was a created race for the expansion of understanding of other beings from outside this world. We were also a created work force. Our genetic expression is less than that of other universal beings. That is beginning to change; albeit in stages. We are a small part of the totality of creation, but we reflect on the ability of our universe. In order for the universe to serve Creator's directive, humanity must rise to the call of our quantum leap forward in intellectual and spiritual understanding. Our humble acceptance that we are not the most intelligent species in the universe is a prerequisite to our reconnection with our cosmic neighbors. This is the first step toward allowing other, more intelligent beings to resume teaching humanity, propelling our understanding to levels beyond what we are able to conceive at this time.

Your Earth is a lab

Diatomaceous—that's what the earth was once—a buffer. Not too much grew.

Genetics came from another...Man will be rearose when all this happens. There will be teachers. You are going to be in a whole new learning experience of a higher level than the last time of man, which would be the time you are in now. Enlightenment will prevail. The magnitudes and universal understanding will create a higher level of cognizance and study value.

The earth today is like an itch that no one can scratch. The only way to scratch the itch is to cut out the itch. It's kind of superfluous understanding here, but the simplicity is being created right now for it.

Kent, visualizing the professor during his meditation, "He is walking back and forth."

Achilles is that part of the earth—and man taps the core. The shift shall take place. Man is too curious; does not take time to understand and perceive his doings. If we did the same thing in the universe that [man] does here on Earth, the whole universe would be one big, black hole with no life. We have learned not to be misguided, to pull back our exploratory values to see things closer and analyze before we misact.

Kent adds, "He says it's hard for him to conceive all the misvalues that humanity has created in the short time he's been here."

2

Man was created as an increasing evolutionary process; a quicker pace to see how development can be handled by a race that has been pushed farther and faster. We have learned much about how this has created a destructive process. Maybe pushed too soon.

Kent continues, "He says he recalls a carcanian atmosphere, talking about injecting atmospheric gases, which changes the thinking process of the culture that's living within that atmosphere."

Redundancy and atmospheric pressures, with the injection of mind-challenging gases, can create the environment that substantiates the changes to a culture or a kind.

Your Earth is a lab to study the evolution of other universal worlds, in its much earlier state.

The origin of man

Your neuronet is a quasi-functional net: not completely developed to the extent of other entities, the human race. In order to expand yours, or to strengthen it, we have to remold it to the configuration to hold a complete vibrational attunement or circuit. Neuronet was never fully completed in human race. Why never designed? Laboratory analysis to see what level the human race can function to a reasonable rate of stability.

The intent of the following question was to ask if humans had evolved from a genetic manipulation of primates:

Q: Were primates genetically altered?
Enough to mimic human behavior.

Q: So humans did not evolve from primates?
Evolved from other species; entities outside this earth. Put here to evolve.

Q: So earliest inhabitants came via vehicle from outside Earth?
Yes! Human species evolved. Many species developed here to study.

Kent added, "Like Earth is an island."

Q: Who were the first inhabitants of Earth?
Irrelevant. Anunnaki.

Q: Who developed the human species?
Various original entities. Higher vibration level of learning. Monitoring stations here at one point—did not work out.

Q: Why not?
Interfered with species evolution.

Q: How long ago?
Before written record.

Q: Was there a reason for the different races?
Magnitude to learning: conceptual agreements among those that differ in origin. [A] learning test before stepping outside of this sphere. Have not done well.

Q: Are the human physical characteristics reflective of the cultures outside of Earth?
More than physical: preference to understanding Self-nature within [a] cultural exchange: paratication to surreal identities outside of Self-conflict. Cannot identify with Self-ideologies until acceptance of

those of another kind. A confluence of Self-influence bestaves away for consequential or inconsequential behaviors. Significance of patterns set, bestowing the true values of a particular culture.

Q: Why were there different species of humanoids living here on Earth concurrently in an earlier time?
Planted here to see which species could exist. Simplicity is just.

Q: How long ago was man placed here?
Thirty-thousand [years].

Q: How many civilizations have been severely demolished in human history?
Not counting.

Our understanding: Are we able to reach conceptual agreements even though we differ in our origin? Or, do we let our differences divide us? This is a learning test for humans; yet we have not done well in this arena. We must first accept our own differences within humanity before we are able to accept the greater differences that exist universally.

But it goes beyond the physical: there is also a spiritual objective here. It is a sequential process: the higher self steps aside to allow the physical self the opportunity, through consequential and inconsequential behaviors, to understand the true nature of the higher self through a cultural exchange with those that appear different than ourselves. Consequential behavior is the resulting adjustment to one's behavior when learning and understanding has been achieved. Inconsequential behavior is the continuance of a particular behavior due to a lack of understanding. We cannot identify with the intuitive nature and the truth of the higher self until we are able to reconcile the inner conflict through the acceptance of those of another kind. This process sets the patterns of understanding the true worth of other cultures, preparing us to accept other, more surreal, entities.

Humanity was a short-term experiment

We were talking about some people who feel they are from another planet, when the mentor chimed into our conversation, Kent hearing:

No, you are not from other planets, your DNA is.

Q: Where does that DNA come from?
Various places, various sources. Not just one place.
Not everybody has it. It's like a time release capsule
for most, becomes relevant when it is time, need be.

For some people, their DNA is activated at a particular point in time to be able to realize certain abilities when they are needed, such as the sudden ability to receive spiritual communication of information needed for humanity at that time.

The human race are not natural here—planted. Unfortunate experiment. Experiment not relative to time and matter, which are dictated by the Universal Laws and Concepts of all material beings. Architectural exposure to the structural makeup of these experiment beings not kept within the conceptual parameters, as agreed upon by other civilizations that were within this sphere. Some disdainment exists by other cultures.

Q: Is it for this reason that there are other cultures that do not want the human race to join the other universal cultures?
Correct. Unverified, immature DNA has not computed to the diameter of other cultures at this time. Gene expression irrelevant. Must materialize

at a higher inference level, or vibrational understanding, before comprehension of other civilizations can be connected. A relevant behavior is incomplete for the human being; markers have yet to be placed where relevancy can occur. Conceptual event will increase these markers, as needed.

Q: For what purpose was it not kept within the structural makeup?
Accidental.

Q: What was the intended structural make-up of humans?
Short-term.

Q: In other words, this experiment was supposed to be short-term?
Correct. Analyze existive value on a fundamental level. Begin to create an exceptional interest for a specific characteristic. Past behavior techniques beyond interpretive thought create an extension for analytical behavior.

Q: Why was the earth experiment not relative to time and matter?
Humans are not going to be a continuance species: *original plan*. Sustain existence only recent on the opt-organic field. Much discussion prevailed to allow continuance of species.

Q: What was the reasoning to allow humans to continue?
Upward movement by many. Congulated effect to traverse field force. Can adjust to molecular manipulation from outside parameters. Interesting, adaptive creatures with beginning intellect; although on a much lower scale. Possibilities exist, showing

adaptive movement to a higher plane of existence.

We were reading the book, *The 12th Planet* by Zecharia Sitchin, based on the translations of ancient Sumerian cuneiform clay tablets that were found in the area of Iraq. We wanted to verify some of the author's interpretations:

Q: What were the reasons for the development of the human race?
Species evolution combined with evolutionary use of a proletarian culture, used for the good of evolutionary process.

Q: So, the primary decisions involved *both* the study of species evolution *and* the use of a proletarian culture?
Correct. Primary evolutionary species thesis pronouncing cultural dimensions under adverse environmental conditions. [A] prelapse to indicators of coming value needed for diametrical correction of upcoming species at that time. A historical judgment in species adjustment to correctional behavior.

Q: Was the great flood expected to eradicate the human race?
Irrelevant to cause. Miscalculation by many; arrogance on their part. More than what the tablets say. This world is a terrarium of many species, some yet unknown by human entity.

Scientifically, the human DNA ladder contains six billion rungs of possible genetic expression. But for the DNA to be expressed, it must first be "turned on" by the presence of a protein marker attached to that particular rung. There lies an elusive answer to the question: "How much of the DNA is actually functional and to what degree of functionality?" While research performed by the *Encyclopedia of DNA Elements*, studying the human genome, found eighty percent of human DNA to have some type of protein marker for biochemical function, scientists at the University of Oxford have determined that less than ten percent—8.2 percent to be exact—of our DNA is absolutely necessary to human development. The problem with this theory is that there is an assumption that, in the course of evolution, only unchanged DNA is assumed to be absolutely necessary to the human genome, and, thus, "functional," and any DNA changes that occurred over the course of evolution was deemed to be non-essential to life. This formed the foundation for the "junk DNA" theory.

Our understanding: The above lessons indicate that humanity was a two-fold experiment. First, that development of the human genome was to provide a work force for others here from outside Earth. Secondly, that the human DNA was altered to express the least amount of gene expression in order to study the evolution of beings in their earliest developmental phase. This seems to have included the study and formal discussion of how the human culture evolved at a particular time and place under severe conditions. It appears they had the foresight of a future decline in the human race and discussed the corrections necessary to reverse our course to correct human behavior.

Humans are not a natural, or indigenous, species here on Earth. We were a created species by those who came here from places outside the earth. It was agreed that the "human experiment" was to be short-term by numerous other cultures who were here on Earth in the promotion of a higher degree of conceptual understanding for themselves. It was an experiment to benefit the greater good by facilitating their more expansive understanding. But the experiment did not follow the parameters set forth by Universal Laws and Concepts, as the human genome was not kept within the conceptual parameters originally agreed upon by other civilizations that were here at the time; the result of an unspecified accident. Our DNA did not materialize to the higher degree of expression that was implied in the experiment, leaving the human race with immature DNA, when compared to other cultures at *this* time. This has caused instability here on Earth due to our inability to foresee many of the problems that we ultimately created.

It is of utmost importance at this time that we learn higher vibrational understanding before the human race can have any future connection to other civilizations outside our own. It is for this reason that those cultures look upon this situation with great disdain. Until only recently, and after much discussion, was it decided to allow this experiment to continue. This was due to many people responding to the molecular manipulation from outside parameters, showing the possibilities of movement to a higher plane of existence, in the form of a higher level of learning and understanding.

Humans one of the youngest races

Humans the youngest kind within all the realm. Under-developed as a cause. Your exploration is appreciated by the Beings That Are. Stay strong in your understanding and consequences of other beings. Be as one to achieve your goals within this life frame, as you understand its meaning. Love of universal values is still a consequence of being.

Q: Are we also one of the youngest spiritually?
Correct. Much to learn. Time has no value on this path, acceptance of understanding does; a cognitive value of self-placement within the spherical changes that are taking place at this position.

You are not *the* youngest of those learning, but you are among the lowest.

Kent describes a vision, "I saw a scale between one and ten, ten being the lowest. I saw us, humanity, at 8.7."

10

Q: Are the spheres for the youngest cultures placed most distally in the galaxy?
Protrusion of fact. A most exact oculation of being reverberates throughout the universal pattern. A consequence of being diametrically opposed to diameter, distallation of being. A lesser being are human; a precondition awaiting to rise.

Q: Was there a point in our past when we had regular communication with outside entities?
Release of energy patterns broken by behavioral concepts of the human race. Reliance on energy patterns have changed; crudacious in event situations. Changing band width to accommodate higher beings—interface with another kind.

Q: These beings will become our preceptors?
Correct. Reliance on others to be established through the veil with understanding the great value of One Being life force.

Our understanding: The "Beings That Are" reflect a higher level of aptitude, intelligence and conceptual understanding. They are the teachers of the universe. They taught humans at one time. But humanity broke the bond when we became arrogant. We have since been in a downward spiral, behaving in a very crude manner in response to event situations. They are now changing the vibrational band width to a higher level for Earth in order to accommodate a greater genetic expression for humanity. This will enable mankind to interface with other beings once again, where others of higher intellectual abilities can share the profound understanding of the One Being life force, or All That Is.

You are being observed for progress, tracked

We had heard that there were tiny lights being observed on the moon's surface and sought verification from our guides:

Q: What are the illuminations that look like lights on our moon?
Beings of another kind: your guidance there.

Q: Who are the other physical beings outside Earth?
Various sources.

Q: Where are they from?
Quantum distance relative to your sun, outside your Milky Way. Distance based on diagonal variance of the sun's projected course, based on the center of your Milky Way. Distance to triangulation. Do not use light years.

Kent injected, "Light years are irrelevant to them, everything is instant." The distance is measured through triangulation, where there exists a variation of the diagonal angle, based on the sun's projected orbit and the center of our Milky Way galaxy, which is an ever-changing position.

Q: What is their mission here?
Observation. Guidance without interference. Hostility abounds here. Perception is misplaced; intent undignified.

Q: You're talking about the humans?
Yes.

Q: Has Earth been quarantined from the rest of the universe?
Release of neurologic studies of Earth vibration upon human race: neurologic studies, a quiet factor.

Q: What has been learned from this?
Control of sequence: neurologic output control.

Q: What has this accomplished?
Release of energy used to control segmented population.

Our understanding: Entities from outside Earth have been involved in a neurologic study of Earth's vibrational influence upon the human race. It seems they are saying this energy controls a segment of the population, possibly by nudging us forward in our intellectual evolution, when speaking of the palakian field. The palakian field relates to the magnetosphere and "helps move the cause of change for specific spheres." See **chapter 3** "Death and spiritual rebirth" in *The Augmentation of Man: A Study in Renaissance.*

Outside thought waves

Toward the end of 2014, and as Kent and Renee began meditating, Renee heard a third breathing pattern. Kent sitting to her left, the breathing sound came from her right. It was a faster and heavier rhythm than Kent's. Renee opened her eyes, searching in the direction of the sound, when it suddenly stopped. Nothing was visible. It occurred again on a second occasion while meditating: the rapid, heavy breathing to the right, while Kent sat at her left. Feeling perhaps there was another unseen being in the room with them, Renee asked out loud if it was possible to reveal themselves. The breathing again slowed and gradually became quiet. A few days later, Renee heard the breathing coming from a different area of the room during their meditation and decided to ask:

Q: Has another being entered the room?
No.

Q: What am I hearing that sounds like breathing?
Pluckarian sound. Not an entity.

Q: What is the sound generated from?
A thought wave outside. You are hearing (a) thought pattern—not physical—a quantarian understanding of perceptual thought-being.

Q: Does this thought wave originate from human beings?
No.

Q: Where does it originate from?
Outside Earth, as you call it.

Q: What is the purpose of this thought wave?
Show not alone. They are with you.

The Pleiadians and the HELL machine

There are books published based on channeled messages from a group of other beings called the Pleiadians. Of course, there is also much chatter within certain groups about their agenda and other communications with humans. We sought answers from our guides as to the validity of this race of people. We didn't expect that they themselves would have come through the communication:

Q: Who are the Pleiadians?
People of color. We give thought to others. We guide intellect and thought-provoking movements to better the human entity.

Q: Are you of physical form?
Projected thought: neuro-stream of intelligent thought, sequential patterns. Neuronical electrical impulses, captured by the brain's synapse of the electrical conductivity. Patterns of thought, that's who we are.

Q: Is there any truth to the story that the Pleiadians altered our DNA?

We are them, the generational representative, the remnants. The remnants of themselves. We are the logic ones: scientarians. We are holding the Light within. The guardians of HELL.

Kent explained, "They equated the word 'hell' with the Pleiades."

Heavy Energy Light Laser. Heavy lasers: war.

Clarifying, "HELL meant Heavy Energy Light Laser. Evidently there was a war and it destroyed a lot of the Pleiades."

The HELL machine. The war was within the Pleiades. HELL: Heavy Energy Light Laser. Created heat and leveled everything it hit—a weapon.

Atlantis experience: just a piece of what that technology can do. Misused, got out of hand. Extremely powerful.

Q: Do they still inhabit the planet?

Kent summarized, "Yes. They learned from their mistakes. We are on a similar quest within our own self. It was destroyed once before here on Earth."

Q: What happened?

Misuse of technology caused the earth to change, Earth protecting self. Thought entity lives within.

Q: A thought entity lives within the earth?

Yes. Help[s] develop new species.

Atlantis

Q: Can you tell us more about Atlantis?
Monitoring city, advanced. Corruption seeped in; overwhelming. Unregulated experiments caused disaster: power grid shift.

Q: What part of the earth was Atlantis?
Now known as Atlantic.

Kent explained the earth shifted, so Atlantis is not in same place as it was originally.

Q: Nearest what current land mass?
Australia. Large monitoring point. Land shifted.

Q: Is this the area that is going to be rising again out of the ocean?
Yes! Separation of land, in your words—the way headed right now.

Thoth, the Atlantean

We were reading a book about the legendary Thoth. Or so we thought. The entity whom we were asking had no knowledge of Thoth. Evidently, he is not known of universally.

Q: Can you explain who Thoth is?
Not familiar with this name. Could be a purple entity of another kind, not of highest order.

Q: I am asking about Thoth, the Atlantean, who wrote on emerald tablets.
There are many emerald tablets by many scholars, a renowned effect of its time. Many pursued this craft in communication. Not familiar with this entity. We

deal outside this realm.

Q: Who are the purple beings?
Ones of another nature outside the earth. Planetarian to this sphere. Created stock for others to negotiate value. Have evolved beyond this point as original aspect, luephorbious, by natural, reoccurring use to perpetuate its species.

Q: What is the name of this culture or race?
First beyond self: first here.

Q: Which planet are the purple people from?
Nibiru; quanticeptual beings of the first sphere.

Q: The first sphere being a planet?
As humans understand them.

Q: Are these the same beings depicted in our ancient artwork?
Spoken of.

Our understanding: We would have to assume "created stock" refers to beings that were created by other beings, just as humans have been. At least some of the peoples from Nibiru are probably purple in color and that they have a history here on this planet. It is interesting that a lot of the ancient depictions of "god's" in Hindu culture are blue in color. Could this actually be the same race spoken of here? It seems the guide is saying that they have evolved to higher states than when they occupied the earth previously.

Nibiru: the Anu and the Anunnaki

Most of the following questions were generated while reading the book, *The 12th Planet*, by Zecharia Sitchin:

Q: Is there any more information about this book,
The Twelfth Planet?
Ninety-eight percent correct. New information will
come forth upon completion of all texts uncovered.

**Q: Are the planets Marduk and Nibiru one and
the same?**
Not relative. No relationship except culture
pathways.

Q: What culture pathways?
Tied to development. Cultures expressing
movement within the salinarian complex—2 percent
of the universal field. Sectional inheritance of gene
complex within the designated field parameters,
cultural complex derived from invasive cultural
forces.

Q: What is the salinarian complex?
A hidden scenario given to those with understanding
complete analysis of sequential values. A complex
of diverse value, sequential in nature, given to those
with understanding quantitative values.

Q: Is one of these planets a balancer to Earth?
Begins process for completion: awakens the inner
self through chaos.

Q: Which of the planets begins the process?
Nibiru: a course corrector. Longitudinal navigation
movement.

Q: Is it an orbital course corrector?
Correct. Carbon unit's transposition coming at
angulation.

Q: What will this create?
Compressed field energy expands upon insonation; an energy consequence.

Q: Is this referring to Nibiru?
A return from many generations. Brings New Age friendship. Most humans ready for cross-correlation.

Q: How long in Earth years is Nibiru's orbit?
Five thousand, six hundred, sixty-two, enter[s] solar system.

Q: When will it reach its closest point to Earth?
When it decides to complete its event cause. Some control of movement.

Q: The Sumerian clay tablets have been translated to say Nibiru's orbit is 3,600 Earth years. Why is there such a big difference?
Not the orbital cycle.

Q: Which one is not the orbital cycle?
Three-thousand six-hundred.

Q: What does 3,600 relate to?
Cycle of a moon—not yours. Smaller planet—non-conductive—follows same path.

Q: Is it a moon of Nibiru?
Precedes. Variation of cycle: a half-cycle of Nibiru—octanian procedure.

Q: What is an octanian procedure?
Looking at all sides of the cycle.

Q: What are the people of Nibiru called?
Octarians: the Anu's.

Q: Can we have a lesson on the octarians?
Eighth planet of the second solar system outside yours. Nepherum.

Q: Nephilim?
Nepherum culture. Your seed of Earth: partial, [a] mixture.

Q: Is there a reference to eight in the name other than "the eighth planet of the second solar system outside ours"?
Eight sides towards infinity. Paraloxical in nature: [a] mathematical equivalent.

Q: Does the word Anunnaki relate to the Anu's?
Proletarians: a created being. Minor planet within circumference of Nibiru.

Q: Can you tell us about the Anunnaki?
The power of knox: they possess the power of hearing the mind without speech.

Q: How would we spell knox in our language?
P-n-o-k-o-x.

Q: Can you tell us more about the power of pnokox?
The power to discern the power of others without verbal conversation; all entities. Discernment of corrective thought.

Q: What more can you tell us about the Anunnaki?
Another race, among many. Advanced intellect: was corrected in time pattern. Now transmental in thought pattern. No longer can abstract consequence of non-correctional behavior. Have evolved and

expanded understanding; a consequence of destructive behavior.

Q: What is their history with early humans?
Celebratory distress. Inconsequential life attributes as not seen, when needed for Self-influence and abductive behavior. A perceptive race of high intellect before correction took place for most [other] entities.

Perhaps this group of beings enjoyed watching the humans suffering. Nevertheless, the observation of this primal state in humans served the higher self and their outward behavior.

Q: Did they enslave humans long ago for the mining of gold, as translated from the Sumerian clay tablets?
For self-aspirations, within their valued system. Misuse, many races. Historical plunderance of value assets of self. Nocturnal effect many had upon other races of entities.

Q: The nocturnal effect spoken of involves keeping others in the dark or from the truth?
Truth not given to true value: useful ignorance. Perceptive promises to many; useful ignorance for cause.

Q: Were humans created as a working force?
Correct. No value when began; still replaceable, if needed.

Q: What else do we need to know about the Anu people?
Not of your choice now; yet will come to your knowledge.

Q: What planet does the Nephilim reside?
Nibiru. Life quadrant five, by your numbers.

Q: What can you tell us about the Nephilim?
Sceupharocal by nature: Self-comprehending
…Planetarian aspect.

Q: Is there a broader meaning of the word sceupharocal than what we currently understand?
The completeness, unending. Various degrees, levels. The lowest being here; the lowest of the highest here. Higher outside understanding.

Quiet your thoughts to what you know or think you know. Quillerian diagram of conceptual events can fill in the blanks to your being, a contemplate to understanding.

Q: What other entities are there?
Innumerous.

Q: How many different peoples are there in all of Creation?
Not relevant to your understanding. Think beyond what you know here; process your mind to higher thought.

Our understanding: The main relationship that Marduk and Nibiru share is their learning pathways. The mentor seems to be saying that, at one time, one invaded the other and there may have been some interbreeding. It appears that Nibiru is returning after many generations, having an orbit of 5,662 Earth years before entering our solar system. It is a carbon-based planet either coming in at an angle, or now coming into view, as in the angle in which something is viewed. A course corrector for other planetary objects, including Earth, it creates a compressed energy field that expands, producing a particular sound, correcting the orbit of outer planetary bodies. Most humans, according to the teacher, are ready for the mutual relationship between the two cultures, bringing a new friendship that shares philosophies and teachings of cosmology and the nature of the existence of All That Is.

The greys

The following questions are in regard to the little grey creatures with large eyes that we often see depicted as "aliens."

> **Q: Who are the greys seen among us and what is their program?**
> Greys are anatomical entities. They're [the] eyes of other entities. They represent information gathering, information gathering only. Conceptual understanding: not.

> **Q: Are their bodies a living organism?**
> Replicators: biomass and androidal.

> **Q: Who are the long greys that were mentioned previously?**
> High-thinking scientific culture. Relationship to universal concepts: understanding universal concepts and beings. The negative concepts of ionic dispersion. Scientific understanding—more than neutrality—making the ionic particle beam scientific.

Evidently, there are two types of "greys," the long (tall) greys and the shorter ones. The long greys are a highly scientific culture; the short ones are an androidal biomass, created for information gathering and not for conceptual understanding.

The reptilians

There is much conspiracy out there regarding another race called the reptilians, so-called for obvious reasons. This communication left us with the impression that much of the information being propagated is false.

Q: Is there a race called the reptilians, as we have heard?
From another planet.

Q: Are they physical?
Yes. A race not unlike yourselves.

Q: Are they as negative as people portray them?
They are a race that is seeking truth, as you are. Their seed was planted here 360 million years ago—unsuccessful. They are learning, as many other races are, cultures are.

Q: So, they don't come in and psychically attach to humans, as some people claim?
No. Many races come here to observe. They are only one of many. Your human attachment is to self-destruction, not seeking peace. You attach your own being of misperceptive provocation of self-worth. There are no attachments. The proclivity of man surrounds the misfunction of their aptitudinal being. A reptilian factor is irrelevant; non-consequential. Self-worth causes the reality of self-perception. Peace and innocence of the heart control the perception of being clarity. Clarity gone, through misguidance and irrelevant consequence.

The following question was asked by a friend, sitting in on the meditation, who had heard that the reptilians were trying to take over the earth. One can almost palpate the irritation in the response:

Q: Are reptilians trying to take over the planet?
No. Your own cognizant ignorance and negative attitudes are causing the planet problems. Your immaturity of thought: adolescent thinking to the value of power because of your inexperience as a race. Your inability to comprehend the value of Self-thought; the cognizant thinking of a unified plane. Unified thought is not understood or reached—a valued concept. Your adolescent thinking is what naturally happens to a young race of maturity. Humans have reached beyond their ability to comprehend, like an adolescent that needs to be pushed back to their point of comprehending their surroundings and who they are. Other entities are here to observe and enforce natural laws of the universe, not to capture human essense. There is no reptilian take-over or event. Immaturity is the culprit of misunderstanding of value.

Our understanding: There are many races that come here to observe and track the progress of humanity, the reptilian being one. This is most likely not the name of the race, rather a description of what they look like. They are on a learning path, just as humans are. They do not attach to humans psychically and they are not trying to take over the planet, as some people are claiming. These claims are born out of our own immature thoughts, our incorrect perception of self-worth and our inability to comprehend the value of one unified field of universal consciousness. Creating peace and innocence within our hearts will open up the clarity in our perception.

The Hathors

Q: Who are the Hathors?
Others that have visited here, as many have.

Q: Where is their planet of origin?
Star system 251-01; category Utarus.

Sirius and the Sharausedhien

The Suraheden are changing the complexity.

Q: Can I ask for the spelling of Suraheden?
Sirius: S-h-a-r-a-u-s-e-d-h-i-e-n.

Q: What can you tell us about the Sharausedhien?
Croptic culture movement, beyond Orion. Creatious attempt to understand human entity's boxed-in understanding, creating capricious difficulties.

A conceptual intercourse between cultures to begin

There is hope. Man will take a place with others in the universe. Man will learn and recognize the good. Love is one of the key words of the universal entrances.

Think about the vibrational levels of existence. The whole of nothing is abundant in the universe. Think about this. All is related to cosmic existence: time perpetration, vibrational atmospheric essence, quintessence of All That Is. Lean toward the lament of purpose. I show you nothing and nothing is full of All That Is.

Kent interjected, "This is the third time I heard, 'now is the time.'"

Ostulation is a covenant between the sectors of a universal dispersion; a prelude to come here. [A] significant responsibility to the continuance of the human race. Release the fracturing of universal ties of consequential cognizance.

A conceptual intercourse between cultures will begin soon: Arcturians and Earthlings. A beginning cosmology interface. Human race, in general, not prepared. Twenty percent ready for exchange of ideas.

It is time that we release the broken bonds between humanity and other cultures to begin a conceptual exchange of ideas once again, starting with the peoples of Arcturus. Twenty percent of humans are ready. Apparently, there is a difference in opinions between teachers in how much of the human race is ready for interactions with other cultures outside Earth, as another guide stated earlier in this chapter that most humans are ready.

You are a permanent experimental race

NOTES

Chapter 2

A New Horizon

Humanity is in a severe Self-identity crisis. Too focused on the material world, we have forgotten our true higher self. The higher self directs our spiritual growth and learning process. Myopic, arrogant and egotistical, our understanding has been boxed-in by our misperceptions. Exacerbating our sleep state, our thoughts are further manipulated by lower-level entities, both human and non-physical, diverting our attention off the learning track even further.

Lacking the ambition to move forward, various energy releases are descending upon the earth to redirect and correct humanity's path. One such release of energy is coursing its way throughout the universes, bringing with it a new and higher numerical expression for all life and all matter. These energies, combined with a human genetic upgrade, will dictate a new organization of the life force field and physical expression to manifest a completely new paradigm for mankind. It is one which extinguishes our current behavior by creating a greater drive within, birthing a higher level of inquisitiveness and intellect by setting new parameters for life expression. We are literally being pushed into the next era, dictated by the laws of consequence, creating humanity's exponential leap forward.

The beginning of All That Is again

From *The Augmentation of Man: A Study in Renaissance*, **chapter 12**, "A collapse of the old paradigm":

> A confluence is to appear, a gathering of souls. New horizons. A confluence of inept matter prelate to a conjunction of high numerical value—human cause not in effect at this time—irrelevance to universal events; a natural movement.

Universal curtain of prelation to understanding is about to collapse, releasing a large neurometrical impulse of knowledge, an electrical impulse far more advanced than the numerical value of all the stars— a collapse of the old paradigm. Release of energy beyond your comprehension, infinite in numerical value by your standards and concepts.

The subsequent questions were asked later, in September of 2015, as a follow-up to the above, after having been informed that a Creative energy was coming in:

Q: Is the Creative energy coming in now the large neurometrical impulse of knowledge?
To those that understand, that have obtained universal knowledge. The beginning of All That Is again.

Q: What is this Creative energy intended to create?
Augmentation of natural Self; a uniform cognizance.

Quintessence of understanding, universal inoculation is coming: behold the inoculus.

Our understanding: An enormous electrical impulse of energy, flowing over the universal nervous system, is penetrating creation, collapsing the old patterns to make way for a new and higher level of understanding throughout the universes. It is bringing an advanced mathematical formula for all matter and life form expression and holds a magnitude of knowledge that far exceeds our ability, as humans, to understand. It will mark the beginning of our learning about all that exists in our universe, once again, to expand the higher self knowledge and awareness. Be prepared to accept an infusion of understanding far beyond what we can now imagine!

A new energy blueprint

Pharoguyance [is] causation for effect that is about to happen; a changer of what is. Ostentatious is the reward for understanding the being of All That Is.

Q: Is this an energy blueprint that is about to arrive in our world?
Correct.

Q: Can we have a definition for pharoguyance?
Exceptional value: extreme Light conditions. Parameter set forth by incandescent stabilization of protracting power. Light given to universal beings of higher nature. External beings of extreme value to universal life force. Life force parameter field dictates consequence of particle beings' organizational structure.

Q: Is a particle being physical or non-physical?
Parameters set for either being. Configuration analysis perform consequential entity or being.

Q: What is pharoguyance used for?
Structural: on-going informational energy is derived from. Manifesting an energy field, called 'manipulating an energy field'.

Q: Is it a part of Source?
All is of Source, causation of *all fields*. Neutronal energy bombardment, quiet, or suropitous, by nature. A natural occurrence. The natural body releases proton energy: consecrated density of matter performing a natural awe.

Q: How will this energy blue-print affect humans?
Not prepared for this. Warnings have been given. Irrelevant behavior to cause.

Q: What will these changes mean for us?
Death in the behavior that now exists. A new cause, a new horizon, a new existence. One unlike this—a new horizon. You will awaken beyond your Now.

Kent, "I keep hearing, 'death to your existing behavior.'"

Q: How will this affect the other side trying to block the changes?
No more. Clearance. Ineptitudes causational to the being: affluential understanding of All That Is *within a limited realm.*

Q: How soon will this be arriving at our sphere?
(5 Jan 2014)
Arriving.

Q: Will this change the projected course of chaos and turmoil?
No.

Q: How will it affect those who seek power?
Ostracization of being: no longer valued. Release all you have, which is nothing.

Sequential movement of understanding prevails—a unitarian process. A natural cause in the human parameter, sequential movement of all things provide access to understanding cause and effect.

Create a thirst for value on the newness. The end of chaos—do not recede to the old. Welcome the gift of life. Establish your understanding of your value in this new sphere.

Consequential beings are reverberating the time shelf. An innocence prevails in understanding; consequence of dyareous events. A perceptual understanding to cause reflection to Self-understanding. Numerious is the cause for reflection at time of need, numerious in a consequential sense.

Q: Does the reverberation of the time shelf cause a quickening of events?
Causation increase. Reverberation influx of numerical value, consequence of dictorial movement by others.

Our understanding: Source is the communication tool of the Creator that higher entities use for high-level information access. It is an unseen network of charged atoms within the atmosphere that channels more expanded concepts of understanding between communicating entities, much like radio waves work, or the fiber optics we use for communication. The charged atoms form plasma cords that carry the informational energy, the Light. The information is then simplified by the communicating entity and passed on to those of lower understanding in a teaching process. It is a transfer of thoughts through a telepathic communication. Source is the beginning of, and combines with, the neuronet. The neuronet is a basic communication network of charged atoms for more simplified information that beings with less understanding can tap into. Think of the world-wide-web: you can type anything into your search engine and come up with a simplified explanation of the search word. Now, imagine that same technology, only you don't need a phone or computer to do it.

The consequential beings—those who understand all laws consequential to an event—affect the organizational structure and atomic spatial arrangement of molecules and are able to manipulate an energy field, called "manifesting an energy field". These higher beings are of extreme value to the universal life force, setting the parameters of organization throughout the universes. They have the ability to be either physical or non-physical.

Much lies in the path of humanity's course reversal: those trying to block the transformation, man's irrelevant behavior, the human-created chaos and the extreme polarization that now exists. Relevant is a man who devotes his time to a greater understanding. A plan has been put forward to bring us back to a time of renaissance, where enthusiasm for learning exists once again. Consequential beings are directing the change and new energies are arriving, correcting our path. As we proceed, each sequential event is meant to cause reflection within the human race, creating a new understanding and a change in our behavior. Each occurrence is a step in the process. It is the cause and effect creating consequences of learning, directing humanity toward the goals of a greater understanding, a more expansive DNA expression, and a pervasive unification. In the end, those who created the chaos, the blocks, and the polarization will have served their purpose in the lessons gained and will be ostracized and disempowered, allowing humanity to move into a new period of renaissance. The gift of life and our true value is always in our expanding consciousness and understanding.

Earth under severe Self-identity crisis

The world has had a rash of mass killings, which have significantly increased in the United States. Terrorism has flared around the globe, seeking to kill in the most despicable and offensive of ways. The first lesson followed one of these tragic events. Respecting the emotional nature of the attacks, and those that have been affected by them, we chose not to identify the events individually. The object is to view the totality of such events in a larger sense for purposes of understanding *why* it's happening and *what* is being done behind the scenes to correct it. Repercussions and corrections are made within the subatomic realm, to be realized later in the physical realm, creating a time-lapse between the energy set forward for change and the actual manifestation of that change.

> **Q: What changes will occur as a result of this recent event?**
> A narrowing of the plasmanic field, causing unequal dispersion of life force, thus making changes in plasmanic field to reshape the guiding diametrical life pattern. Must make changes in global atmosphere of unsaid planet. Behavior not acceptable to life pattern. Changes will affect many within their field, equilibrium adjustment forthcoming. A neuronetical recharge-up, causing atmospheric change, stabilize[s] hologram particle and environmental pattern change.

These horrific acts have initiated a narrowing of the plasmic field parameters, impacting the life force energy that emanates from Creator, as it passes through the plasmic field of charged atoms. This will change the pattern for how life is expressed on Earth. Part of our transformation, as a species, includes the change in the gaseous atmosphere around Earth and the reconstruction of the neuronet to allow a higher degree of intellectual energy to envelope humanity. These changes will push mankind forward in our understanding and stabilize the environmental field in which we exist.

The next lesson followed another shooting. This event created more intense repercussions and initiated a process of having all fields corrected.

> The taking of innocence today will accelerate the effects that are going to take place. The innocence of the universe has a replay effect.

> **Q: How does the replay effect work?**
> Higher, more intense degree of repercussions.

Q: What happens to those who commit such atrocities?
They are put on a variance board.

"Like a platform called a variance board," Kent added.

They are weighed by their parameters.

Q: Is this a way of measuring parameters of their vibration?
False parameters [of] a magnetic field wave—aura in your words.

Q: What follows this procedure?
Magnetic field set-up procedure set forth. An understanding of magnetudinal force proceed[s] by each individual entity. Correction of *all* fields under way.

The variance board is an area in which the entity's deviation from the allowable parameters is measured, or evaluated, in order to diagnose problems in one's magnetic force field. The corrections are made on an individual basis, within their subatomic and magnetic fields.

The following lesson came after yet another event, in which several people were killed, many more injured. The higher self is expressed as Self, capitalized; the physical self is uncapitalized.

Earth under severe crisis of Self-identity. None can judge the other: all fit within the criterion box. Constance of inept judgments upon each other constitutes irrationality on the human plane. No value on all sides, feeding each other misery of misconceptive truths. All are equal in the corruptive behavior attained in this situation, no one individual outstanding. Percolation of malcommunication exists on all parameters. Act caused by delusionment and loss of value on all planes of the human existence; not one individual cause. Human evaluation disintegration, completing itself.

Kent explains, "It is the totality of what we have *all* created. It felt completely non-judgmental."

A war is coming.

Q: Who would this war be between?
Self, within self. Quanticeptive judgment. Qualiceptive judgment: quanticeptive judgment.

Q: What can we learn from this war?
Self-attainment.

Q: Can you help us understand ideologies associated with terrorism?
A magnificent misfortune for humanity. Clarity unbeholding to the understanding and the reasoning of humanity—no longer acceptable. Prolific culmination of self; unrealistic by natural law.

Our understanding: Humanity is under an identity crisis. No one can judge the other: we are all implicated; we are all intertwined. Where we are currently, individually and collectively, in a general sense, is the sum-total of all previous decision-making. The manner in which we are treating one another affects the reality of who we think we are, resulting in the disillusionment and loss of value for the entire human race, causing our implosion from within. The war is within ourselves. It is the disconnect between the higher self and our physical self playing out on the world screen with the culmination of the lower physical self, unconcerned with natural laws.

The goal now is to come to know, align to and attain the higher self. To understand who we are at our very core, why we are here and to see our mission with clarity. This *is* the Self-realization.

The fight between the light and the dark

There is a fight on both sides.

Q: Is this a fight between light and dark?
Yes.

Q: What is the dark side trying to accomplish?
Trying to stop the opening.

Q: Why do they want to stop it?
It will further the closing of this world and begin the transformation of the next. 'Preventing the God's return, that's what we are trying to do.' The ones that used to be here, the new ones have taken their place.

Kent elaborates, "When the opening occurs, they can no longer come here. It will shift to a higher form and they will lose their power."

Lower level vibration entities trying to interfere with the enlightenment movement out of fear that they won't be able to reincarnate back to Earth. Many are trying to move others in the wrong direction—they are being used.

Q: Who are they being used by?
Vibrational manipulation without their knowledge, due to the lack of understanding; a continuous event operation...Lazy to cause. Happy in a box, in a bag, on this sphere. Evidence of insignificant value given on a magnitudinal concept on this planet. Duality of singularity is not apprehended, except by conceptual beings—very few here. Human arrogance devoids this concept.

Q: Will this change in the near future?

Only upon severe thunderings of events, creating humbleness required to understand universal concepts and equivalence that hold these concepts. Not many—prevalence of attitude is wrong, or encouraged, and incorrect.

Q: How would we explain the universe is neutral, yet there are positive and negative entities?

All the universe are *not* neutral. Neutrality exists on a plane of understanding; [an] on-going process for *all* cultures.

Wrong is he who deceives all that want to learn. There are those in the field that want to detain the thoughts of others.

Q: How can humans ward off entities who control their thoughts?

Absolute truth-finding. Given the consequence that those that live in a fabricated world, they hear nothing but their own thoughts. Absolute detention of proverbial thinking process. A lubrication of self-thought. Stay with truth; it deflects all other beings.

Q: Why have certain populations declined into violence, crime and non-progression?

Meaningful task for self-annihilation within their sphere of understanding. [A] consequence of self-mutilation to release cause and effect. Varying level beyond recognition of value within this realm; only magnified on spiritual level. Physical non-compliance with spiritual understanding; not belonging here beyond this point of conciliatory progression to understanding. Purpose: to relinquish physical constraints provided by others outside their parametal sphere in this conscriptatory place.

Release of themselves from unrealistic parameters born within this sphere.

Ramification of understanding with the profusion and injection of quantification, with the physical being and enlightenment of man, soon to be.

Kent comments: "Man thinks he knows it all. The negative vibrations, which continually flow from mankind, has expanded, like the ripples from a pebble dropped into the water, to the point of affecting the universe and its vibrational symphony."

Our understanding: Ignorant to the universal consciousness and the higher level of truth available, man's thoughts are further manipulated by negative entities. Positive entities seek to expand universal consciousness; negative entities try to block it. Happy in a box, people are too lazy to put the effort forward to gain a higher understanding. The evidence lies in the extreme value man gives to the insignificant and the material world. Most humans believe that we are autonomous individuals. Very few understand that we are all a part of one networking conscious field and that everything is connected. Arrogance does not allow the human race to understand this concept. The priority of truth-seeking acts as a deflector to the manipulating entities. Even so, it does not guarantee that they will not try and we must always be aware of their possible influence until the vibrational changes are complete and they are pushed out.

Within the inner cities, and some other areas as well, we see a rise in violence and disintegration of society. Have these people unconsciously decided to self-destruct to release themselves from the unreasonable life parameters put upon them? Their true learning will be magnified only within the spiritual realm, as they are unwilling or unable to overcome their own hostility regarding their circumstances to gain the higher understanding while here.

On the horizon, a new period of enlightenment is developing, branching out and injecting a massive amount of understanding into

40

the human race. A new paradigm is manifesting itself.

Man has options

The sky, an infinite tranquil cover; besieged by man's incessant curiosity to explore.

Man has always been given options but has not been prudent with them. His dusty feet are steadfast. His movements are not precise; they are slow. Perceive[s] things as undertakings, other than an opportunity. Quest and thirst can be one. Ascertain your abilities. Project the understanding. Manifest your sights. Leave what you have.

Quintao: the course to gain access to the inaccessible. Chivalry was a misperception—it never has existed. Man is too obsessed with his oneness, does not know how to bequeath his love to others.

Alchemy is a method to reduce something, which covers up the truth. Deception of the truth to get you to look away on another path. Alchemist is a deceiver; make[s] you feel and give[s] you a perception that things are good—a cover.

In this sense, the alchemist diminishes the value of the truth, guiding others to look in another direction, away from the reality of the situation. The alchemist gives the illusion that things are good, masking what is really happening.

Man should blame self

Pervasive intelligence is a prelude to stop judgments. You are caught in the ecstasy of abundance. Tribulation will bring evasive judgments. Many will make wrong choices. All will have a chance. Creatures are smart: they follow the life's pattern. Connective cognizance is a pervasive congruent judgment. Ridicule will be exact; ostracization of many will take place.

Kent describes a vision, "I saw people criticizing others, causing turmoil and violence. People will turn their backs on each other. Help is not to be found. Many of the original cultures shall unite. They still have some knowledge of ancient ways in books and mind."

> Strength is in the cognizance of recognized perception; purveyance of/per fortitude. This is to stimulate perception of incongruity. All are displeased. Congruence of/to realities: hide the truth by many government's purveyance and the aptitude of ignorance. Shift to the Light.

Our mental and emotional strength will arise out of the recognition of our misled perception, shining a light on the inconsistencies. Consistent with reality: the government has been hiding the truth and we have been ignorant to it.

> The threshold of ignorance is about to be met. Man's propensity for misguided understanding will face awakening from within—will begin to prevail. Neonatal positioning will not prevail, although used. Man should blame self for allowing those in government to supersede all universal concepts of living things. You have choices. Concepts are distorted to relevance to self-interest [and] speak of the wave of conscript; conscript of distortion. Platitudes surpass evidence—will mislead by all. Waves of distortion provided throughout, separating all living things.

Our own self-interests are compelling us into a distorted view of concepts. We have allowed those in government to replace the supremacy of the universal concepts that govern all life. This imbalance exists throughout our world, separating all living things.

> Movements within this sphere will begin to materialize. Young ones can tap the understanding of higher dimensional vibration. The seventh dimension will come into being for understanding conceptual relevance to man's advancement.

> Destruction of Earth is irrelevant, nor will it be. A distortion wave that hits the earth will cause man to fail their minds, their minds depleting themselves of life as you know it. But not the end of the essence. A new learning they must go through in order to bring correctness to the tonial vibrations, which make up their essence. You are but a very tiny part of the concept of existence.

> Eagles flourish beyond your particle self in the overall realm of ongoing events [and] perpetuate vibrational movements throughout the universal systems. You put too high of a level on your very small understanding, very small of the whole.

The spirit world designates those who are of the eagle essence: those who have the ability and the desire to go to a much higher level of vibrational understanding of All That Is.

> The creeping disease will over-take the concepts of man. The disease is self-perpetuating oneness. Oneness of self-indulgence, not the Oneness of universal connectivity.

> Humanity is moving to a crescendo of emotion, at which time the gods will intercede.

Kent clarifies, "They call themselves gods because we called them gods. They are trying to protect this planet. It is the ignorance of the humans that called them gods, rather than respect the higher intelligence and learning."

Our understanding: Humanity is now moving toward a crescendo of events that will be allowed to play out to push us into the next level of vibrational understanding. We are here to study vibration. Everything is vibration: the material world, energy, light, events and our thoughts. The events that manifest are the result of our own decision-making, based on our current comprehension. Cause and effect create the consequences that, upon reflection, create a new conscious level. The new understanding opens the door to our awakening and a reconnection with other beings not of here, who are waiting to deliver a new teaching for man. This will begin the new cycle of conceptual learning, pushing man forward and reuniting humanity with other universal beings in a teacher-student relationship.

A change in the hologram

Truth to the realm of being: causation understood by only a few. Truth is desirable only on an unrealistic plane. Humans live in unreality, where untruth survives. Experimental damage has been completed to the human consciousness. I have beset the truth of unconscious behavior. Humanity is beset by the untruth of All That Is; have beset the untruth. The crystallization of mankind into conscious behavior of truth has missed their mark. The power of greed has become more generating.

Q: What caused the damage to the human consciousness?
Not to those that want to learn. The lower beings' DNA forward lapse retrieved: a lapse in consciousness prohibited learning.

44

Q: Why do some people have a lower DNA expression?
Experimentation in each kind.

Q: Does this go back to the original making of mankind?
No, recent movement.

Q: What caused it?
Repercussion of human. Relapse in understanding the value of Self. Perpetration needed for curvature of a DNA procurement.

Q: What has to occur to procure the DNA?
Truth is accepted.

We will help retrieve this planet back to animal desires—excluding humans. Scherlong, scherlong to atmospheric conditions—will prevail. The waters will widen. Many species will fall in numbers, while others rise in numbers.

A balance is proceeding: The crumbling of courts, giving way to new waters; many lost in their sphere for abundance. Acularian process—in denial—will accomplish the residual task in Creative influence upon man's path, man's pathway. Ocularian at hand to intercept the event cause; a complex situation made simple.

The exposition still continues, eradication of the program will cease. Feed the program—exponential results.

Q: What is the program?
Hologram. Humans create their own hologram from their perceptions of what *should* be: illusionary of thought.

Q: How do we feed the program?
Positive thought patterns: introduction of new material.

Q: Are we to increase the release of information?
Dissemination of information is important right now. A concrete inhabitance of information is at hand.

Q: Which topics are most important to release at this time?
Topics of inquiry: illusion of the value here on this plane. Triceptical in nature: illusionary as perceived by the perceiver, authoritic in written form, a perception of non-truth is achieved for the unbeliever. Acquiesce to the truth of this perceptive value.

Our understanding: A multitude of events are unfolding in our field of vision, soon to destroy our misperceptions. Positive thought patterns are those that bring a new and truthful understanding. It sheds light on our misperceptions, written works and our own denial of truth. A new organization of atomic structure, starting with a change in the atmosphere, begins the process. It will change the template for how life forms are expressed here on Earth, causing many species to die off, replaced with a rise in new life forms, genetically attuned to Earth's new vibration. Many will be lost within their sphere of abundance, not aligned to the true purpose of being here. The muddied waters will be replaced by clean and pure water. Our denial of what we hear will accomplish the final tasks, the Creative influence intercepting to redirect humanity's path back to the true course of learning.

Release the bonds of distraction

Humanity has lost its purpose in the distraction of the material and political worlds. This distraction has caused the division world-wide within the human race. You cannot change the world's perception of these distractions. But you can begin to understand why these distractions occur, which increases your understanding of why you are here. Why is mankind still not believing in themselves? The exponential treatment of each other creates a learning diameter. When the understanding is not learned, chaos ensues.

We do not expect the civilized world, in general, to know why they are here. I used the word *civilized* because there is a variance between the natives of countries and those that *think* they want to be better. The indigenous of any country, who are still attached to their cause, know the understanding of man upon this plane. Those indigenous who understand are two percent of the world's population. Has this always been like this? No.

The human race has boxed themselves in to only understand the perception of another. The truth is trying to raise its head, but perception prevails, creating uncertainty, division and chaos within the human race. Are you willing to step forward? Begin releasing yourself from the chaotic bonds that surround you and begin to understand and act on why you are here on Earth. Think about this. Are you willing to follow the guidance that is given within you to a higher level of understanding within yourself?

I'm not here to change your minds; you must change it within yourselves. I'm only here to awaken you.

Human arrogance

Love All That Is and humble yourself in front of All That Is. You cannot influence the Creator's path. You can only adhere and flow with what is and what is to be—[a] constant reminder on how small but significant to the continued process to universal progress—[the] production of matter and kind.

Arrogance of self is taught, but other's views of your existence [is] contrary to the readologies given by humankind. You are a virus, as compared to the complete universal microcosm. Don't let yourselves be bigger than your actual value. Your conceptual understanding of who you are, the human race, is not complete. An occultarian view is sustained by the perceptual matter of self-indulgence, placating your own humanity and strident pleasure. We are speaking of the human race in these concepts. Love of All That Is, is important. Understanding of All That Is, is important.

Reality-based perceptions of universal law and self-indulgence of a higher perceptual value do not correlate. You cannot change what is to be. Fear is an indulgence in self-flowing myopic structural concepts. Yours is a riddle of time for all races and cultural aspects. Time is valueless with meaning of worth and the value of self-power, which do not exist except in the neuronetical field of others' perceptions, based upon the view of their literal, not ethereal, surroundings. Propagate away: of the self-thought.

The hard-line viruses will conjugate the flow of this perception of value, stroking the human ego, fraudulently derived of a higher Source. Source is actual only on its terms, not human identity to individual thought of self. An occultarian view from pretentious instinct can occur if not attached to a plasmatic field of a higher geometrical pattern, which includes the concepts of all universal laws of life and thought.

Rely not on human theology-incorporated self-worth—we will call this 'religion of self-value'—to ascend and descend upon others with misguidance and non-credence to the values of the universal etheric flow of energy patterns. Self-indulgence precludes these false-realization shadows: the true value of spiritual exploration [is] within one's own experience. Crustacean progress covers one's own ethereal existence, when relying outside self-realization and allowing other myopscopic viruses to invade their space and neuronetical field with unrealization patterns of self-thought.

Pretentious humans cannot change what is. Though purity is obtained within this planet, not enough purity [exists] to sustain a correctional redirection. Pretentious, egotistical hope is maintained at a constant processive level by the unrealistic mind-set, preserved by unrealistic higher self-value. This does not exist here. 'Look at me.' 'My' importance is valueless. Beyond value precedes this concept. This is not from universal concept of All That Is.

Ready your serenity. Bow to a conceptual behavior of all those that oversee the universe. Release your myopic thought of who you think you are. Love is essential outside; bring outside in this sphere.

Sagarian aspects—on a subterranean culture—are important to a valued existence of this sphere; planet by your words. Speak the truth, adhere to the thought of truth. Waver not in these concepts.

There exists a subterranean culture on Earth—the true indigenous peoples—who possess a much higher degree of understanding than humans. They are the ones who create the value of this planet. In the future—providing we give up our warring ways—they will become our teachers.

Separating the human consciousness from the ego

Be sure to mention the Native American—Lacota, Hopi, Apache, Mohawk, Iroquois—their leadership [and] importance of leaders in teaching those that don't know the way in the coming trials. Be sure to instruct the importance of their relationship to the ancient ways and the Creator, to instructing the whites.

A connective distillation of the spirit from the human ego, the spirit has to manifest its own reality in connection to the vibrational resonance about Earth. Protective shield will manifest, brought on by indigenous throughout the earth in many places. Distillation of human consciousness and human spirit, separated from the human perspective of dignity, which they have contrived [to] meet their existing level of egotistical behavior. Letting go of who they see and bringing forth of their ancient essence; a conjugal of consciousness by itself. An essence of spirit cheats the intertwining of the corn and bean; connection of the earths' spirit releasing the essence of their captive behavior.

The flow of the spirit behavior must be smooth and rippleless, must be subjective to learning and teaching to the very core depth of the human spirit.

We do not want to speak to all who meditate. Their subjective values are not relevant to the core precepts of what they want to discover. So they manifest their own phraseology, thereby falsely increasing their enlightenment: of self-worth. Continue your analogous analytical behavior. Create a consequence of understanding. Do not be trapped into human characteristical behavior as an understanding or relationship to spiritual magnetical behavior. Creation of the self-vibrational field outside their spiritual essence [is] a strong consequence of egotistical influence on their vibrational field. Self-indulgence, unrecognized by many, is perceived as spiritual. This vibration can be increased through the manifestation of the mind precepts. Not [a] truthful consequence, a form of manipulative manifestation.

Two knives: one serrated, one straight. When someone is not aligned: tracing the serrated edge. When aligned: trace the straight edge. Man creates their own entities to go against their own transformation.

Our understanding: Humanity is influenced greatly by the ego. This egotistical vibration is cast upon the field around our physical bodies, disconnected from our true spiritual essence. We create our own words and concepts to stoke the ego, magnifying our importance in our own minds. We are manifesting our goals in a manipulative way. Though done in the name of spiritual growth, the behavior denies our true enlightenment. The true path is possessing the humbleness required to seek guidance from our higher self and the universal beings that are beyond our scope, while, at the same time, connecting with the vibrational resonance of Earth.

Earth will be pushed into the next era

Who are we but lesser of many? We hold the truth in our hand. Precarious results be derived from suspicious behavior. A new dawn—the challenge! Enlightened ones help those without. Create your own destiny through auspicious behavior. Graveyards will arise through resuscitation of the spirit.

Peaceful, quiet, heat vibrations. Like a tornado, but it is not fierce. The vortex will arise and spread over the land and calm those that are not. The energies will replace the negative vibrations created by those that are now gone. Serenity will prevail. Auspicious presumption.

Man will perceive one another as an extension: existence of their past from other places. A new reality will prevail. Pretentiousness will no longer arise. New values are conceptual to the realities of man's true being. The effervescence of perception to the truth will flow in the veins of man, creating a new concept in appreciation of who they are and where they come from.

Negativism will not be tolerated. It will be dealt with by outsiders directing the change. Part of the universal change for the enlightenment of the universe. A connective tissue of the whole—not standing alone—a small part of the whole. You are but a small sequential item of the whole, but you reflect on the ability of the whole universe. Man has turned his face from the Creator of the universe. He believes nothing. The quintessence of his arrogance creates a vibrational disdain of taste.

Rise to the simplicity of innocence. Rise to the consequential being. Rise to the value of Self-worth, the truth of inoculation, a being of just. Peace be around you and justify Self as One. Listen. Do not perpetuate misunderstandings or misconceptions. Peace be with you. The inoculus is the understanding of the Great One; serendipitous behavior of all that surround the energy of the Great One.

The consequential being

The proclivity of man is at hand. His ability to destroy himself equates to misperception of truth. Serendipitous by nature; serrated by character. Man's discontent on self, projected in the world screen; disingenuous to all. Man has shadowed the Creator to a second level of diety. Cornucopia is within—the Creator is the basket. Horrendous are the diatribes given by man's affluence over each other.

Ardent behavior: a consequence from Universal Law and Ordinance. We have captured the essence of various entities to arrive the DNA that will propel an understanding with community. The laws of consequence will prevail the new species. Welcome to the next emergence; we will be waiting.

Astuteness prevails. Prepare a place: your understanding is consequential. Learn the wisdom of natural law. Keep truth at center.

Seeking is the virtue to learning. Open to those that are seeking. Knowledge is abundant only when applied to one seeking the truth. Seek those looking for answers. Relevance to abundance is questionable. Abundance does not equate to the amount of those around you, but to the purity of the souls seeking the right way. Importance is your teaching to new seekers, not quantifying yourselves to those that follow with already abundant knowledge. Time to move on to new understanding.

Kent further explains: "The group of those who somewhat understand, but think they know—it's like preaching to the choir. Their energy as a group is over-shadowed by the intense energy of the one seeking the truth with an open mind—they are thirsty."

The above was our personal guidance, but we believe it delivers a valuable understanding of how other entities recognize when one is ready to learn, and so warrants being included in this book.

Verdiance: thirst for truth.

Q: Does the word verdiance mean truth?
Correct! Hold true to the meaning. All truth should be held to the true value that truth is. Consequential behavior will succumb to non-truth teaching. Stay with the values of intellectual understanding. Time is short, as time is measured by man's irrational thinking. The value of time is only of value to oneself that relates to a particular event dictated by oneself.

Consequential events create the appropriate flow of energy that can compensate for all directional corrections, as needed, to accomplish required tasks. Do not preclude options of understanding. Negative can mean a positive to flow values, as seen from the whole. Do not preclude presumed negative options. Obstructing the flow is the only discourse, creating no value to any procedural event. Confirming an outcome helps create directional flow to final completion of needed requirements. Over-analysis can be dangerous, superfluous to the outcome. Simplicity rests on the backs of *neutral* behavior, relating to the flow of energy; the path to be completed by all those attaining the needed end. Narcissistic behavior of carefully created thought no value here.

Every time has its purpose of beginning. Help will be evaluated when it is needed. Help will be given when time is adjusted, not before. Must adhere to the rules of consequence. Consequence of events must take place. This is as before, millennia ago. A cycle will reappear, giving birth to causation and effect.

Our understanding: As we enter the next cycle, the laws of consequence will guide our growing understanding and developing astuteness. Our learning is consequential *and* sequential, each event building upon the last. The learning must include an open mind and an acceptance of truth, the whole truth, irrelevant to what we *want* to see.

The next cycle of conceptual learning will include the laws of consequence. These are universal laws that ensure the appropriate flow of energy through corrections in our directional behavior. It is necessary to accomplish the tasks for why we exist: our ever-expanding conscious development. Obstructing the flow of consequences only serves to divert us off our path, creating no value to any event that occurs. Reflection upon the outcome of an event—born of our own decisions—allows for a greater understanding and subsequent correction of our thought process and behavior. The new cycle will give birth to a restoration of the true learning field of cause and effect.

Beginning of the next phase

Exonerating platitude will be the misfortune of the calming concepts of the people: serendipity of [the] government's misfortunes, of allegations quantipitous. Man needs to exonerate the Omniscient One from cause. They say *He* causes. Not true. *The cycle causes.* Legends abound. The Omniscient One *oversees*.

Perceptions of stupidicious overrides the realities of perfect intact quiescence: liability of none, to the pervasiveness of many to the reality that will set in when the oscillation of perpetuousness begins.

Perplexing behavior of man makes it difficult to direct the changes ensured for man. The enlightened ones will guide. Man be hated, man be hunted by those of disdained vibrational occurrences that surround him. They are the perplexing, disconnected culmination of negative vibrational occurrences that are happening today. They boast of their insincerity and their courageous deceit. They defeat their intent to live: pseudo-essence.

A serendipitous attitude will quell the awakening of others. Sarcaustic sleep is an aptitude of mankind, the human race. Narcolysis presenting himself to the quantum understanding of the universal conceptual being that will be arriving soon to perpetuate the coming change of the beings on this sphere.

Q: Does sarcaustic hold the same meaning as sarcastic?
Same relation, meaning caustic in nature.

Tremendous opportunity for change; lackluster performance. Thought entities will be pushing forward to increase those with reception, perceptual rehabilitation of the mind thought, new concordance of understanding.

Our understanding: There exists an attitude among some people that the transformation will be quick and easy, transforming our world to a state of Utopia almost overnight, serendipitously. This attitude is incorrect and will actually impede the awakening of others. We are presented with much opportunity for change, yet lack the enthusiasm or the work ethic to make it happen. The human race is caught up in a caustic state of sleep, soon to be released by Narcolysis as he perpetuates the coming changes to humanity, awakening us to the reality of what exists. Other entities will increase the numbers of people who will be able to receive communication, rehabilitating humanity's thought processes.

There is a developing field and much is changing without our notice. It is a laborious, concerted effort among many in the universe to make these changes. It is only when all is complete that we will suddenly take notice. This will seem to have taken place overnight and effortlessly. But, we assure you, it will not have; we will have just awakened.

A new dawn

A quanticeptive agreement has been reached. The new dawn approaches. Co-lingering among those that dwell within the longerian sphere—which is the influence of unperceptive values—fifth not to fold within itself. Acceleration [of] astuteness, hold to its comprehensive value now.

Kent explains *unperceptive*, "It is not based on perception."

Q: What is the fifth in reference to?
World; octarian by nature. Laborious will prevail its natural way of Self-infusion of the Self-diagnostic entity to exist. A diagnostic of the internal being is coming to the new order. Movement beyond recognition of now-circumference dictated by human race. Cross-contamination of species a laborious

effect upon the close of this cycle.

Hold your course, Creative aptitude will begin; causation to understanding prelapse.

Non-communicative abilities by humans increasing, open parameters to next step. Slow dictation of variances angulated to complete concept.

Q: Non-communicative abilities open parameters to which next step?
A communicative process directing all entities to a conceptual movement.

Our understanding: The fifth world, according to the Hopi Native Americans, is the next cycle humanity is moving into. Each previous cycle ended in a major catastrophe, closing the door on a society that had morphed into corruption and forgotten its Creator. Those who had followed the spiritual path and listened to their guidance survived to start a new cycle, where man, once again, placed their focus on the Creator.

We will have to spend much time reflecting on the past, and our part in it, so that understanding of all factors leading to the culmination of the state of our society today is well-understood. Much work is being done to bring human genetics forward upon the close of this cycle so that a higher conceptual value can be realized in the human race.

Understanding must be brought forward

Rapidivious, rapidivious: the movement of a rapid-spreading word with a caution of understanding. Solace, solace to the individual that mourns Self and pities denial of its own conscience. A crusade of afterthought will prevail the upcoming events. Serendipitous behavior continues to the end; farcical as to the understanding of the character of those that will try to prevail. Man is too close—like an ear is too close to the drum—cannot hear the true beat: rhythm of universal vibrations.

All is the creators of the world—worrisome. Man is creating the world he lives in. This is not negative, *this is the positive change.*

Precarious times are ahead—irrelevance prevails. Even the enlightened ones have ignorance. The innocent ones are the ones to teach. The enlightened ones are too caught up in their enlightenment. Enlightenment is a cause, not a responsibility. To be one with enlightenment is a cause to [be] one with a group, but is not responsible for true universal enlightenment. Many are cause but no effect. Bragging rights prevail. Uniform materialism is at hand. Quasi-fractional understanding is a common moment among those who are impervious, except to their own limited thought.

Horrendous appetites are those that refrain from the truth. Experience the love that surrounds you, saturate yourselves of the true vibrational nature of Earth Mother. Welcome the experience of exceptional understanding. Your hearts must be free of thought [and] cumbersome values of a materialistic nature. Success is based on your ability to freely flow the vibrational entities that surround you. Bring forth your inquisitiveness. Create a cornerstone, a cognitive influence to the understanding of the dimensional change that will be influenced by the magnitudinal shift to come.

The pond of life will expand to mirror the vibrational output of universal reflections to absorb lost times of consequential information that must be attained to continue the pattern of life itself, a reflection on DNA past.

Our understanding: Our survival as a species depends on our ability to change, to constantly evolve in our level of understanding, modifying our behavior as we go. The absence of the laws of consequence requires we must make up for lost time to bring our consequential understanding forward.

Truth changes with events

Truth: there is no future truth. The truth is what is happening right now. It's like a map of the past to see the truth and non-truth. The truth is what is happening at each moment within the time continuum. There is no future truth because truth has not been designed until it happens. Truth is a fleeting value based on each event that happens, whether it be a large event or individual event. Truth is as each individual sees the event. Therefore, it is a fleeting value based on each individual's perception.

Q: How would you recommend an evaluation of truth?
It's an individual's perception of what they see or hear. You may agree with all the event. You may agree to partial; what you are seeing here to the event. You may not agree with any of the event. That's why it's perceptive.

Q: How do other universal entities evaluate the truth?
All are different. All based on perceptive value, except for a small, very small, group, which bases what they see and hear on the Creator.

Q: Does this small group communicate directly with Creator for their understanding?
Yes, higher value of Source prerequisite for understanding. Cognizant value of Self determines the value of your truth.

Q: Can you elaborate on the cognizant value of Self?
How you feel your value is within this sphere; abstract at best.

Q: As cognizance expands, do we see a greater depth of truth?
No, a change in its value.

Q: So, the value we place on the information changes?
Changes with events.

Our understanding: With the exception of those that communicate directly with the Creator—the Ancients—the rest of creation views truth through the eyes of perception, with various degrees of accuracy. We analyze the truth of each unfolding event based on what is seen in the current moment. Along a linear timeline, as events unfold and as we add to our data collection, we discover a more expanding picture. We may choose to agree with all, part, or none of the event, depending on what we are willing to accept. The data we have already gathered is influenced by our background environment—the way we were raised and what we have been exposed to—and dictates the basis for how we perceive events in our life. Truth is also dependent on the understanding of ourselves, our neutrality or biases, and what value we assign to our conscious understanding.

Finding the perfect truth

Go quietly, walk in peaceful steps. Surround yourself with a vibration of truth and quiet. No matter where people are, they must start to recognize the value of the environment and what's happening.

Quit listening to soothsayers. Too much attention is being given to soothsayers. Look around, be inquisitive and be within. Quit looking for answers with the soothsayers. Your perfection cannot be completed by using the imperfect people. *Your* imperfections are good because it will propel you toward finding the perfect truth. Read books of knowledge and wisdom of ancient cultures that still created their corrections through the Omnicient One. The ancients were guided on correctional paths through ceremonial ordinances that have been lost by most.

You have relived your anxieties by releasing your connection to the Creator and the Laws of Ceremonial Credence. Ratify the ancient ways, regain knowledge of ancient events. This a precursor to universal *and* Self-understanding. Wisdom does not come with understanding; understanding comes with wisdom. Fortuitous events will happen for all. Replenish your gourd with the liquid truth of the universal essence, of all humanity and entities that connect all together. Lies have become truth and the truth have become lies.

A consequence of misunderstanding is also a consequence of self-indulgence of misperceptions. Prognosticators abound as a result. The value of truth becomes irrelevant to their objective. A manipulation of time-thought.

You need to back away from the world that inoculates you to misunderstanding, that does not give you the truth—the everyday world.

Prepare and know the words. Stay within the frame of knowing and understanding. Perpetuate Self-confidence and rise your vibration to a higher level constantly. Peace will be with you. Do not back away from obsurdity; face it straight on. Truth must prevail.

Kent, "One professor keeps saying:"

Perception, perception, perception. Negative perception. And truth is so easy. It's easier to practice negative than positive, it takes work otherwise. Man is lazy.

"He says we can recreate the rings around us and everything and strengthen them; the rings of white consciousness."

Reach out to Q. The truth is the narrative of Gods' Self. Besieged, the oppression of man. Counteract with love. We cannot stress this enough. New peoples of truth rise. Quenine: the elucidence of affinity. Renaissance is inevitable.

Truth is a consequence of understanding. Acquiesce to the truth. Your perception is what you make it, causing delusion. Truth, a consequence of indirect behavior.

Kent explains, "You can only be neutral if you understand your surroundings and watch. You cannot be neutral just by not being political. When they talk about being neutral, they are talking about life in general. You have to look at everything, the whole environment around you, neutrally."

Neutrality and love procure truth

Q: What do we teach others who are looking?
Neutralism—between truth and untruth. It captures the essence of reality.

Q: How is that?
People live between truth and untruth; a constance of life's reality.

Words should not fall upon deaf ears. A portrait should be painted of surrealious understanding. It has to have a credence of the flow of information to create an understanding of value and significance. One paragraph is more valuable than a complete book if the only concept understood is the one paragraph, which completes the understanding of the new value of the complete book, which may fall on deaf ears.

Q: How do we handle situations in which people are confrontational to the information we are teaching?
Teach neutrality, because there are no winners. Only neutral. Teach neutrality. Teach the understanding of love, how to understand it. Be prepared to teach understanding. Deflect. The truth is open to understanding. Deflect those with truth *to* understanding. A valueless society is overtaken causing nomeric understanding to, a principle cause of their plight.

Neutrality of nature brings cause for perceptual agreements to your being. Humble your attitude toward Self.

Truth occupies all. Love beyond seeing—your variance in conception not yet attained by humans.

Q: What is the universal definition of love?

Love All That Is. Not emotional. Must be neutral to love All That Is. No field can penetrate this cause. Penetration of incident will cause human distortion of truth—[a] pervasive augmentation of fact—a perceptual ideological creation of self. Incidental decision is causing a procedural event in human society. Neutrality only existence for this race— quanticeptical. Fear is overtaking the presence of neutrality among the culture.

Q: Does this accentuate the polarities?

No, neutralizes their value. Accentuates the Self-worth as a reflection of a society of worth. Neutrality becomes a complex issue when one is polarized, even though it is simple. Complexity of natural law is given to those within the neutral realm of understanding. Open the theoretical discovery. Those that practice neutrality of self are the true leaders of mankind. Provincial influence is evaluated at the cost of human lives. Rest your thoughts this day; you'll procure events as they happen.

May all understanding be with you and keep you strong in your quest through peace.

The intent of the last question was, "does fear accentuate the polarities?" The answer, however, was based on the word *neutrality*. It is only when we remain neutral enough to be able to study the entirety of any given event that diffuses the polarities and accentuates the conscious value of the higher self. It relates to our cognitive ability. It is a reflection of a society that values the higher understanding. Polarity develops when we only see one side of any given issue, refusing to see the entire picture. Neutrality opens the learning field and brings peace. Neutrality and peace allow us to love everything and everyone that exists. This enables us to view everything as a learning opportunity and everyone as our teacher, regardless of how different from us they might appear. That is when our real learning begins.

Don't expect the Creator to change the world if you are not willing to change yourself

NOTES

Chapter 3

✦———•••———✦

The Shift

The following inquiries about the universe sought to answer some of the questions generated since the printing of *The Augmentation of Man: A Study in Renaissance*. Our spiritual guidance answers those questions, then takes a turn, revealing to us the magnitude of changes affecting not only the earth, but the entire universe and beyond. The transformation is far more than anyone could have guessed, supported by a labor-intensive collaboration of other beings.

The universes: a correctional understanding

Q: Has there been more than one "big bang," as some scientists believe?
A progressive appearance: only one, creating a progressive appearance of more than one.

Q: What is dark matter?
The core of the universe. The universal correlation of the communicative process. All flows through a pattern of understanding a communicative Source to those who perceive it, given the rationale of universal substance. A Creative energy is set forth as what is known as the black hole of matter and communication—matter being a conductive material for the communicative process to take place. We are here to substantiate the existence in the universe—more than one. Beware of the holdings that last but an eventful period. The communicative process is everlasting since the beginning of All That Is.

In the meditation that follows, May of 2018, Kent describes seeing groups of universes. He could not determine if it was groups of seven universes, in larger groups of three, or groups of three to seven universes; multiplied by many times. We had previously been told there were seven universes, as was printed in the first book, *The Augmentation of Man: A Study in Renaissance.*

Kent began, "We are smaller than we think."

Q: Are there more than the seven universes, as we were previously taught?
Yes. You are not ready for this; a correctional understanding within your field.

Q: Do they work in groups of three, like the galaxies?
Correct. Do not go beyond your comprehension.

Q: What are the total number of universes?
More than you can comprehend at this time.

Q: What are the other two galaxies in *our* triad?
Voltarean region.

Q: What occurs in the galactic center of our Milky Way?
Proton release, isospheric particles: [a] mixture. Random set of numerical values released.

Q: What does this create?
Change of address.

Q: An orbital change?
Correct.

Our understanding: We often have been introduced to new principles, believing it to encompass the entirety of the subject, only later to discover it was only the beginning. Learning comes in sequential steps. We are given basic building blocks of information and more is added as we comprehend and assimilate what had previously been received. In this case, we were told there were seven universes and, within each universe, the galaxies are grouped in sets of three; two galaxies rotating in one direction, the third rotating in the opposite to create balance. We came to understand that the seven universes comprised the totality of Creation. That was only the beginning.

All structures within the universe support the movement of universal consciousness in a propagation of Creative energy, the Light, that passes from one structure to the next, one entity to the next, through connecting charged atoms within a vast communicating nerve-like network known as Source and the neuronet. These structures include all the universes, the nebulae, comets and, yes, even the black holes. Creative entities and Creative energy manifest the Creator's directive for expanding consciousness through this communication network; fulfilling the purpose of All That Is.

In **chapter 12** of *The Augmentation of Man: A Study in Renaissance*, the lessons tell us that the planetary orbits will change to some degree, based on mathematical calculations by ciphers of the Creator, to reinstate balance in the universe. There will also be a change in Earth's axis to correct the wobble. Of course, when this happens, our viewing of the sky above us will change, thus explaining the biblical meaning of "a new heaven and Earth." The new planetary alignment will change the vibrational resonance between the planetary bodies, creating new and higher vibrational learning fields throughout creation.

Star systems taking their points

We will occasionally give the dates of the reading so that the reader can gain an understanding of the timing of the process taking place. In our personal experience, we generally are given notice when an energy is released, but do not see the manifestation of the event it creates until later. This creates a time lapse. The following message was received in February 2013:

The octagon is being set in place.

Q: What is the significance?
The stars have aligned to themselves; the galaxy is shifting. The octagon is being set in place.

Kent added, "It has something to do with everything lining up."

Q: Can you tell us more about how this octagon works?
Star systems taking their points. Each system sits on a point that forms the octagon that begins universal movement.

Q: Is this within this universe only?
No. Representation of *all* universes. Shift magnitudinal power—all systems. Prophesy: a new quadraplex. Research strength of the galaxy. Stay focused—major gains to come—be, stay focused. Pyramids more important than Maya legend and prophesy. A complete solarization of the planet: The Light that gives this planet the direction it flows.

Our understanding: A shift of star systems within the universes is taking place. Within the new alignment, each one of eight star systems is moving to an assigned point that, collectively, form the eight points of an octagon. The new arrangement has a direct vibrational influence on Earth and her inhabitants—and possibly other planets within the universe—in the form of a higher degree of learning within the new cycle. This creates a new structural network that directs the flow of energy to a higher level of universal consciousness. The mentor is telling us that prophesy has spoken of a time—a new heaven and Earth—where our view of the sky will change in respect to the changing orbits and axial shift of the earth.

In our research, the strength of the galaxy might be measured in the amount of hydrogen it contains, which is about 92 percent. This hydrogen provides the fuel for the suns to create thermonuclear fusion, ejecting an enormous amount of energy into space. Our guides have indicated that increased activity of our sun produces changes in our gaseous atmosphere, forming a new template for all life expression on this sphere. This template has a direct impact on gene expression that varies depending on exposure rates, as we will see later in this chapter. The pyramids may have something to do with this event and are more important than Mayan prophesy and legends.

A cosmic momentum is developing

There was much speculation about December 21, 2012, and the Mayan calendar. The Mayans were great keepers of records and had been taught a complicated multi-calendar system, based on cogs and wheels by an often-cited deity, whom they called Itzamna. Noting that certain types of events had occurred on certain days of the calendar, they were able to predict future events based on this correlation. But all the predictions abruptly came to an end December 21, 2012. A great fear was developing about what it meant, much of which was based on the speculation that the world was coming to an end. This section starts from January 2007, just as our journey had begun:

Supernova will tremor the universe; Earth is in path.

Kent injects, "Vibrational things will help move or tilt something. They are preparing for a supernova. They said they cannot stop a supernova, but they can help direct its path when it explodes." In May of 2008, we were informed that a starburst, an assumed supernova, had occurred:

A starburst has happened and is in view now. No dates; dates are irrelevant. Time is irrelevant at this point.

Orion will align with Sagittarius.

Q: What is the significance?
Points our way: directional. Part of recovery.

Q: Is there a date associated with this time?
Fifty-one twenty-five; when the north turns east, moves toward the east two one-hundredths of a degree: 0.02. When Polaris is at its top, on the back side of the equinox. An evisceration in the time continuum will occur about the same time. The moon is broken up.

Kent clarifies that the moon is not actually broken up, but, rather, is not shown as a whole.

When we researched the date, we found the Mayan long count cycle to be 5,125 years long, ending on our calendar year December 21, 2012.

Q: What specifically will occur on December twenty-first?
A core breach…The beginning of realigning. Neutron explosion; minor at first.

The neutronal field accentuates your cause given: the severity of your understanding, retract events to come before you. Fluctuation of energies will protrude the interior realms of understanding who you are here.

This is an aligning of events to come: the supernova begins the process, possibly creating the evisceration of the field that corrects the time-space continuum, discussed later in this chapter. Orion aligns with Sagittarius, and Polaris is at its top, all taking place around our time of December 2012.

Q: Does this cycle start with the sun in the universal equinox?
Ends in the equinox, begins when the *system* reverses polarities. Others have already prepared. Your place is ignorant to cause, speaking of the earth.

The brightness of the equinox shall prevail to the vibrational activity in each who follows the true path.

In January 2013, we had read in an Earth changes newsletter that a huge blast of charged particles was coming from the galactic center, five times that of a supernova. In July of the same year, we asked about it:

Q: Is there a supernova headed our way?
Begotten already: particle path.

Q: When would we expect this to arrive here?
Now—beginning—increase to come. Change behavior of many; increased.

Q: Are there any precautions we need to take regarding this supernova?
No. Understand its value.

Q: Are our scientists aware of this?
Correct.

Kent tries to explain, "It's like a beginning. There's no time, no dates; there's a window in this time frame. It's a minor core breach. It's like a minor core balancing to begin."

Kent opens the following communication, November 2013, describing a vision, "I'm not sure if it is an ionic or magnetic belt around Earth. This belt is a protective layer that helps deflect incoming matter. The belt is deteriorating, like a belt that encircles the earth."

> Synacious causation to placate the higher beings:
> rapid movement in fluxation; the cosmic momentum
> [is] developing. Energy has been supplied by others
> to keep it intact, but no longer.

The following message, received in January 2017, speaks of a pulsar release coming in. In a summary from NASA's website, pulsars make up the majority of neutron stars: A giant sun, with its energy spent, exploding into a supernova, blowing off its outer shell and leaving the remaining protons and electrons to collapse into a rapidly-spinning inner neutron core under a massive gravitational field. The new pulsar projects gamma ray particles and light out of its two strong magnetic polar ends, which may not be the same as its' axis. Acting somewhat like a lighthouse, the projected beam of gamma radiation and light spins around, appearing as a pulsing light as it crosses our line of sight on Earth. According to the *MIT Technology Review* website, "When cosmic rays hit [Earth's] upper atmosphere, they send high-energy particles, such as neutrons, showering down towards the surface."

> Redundance is happening. A credence is about to
> happen: understanding the beginning of All That Is.
> Recurring; a pre-tense of the beginning.

> **Q: Is the redundancy referring to a recurring
> energy?**
> Correct; incoming neutronal access to a living
> organism. Betrayal of happening: pulsar release
> coming in. Truth squeezed to augment its value.
> Auguration recommended for cause.

Our understanding: We assume the core breach is within another galaxy or universe, based on other lessons we have received, printed both in this chapter and in **chapter 12** of *The Augmentation of Man: A Study in Renaissance*. This core breach may well have been a supernova or a neutron explosion that began the domino effect. The gamma rays it produces collide with other particles in the atmosphere, fracturing atoms to produce neutrons. Supernovas often create new pulsars that channel neutrons out its polar ends. Others outside of Earth have been preparing for this event, but Earthlings are ignorant to what is coming. The new cycle for Earth begins when the *system* reverses polarities, not just Earth's electromagnetic field. At the behest of the higher beings, a unified cause is developing a cosmic momentum, a rapid movement in energy—still in flux at the time of this reading—to withdraw the energy being supplied by others to keep Earth's magnetic belt intact, no longer deflecting incoming matter.

Piecing both the channeled message and our research together, the incoming cosmic rays, remnants of a supernova, are working in synchronicity with the solar phases of our sun. Normal solar activity feeds the strength of the ionosphere. It may well be coordinated with the solar minimum, beginning around 2019, to allow the gamma particles in, which will function as one aspect of the planned genetic change for humanity. When the sun has a hole in its' corona, or outer region, it allows charged particles to escape in a solar wind. That solar wind, if directed at Earth, causes a disruption in our electromagnetic field, weakened during a solar minimum, as it is being blown around. The solar and cosmic gamma rays are normally captured in Earth's upper atmosphere. Neutrons, protons, x-rays, and other particles are released through cracks in our electromagnetic field caused by the solar wind, which then shower down on Earth. The recurring release of a pulsar bringing neutrons to Earth, a living organism, accentuates our understanding of who we are and what our purpose is, giving us direction. The truth is being squeezed, increasing its significance for humanity. At the same time, the gamma rays are creating our genetic change, if our exposure is limited, through a mutation process. Of course, large exposure rates can adversely affect DNA, leading to cancer. This is discussed further in **chapter 4**, "A gamma species".

Orion leads the way

Dimensional change: Magnitudinal direction seven degrees, based on the triangular distortional magnitudinal variance of Orion. We are at three degrees. A deviation of variance is in direct proportion to the magnitudinal degree that is based upon the distance, which is in direct proportion to the circumference of the diagonal, or the magnitudinal flux at seven degrees. We use this as a beacon for guidance. All magnitudinal changes are subject to polarization of the planets. A curvature will create a distortion of the travel distance. Ionization propulsion is an old way. Each planet is related to each other on a diagonal transcourse of dimension. This course can create a perception. It's not a true travel distance.

The vibrational rings around Orion will create a manifestation among the native people: indigenous. This manifestation will create a new excitement among those of higher vibrational levels.

Rite under Sirius, rite under Sirius. Rite: the beginning of the node. The fires of the Ancients will begin.

The triangular distallation of Sirius will be part of the new concept given to the understanding of the universal vibrational acceptance.

Kent explains, "It's an actual fire of spiritual use." It seems we are being told that the fire of the Ancients will set forth the energy to start the correction of the beginning of the node that exists under Sirius. Sometime in 2017, we noticed that the Ancients had not been as available for guidance and later learned they were involved in setting the new vibrational parameters for Earth.

On January 2, 2011, we were informed by our mentor of a disturbance viewed southeast of Orion in the X-215 system, which has a direct link to Sagittarius:

> Sagittarius is a direct link to system X-215, an influence of great magnitude. Parallels will be divided. Normal becomes the absurd. Nostarius—a system to be reckoned with—points southeast of Orion: a disturbance.

The guide is telling us that this disturbance will have a huge impact on Earth and her inhabitants, causing a great divide, where normal becomes the absurd.

In October 2013, we received the following message:

> Constance of Orion seen: watch for change.

Q: What does Orion's position affect?
Earth structure, vibrational character of inhabitants. Sequence of events contribute to vibrational cause and effect.

Fourteen months later, in December of 2014, we were told to watch for Orion's change in position:

> A constance of Orion will lead the way, preverbious to its nature.

By January 2017, we were informed that the correctional shift of planetary orbits, including Orion, is beginning to accelerate due to the thought patterns of the conceptual beings involved in the change:

> Magnitudinal change accelerates its capacity to include the Orion constellation within variance of amplification parameters. This is due to the conceptual being of those involved in the change; a

thought pattern initiated through the variables of understanding the parameters of the event to take place. Astrological effects are in place to begin change in universal conditions, including atmospheric reductiation.

Our understanding: Here, dimensional change is referring to the change in the angles of the spherical orbits in space. It is assumed that the mentor is talking about a change in the angle of the earth relative to Orion by seven degrees in space. This calculation is based on a variation caused by a distorted view of the triangulation with Orion. We are at three degrees in that shift, as of March 23, 2007. The angle of deviation is the bending of light away from the straight line of sight, directly proportionate to the degree of the angle and the distance being measured. This is in direct proportion to the parameters of the moving angle at seven degrees.

The lesson tells us that Earth's location is relative to the placement of Orion. All distortions of the actual placement of the spheres are subject to the various properties of each planet and how each deflects light. The curvatures in the field (created around a sphere) will create a distortion in the optics, bending the light and changing the view of the true travel distance. The planets are related to each other, based on the angle of the orbital path of one planet in relation to another planet. The orbital course can create a perception, based on the optical distortion, and is not a true travel distance. The guide interjects that ionization propulsion is an old way of spacecraft propulsion.

A vibrational triangulation, to include Sirius and Orion, will establish the circumference of the vibrational influence, which includes our Milky Way, affecting the charged atoms within the atmosphere to direct the flow of conceptual energy for Earth, bringing a higher value of learning to our sphere.

By the spring of 2019, as we enter the final stages of this book, we are seeing a great polarization of people across the globe, many behaviors becoming absurd. This did not happen overnight; a crescendo has been building over the past several years.

The crossover of the galactic meridian

Ten to sixteen inches of rain came down overnight in Houston, on April 18, 2016, producing massive flooding. San Antonio was hit to a similar degree; Dallas, to a lesser degree. Several major earthquakes happened over a few days just prior to the Texas rains, ranging from 6.9-7.8 magnitude in Ecuador. The close timing of the events caused us to wonder if the earth events were related to the crossing of the galactic meridian, mentioned in **chapter 12** of *The Augmentation of Man: A Study in Renaissance.*

> **Q: Did the crossing of the galactic meridian trigger the massive flooding in Texas and large earthquakes in Ecuador?**
> More to come; eclipse of the equatic center will happen, magnitudinal shift of the variance.

On June 5, 2016, we asked:

> **Q: How long will it take Earth to cross the galactic meridian?**
> Approximately one year, your time from here. Eight months minimum, your time from here.

By August 8, 2017, we were being warned of the impending crossover:

> Prepare yourself for the passover of the galactic field.
> Reverberation brings cause of event. Reiterate.

In reality, the heavy rains and the large earthquakes were not related to the crossing of the galactic meridian. We really did not know what to expect at that time. In **chapter 12** of *The Augmentation of Man: A Study in Renaissance,* "The crossover," describes a

"Collective movement of planetary bodies' orbital path—planet's reconfiguration. Magnetic pole shifts of each sphere, molecular movement of atomic particles: converse relationship to magnetic field." This crossover would last a short period and the new planetary alignment and change in orbits would create the vibrational conditions for a higher level of understanding—the beginning of the transformation on an accelerated level. Although, by mid-2019, we have not seen Earth's anticipated electromagnetic pole reversal yet, the magnetic pole has significantly increased its wandering speed, headed for Siberia, with the electromagnetic field losing strength.

Orbital shift triggers an ocean shift

As mentioned above, the crossover event is described in **chapter 12** of *The Augmentation of Man: A Study in Renaissance*. It tells us that this is an event that coincides with the crossing of the galactic meridian, triggering a movement of planetary bodies in their orbits, dictating a rebalancing of the universe. We are told that there will be a slowing down of outer planets, creating stress on the core planetary system, then releasing to allow planetary bodies to move in their orbits. An accelerated spin, as well as the shifting weight from ocean displacement, will allow the earth to balance in her new orbit. We pick up where we left off:

> There will be an ocean shift.
>
> Temporary display: coagulation of atmospheric conditions. A movement of twenty degrees east, ten degrees south will take place off of meridian. Hold core in place. Orbital change: expansion, tighter field. Magnetic energy increase[s] to fluctuate neuronetical fields, strengthen. Causation a must.
>
> The winds of change precede the coming. Soon nappeletts, the correlation universal bodies in relation to each other, begin events of directional

change. Influential mass to coordinate directional patterns of orbital patterns.

Q: When can we expect the movement?
Sooner than what's expected. There are still variances allowed, based on behavioral structure: based upon behavioral consequences within a specific field or structure. Very soon; the patient is anaphylactic, needs shock treatment to stabilize Earth Mother.

Q: Will there be a change in the appearance of our world?
Yes, the water stabilization will correct the orbital path.

Q: Will the earth move closer to the sun?
Elongated orbit.

Q: What will create the heating up of the planet?
Narrower projection of movement.

Q: How correct is the map of the future U.S. by Gordon Michael Scallion?
Movement close to original project.

Aquafier to come; dianectical divergence to orbital effect.

Q: Will this have the impact on the oceans?
Correct.

Nordactic procedures: ice will melt.

Q: May I ask for a spelling for nordactic?
N-o-r-s-d-a-t-i-t-i-c-s procedure: a survey assigned to gaseous analysis relating to the deconstruction of

the ice fields.

Q: Would this be the polar ice caps?
All.

Earth changes to come; world does not recognize. Elevoracious, elevoracious in concepts; precursor to disastrous events for their world realities.

In April of 2016, Kent reported hearing, "Are you ready? Are you ready for the transposition?" Renee followed up with the following question:

Q: How do we prepare for the transposition?
You are preparing: your understanding. Conceptual reasoning a must.

Our understanding: A coordination of atmospheric conditions will begin the process of an orbital shift of twenty degrees east and ten degrees south. Earth's orbit will also become tighter and more elongated. The magnetic energy will increase, causing a fluctuation in the neuronetic fields, strengthening them.

All ice caps are expected to melt, including the glaciers. There are many Earth changes to come and people are not paying attention. Humanity is to develop a passion for understanding the concepts involved in these changes—why they are necessary—before the reality of the disastrous events occur.

A correction in time

Q: We had been told of a previous time adjustment. Can you explain?
Universal movement not coincidal with planetary movement. Time not [an] option. Event cycle overlap to consequential events, the universe cycle; therefore, magnified in this spherical plane—Earth,

as you refer to it. Consequential linear acceleration of events, magnified by processes universal, control the ability of this sphere to over-come forces of unnatural beings.

Vibrational surveillance: must understand. Correlate a universal analysis as a rippling effect: waves of dispersion on the time line. Truth and perception is only the beginning—a far point. Congruenial coexistence of opposite effects—the vibrational strands as they relate to the linear time frame— nebular region transpose[s] the particles. The universal creation: [a] rapid-evolving neuro-electronical electron-base net system. Particle configuration through abstinent space and time is a non-lineal time configuration.

Who are the ascenders? Those with a hyper-bolster system, creating particle infusion—a hyper-space tunnel of time and motion. Instantaneous curvature of the time-space continuum, ascending to the star side of the time quantarium. Provider of the quality of iridational metal, such as iridium, a base for universal coagulations and stability.

Kent explains, "It's like the planets move in a plane to create the time-space continuum. The earth is becoming really unstable from what we've done to it. They are going to restabilize the earth."

Octuarian: a relapse in time.

Q: What is the purpose of the octuarian?
A time frame reformation, equivalent to exacerbation of events to come.

Q: Does this relate to the correction in time?
Correct. A quasar event, this will displace energy in

the formic field.

Q: Does the correction in time relate to the changing orbits?
No. Time as it exists, as a variable.

Time frame bends to the coming occurrence of the diagonal convexes, is relevant. Concave dispersion to the points of time in a magnetudinal flux. Surreality understands: simplicity a must.

Q: What is it relevant to?
Relevant to the consequences.

Q: Can you explain the concave dispersion to the points of time in a magnetudinal flux?
Outcome will behold the answer to your question soon. Outcome is in the equational answer. Watch for the outcome. Your science is moving quickly.

Our understanding: Time, in a universal sense, relates to the movement of energy—and mass is energy—through space. It is also the perceived pause between events related to the movement of energy. But, in the above message, the universal movement is not related to the movement of planets. Over-lap, in this instance, may be used in the sense of overlapping universal cycles that produce an acceleration of events, magnified here on Earth. The linear acceleration of events suggests events occurring one after another in an accelerated manner, having been magnified by universal processes that control the ability of Earth to overcome human activity.

The momentum of energy movement creates the "building up" to a final event. Within the energy flow lies a pause between one event and the next: the lapse between the energy release and the actual event as it unfolds. The speed of the flow of energy determines the length of what we call "time." If the sun released a solar flare, spewing charged particles toward Earth, it would take roughly two days to arrive, based on the average solar wind speed. But this time lapse only applies to Earth and its inhabitants because our measurement of time is based on Earth's unique axial spin and rotation around the sun. If that *rotation* were to change—and our mentors tell us it will—our measurement of time would also change. Therefore, time exists as a variable.

It would help to do a little research in physics and the bending of time to understand this concept. We will attempt to provide a brief explanation, based on our research and limited understanding. Mass occupies and bends the space around it, forming a convex surface on the outer side and a concave surface on the inner. Within the inner concave surface, lies a dispersion of points in time relating to the flux of the magnetic field. Think of Earth, spinning in her rotation. The space around her would be bent in a concave fashion and under the influence of the magnetic field. If you were to draw points on the inner, concave surface within her atmosphere and, as she rotates, specific points on the globe would change relative to the points on the concave surface, creating time. Are we being told that something is coming, creating a convex surface—possibly an event arising from a quasar—that would alter the atmosphere around the earth, bending the magnetic field and distorting our time? Perhaps we just don't know enough about quasars at this time.

We must come to comprehend what we are observing in the vibrational field. The universe is a rapidly-evolving electrical system, running upon the electrons of a network of atoms within the atmosphere, behaving much like our bodies' own nervous system. Vibration is the basic building block of all atoms within the fields of both the seen and the unseen worlds. Our observations of the field around us can give clues to the coming domino effect occuring along a time line: one event setting the stage for the next. Humanity's expanded understanding of the truth is only the beginning of the events to come. All events are intended to create an effect. The effect is a new understanding and the subsequent change in our behaviors.

There are many questions to be answered about the nature of black holes and quasars. Black holes, until very recently, could not actually be seen. What has been observed is the field around them— the movement of matter around the immense space it occupies— suggesting an immense gravitational field. Only presented in 2019, scientists have pieced together over the past two years a torus representation of a black hole from the Milky Way center with the use of eight high-powered telescopes over the earth, using background radiation to outline the theorized black hole. It is believed that black holes can contain up to 3 billion times the mass of our sun and possess a gravitational field of such great magnitude, that even light cannot escape its clutches. Quasars are believed to be related to black holes, in that the vacuum-action of the black hole funnels energy to the quasars, which, aside from supernova, are the most luminous, yet distant, objects in the sky. Both black holes and quasars are currently found to reside at the center of most galaxies and the size of the black hole appears to be relative to the size of its galaxy. Quasars can be larger than our solar system and are found to emit a faint radio wave and visible light, as well as ultraviolet, infrared, gamma and X-rays. Our guide suggests that some type of quasar event will displace energy in the formic field to create a time frame reformation.

Chapter 11 of *The Augmentation of Man: A Study in Renaissance,* "An iridium hit may be necessary," describes how iridium creates diameter points that give the stability of the magnetic field curvature around Earth. It also states that our mining and stripping away of the iridium has created an instability in the electromagnetic field, moving the directional flow and creating an unstable wobble. The mentor went on to reveal, "An iridium hit may be necessary for stabilization." If iridium creates anchor points to the magnetic field curvature, how would it affect other universal orbits and the time-space continuum that are also based on curvatures? Iridium, of course, is not indigeonous to the earth, it showers down to Earth on meteorites. Is it possible that meteors may be the only way to replenish Earth's iridium in order to also correct the time-space continuum?

Nibiru: the octarian entrance

The following message was received in February 2014:

> The octarian effect will begin—constance now—apprehend the values.

> **Q: What impact will the octarian effect have?**
> You know: the beginning effect, slavorious in nature.

Five months after the above message, July of 2014, we had the following exchange, giving us a clue:

> The bending of light can help you see.

Kent explains in his own words, "The bending of light creates a shadow. Looking directly into the light, you cannot see what you are supposed to see. To see the whole of All That Is, you need to look at the light and then bend the light so you can see the shadow."

Q: How do you bend light?
Kent, "By putting something in front of it, like an eclipse or partial eclipse."

Q: Would it have to be eclipsed with something round?
"It doesn't have to be round. Triangular."

Q: So, does this apply only to looking out at the cosmos?
Kent, describing his vision, "Yes. It's not the sun. I'm seeing when looking at the cosmos."

There may be a reason why we were told how to visualize a planetary body that is being obstructed from view by another cosmic body. Nibiru may be one such reason, giving a hint at how to visualize a planet just returning from its long orbital journey, still hiding behind another sphere. Perhaps this is a heads-up to the massive changes that Nibiru brings, mentioned in **chapter 1**, as

Nibiru is known as the balancer, "a course corrector" and one that "awakens the inner Self through chaos." The planet will have an effect on Earth and its' inhabitants. The people of Nibiru are known as octarians, those who can see an event from all eight angles. The Nepherum culture, one of our genetic predecessors, are also referred to as octarians. The Nephilim, mentioned in Genesis of the Bible, are the children produced by "sons of gods" and "daughters of men."

In March of 2015, having had much difficulty trying to communicate during Kent's meditations, Renee started the session with a question, "Are we going to be able to communicate this week?"

Difficult. Protracted atmosphere: Nibiru in charge.

Kent explained, "Nibiru is on the dark side or behind the sun."

In June 2017, a report came to our attention that there was an atmospheric disturbance that behaved like a solar wind, but was not the result of the sun's activity. This prompted the following question:

Q: What is the atmospheric disturbance coming in to this system that behaves like a solar wind?
Octarian entrance; a disruption in kind. Precognizance to the event. Malfeasance is the cause of the event. You are protracted between two sides of an event. We will further cause disruption to bring on cause.

Were we being informed that Nibiru was ready to make her entrance? Have humans brought this on themselves by not adhering to universal laws? The disruption has begun and we are caught in the middle of a long, drawn-out event bringing further disruption and chaos with the goal of awakening the human inner Self.

A little more than a month later, a friend asked about the impact of the upcoming eclipse on August 17, 2017. We, in turn, asked our mentor:

Q: What effect does this solar eclipse have on the earth?
Havoc; consequential circumstance will be prevailed. Unplugging those events about to happen, a Creative influence. A shadowed event known by those ancient cultures, the natives of this area. The legends of land is spoken.

Q: Do the Creative beings influence the events about to happen?
Creative by others outside this parameter.

Q: Would that be from Nibiru?
Yes; possibilities are high. Angulareus, the provider, is given cause for the event to happen: non-consequential being.

Q: Is this being from Nibiru?
A directional aspect.

Q: Can you define how this being is different from the human perception of "beings"?
Narrower parameters for just cause.

Q: In other words, this being is created for imparting a certain purpose or cause?
Those that are involved in this purpose. Elate: justification for purpose.

Our understanding: We are often told in advance of coming changes. As mentioned earlier, a time-lapse occurs between when we are informed of a coming event—at the release of energy—and when the event actually occurs. In this instance, we learned that the eclipse would release the energy, coupled with the Creative influence, that would unplug future events to come, perhaps correlated with Nibiru. It seems that the Native Americans may have foreknowledge of this event through their oral traditions and legends. The above mentioned being comes from a visual direction near Nibiru, working together with other beings involved in the cause, with justification for the task at hand upon Earth and humanity to correct our course.

Solar activity influences ionosphere and magnetic field

In August 2012, at the height of a solar maximum and its solar flares, we were told that the "havalarium," or atmospheric gas restructuring, had begun, dispersed in eight directions, shifting and creating a triangulation of the grid with the magnetic and electric fields of the earth. See **chapter 12**, *The Augmentation of Man: A Study in Renaissance,* "Atmospheric gas restructuring."

The following messages begin in April of 2007, with the announcement that humans are mismanaging the atmosphere around Earth, followed by the coming changes and showing, in successive readings, the developing stages that present a timeline of events in the correction.

27 April 2007
Kent starts with describing a vision, "I am seeing a change in the atmosphere over the earth, way, way up, outside the sky; like layers are being compressed, creating pressure on the earth."

> Atmospheric conditions will prevail to the mismanagement of mankind. Vortexes will begin to destablize. Many people will feel confused. Serendipitous behavior will be felt by many and will prevail their lives.

12 Sept 2008

Arcturians are preparing for an all-out push to start clearing the atmosphere of the earth for the movement and also start clearing the negative atmosphere. The colors in the universe, the galactic fields, will start to change.

6 Feb 2009

The shift will release the energy: prelude to vibrational shift. Consequential outcome to understanding the trudence for required correctional behavior. Quintessential beings will begin to correlate with universal connection. Astute behavior: man's perception of distriangular dispersion of truth. Nocturnal events to happen.

A dispersion of solar infusion into the atmosphere, bending of magnetudinal field creating vibrational imbalance within the core of the earth's magnetudinal shift—accellerates volcanic events. Ocean flows shifting, attempting to stabilize human magnetudinal field, causing confusion. Hole in flux: isolated solar activity.

Q: What is distriangular dispersion of truth?

An angulation of consequence relating to thought truth. Not a variable to understanding—actual consequence. A variable to understanding its value, recipical in nature.

10 July 2009

Proximatal: an increase to the understanding of parameters to the coourzonian of behavior aptitudes.

Q: Can you explain the coourzonian of behavior aptitudes?

A nefarious coagulation of atmospheric effects:

Centralized plane to the neuromagnetical field relating to consequential behavior of various energy sources, coming soon to affect a single body of this planetary field. A numerical value to be used as a source of concentrated energy: n-5.

Q: Is n-5 in reference to nitrogen or neutrons?
Neutronal display: gaseous makeup astronomical display. Neutronal atmosphere within the gaseous parameters that make up the display. Virgocious is the display: neutronal gases displayed across a field of anti-matter.

Q: Does virgocious refer to a rod?
A type of lineal progression within an anti-matter field.

23 April 2011
Particles of light are growing dim; atomic structure is changing. Molecular interpretation is a condition of self-illusion. Self-illusion is the concept that is sought after; a false importance of being.

Q: The atomic structure is changing within which field?
Electromagnetic field: stretched out and condensed.

Q: How does this relate to the dimming of the particles of light?
From within your own system: they're blocking. A systematic, created, vibrational field blocking resonance on a multilateral plane.

17 May 2011
Tell them the flow of energy is quickening. Events will precede the action for the change. Be awake and aware of all that prevails around you. Do not be

myopic of the horizon setting. Stratospheric conditions contain a just cause to create a new path of adjustment. Those that know will hear. Those that are captured by self-importance will not hear.

19 Feb 2012

The shift is building amplitudinal tonic wave vibrations to a point of discharge value: Light Beings released from crystal chambers organized 65,000 ages past. Happened before then-period to be released again as molecular consumption of particles increase, creating a density needed to release the shift again.

Q: How many shifts are there going to be?
Two shifts will occur, close to each other. Preparation at hand: obedience to self-annihilation of what was will be the beginning for those. Shift to cause disruption of being, absolute in cause.

Q: What are the precipitating forces?
Cause for electromagnetic field pole to move. New cycle to begin, opening Creative cause to justification for balance in the electroplasmatic field of the upper shelf. Creative influence at hand in the electromagnetic field, causing molecular dispersion of matter on this entity field called Gaia. Severe misuse of field mathematics creating astronomical distortion of field complex. Severity of cause in relation to distortion. A meteorlogical event take[s] place.

A correction is at hand for a neurological inscription upon this entity plane—a Gaia understanding. A field arthropic to cause. Dispension of matter along the stratospheric line—a causation of understanding is at hand—triacular in cause for dispersion of this matter.

Q: Does triacular mean three-pronged?
Triacular integration of the pod; a stand-alone configuration.

Q: Is it similar to a tripod?
In form.

Q: When the first shift releases the energy, where is the energy coming from?
Outside your galactic system; a key variance associated with arvadarian galactic field hole. Nupharous principle holds the field together.

Q: Does it have anything to do with our sun?
No. Non-sparing aspect of our system.

Q: What is nupharous?
New formulation; a multiplex unification of existing natural law.

Q: How does this release of energy affect the second shift?
Coagulation of atmospheric variance within the outer planets of this galactic system; outer planets only— the perimeters of pass-through.

3 Feb 2014

Exotic influence on the magnetudinal field: CME disruption of particles. It will cease: pattern reverse soon to come.

Q: When will our atmosphere become more stable?
Logarious: after instability.

Q: Does logarious refer to logarithms?
Those that have the mathematical codes; the release of vibrational underpinnings.

26 July 2014
Q: Why have the number of sun spots declined?
Correcting balance—will increase again.

Q: Can we expect a large solar storm in the near future?
Yes; all is not done. The cycles cannot be changed. They set the parameters of existence throughout the universal being.

5 Nov 2014
Q: What can you tell us about the large sun spot occurring currently?
Precarious by nature. Hold position; play the cards. Relationship: ascension.

Q: How does the large sun spot relate to ascension?
No ascension, as relating to your definition. Cause parameters of this system to shift. Not individual purpose. Universe more important than those on this sphere.

Q: So, it was an upward shift in vibrational parameters for this system?
This system *and* universal parameters adjustment.

5 April 2016
Quasi-magnitudinal shift of atmospheric gases is taking place, causing the beginning shift and vibrational energy on this plane.

Q: Does the shift include magnetics?
Not yet. Magnetudinal correction to come—later date within the human time frame—exceptional energy release from solar phases.

Q: Will the energy release from solar phases cause the quasi-magnitudinal shift of atmospheric gases?
Part of the realignment phase within this quadrical system; coursational by aspect.

6 Sep 2017
Q: Is this solar activity going to change the gaseous makeup of our atmosphere?
Ionic structure change: small, beginning. Increase on rise of atmospheric conditions.

Q: Is the change in gas in our atmosphere to include a higher level of oxygen?
Eventually, 22 1/2 percent, up to 26 percent. Less humans, more pervasive creatures.

Q: Does the change in oxygen change the grid geometry?
No. Species change: octarian-type creatures. Not creatures: living organisms. Targnarius is the type of animal: new species.

Our understanding: A wicked combination of atmospheric affects is coming to Earth from various energy sources. There will be two shifts relatively close to each other—at least in universal terms. It begins with an event from outside our galaxy that creates a molecular consumption of particles, releasing a vibrational sound wave through a hole in the galactic field, triggering movement in the electromagnetic field. This will cause a molecular dispersion of matter in Earth's atmosphere, correcting the field mathematics that has been distorting the astronomical field complex, caused by man's activities. Our guide is saying that the field will be held together through a new system of multiple unified networks. The first shift triggers a second shift of atmospheric variances around the outer planets of our galaxy as these planets pass through the field affected by the first shift. Earth resides on the outermost tip of the Orion arm; the outermost part of our Milky Way galaxy.

The initial shift will release an energy, creating a vibrational shift, delivering a new understanding of the truth, shaking humanity to its core and destroying the paradigm that now exists. A new consciousness will be born out of this event, which is going to create a consequence of seeing the truth through a direct route, possibly producing a consequence of being to view all angles for a more complete truth. This is required for man's behavioral correction. Astuteness is necessary to be able to *see* the truth. The term "nocturnal" is often used to imply "being in the dark," as in not being able to see with clarity. It also implies that we are being given false information and/or events are occurring without our knowledge.

It was predicted that solar activity would significantly increase. Our mentor is saying that the bending of the magnetic field, usually caused by solar wind, interacts with Earth's iron core, creating a vibrational imbalance and friction within that increase's volcanic activity. This is an attempt to stabilize the human magnetic field, resulting in some confusion for people. The submarine volcanoes are heating the oceans, changing the direction of the ocean currents, which, in turn, changes the weather patterns.

In February, 2014, we were told that the then solar maximum was going to cease for a time, reversing its pattern, balancing, in an assumed solar minimum before returning to a period of increased solar activity. The solar maximum reached its height in April of 2014. By 2019, we were well into a solar minimum. It seems that the release of the vibrational underpinnings causing the atmospheric instability will occur after a mathematical correction. The cycles cannot be changed, they are what set the parameters for maintaining balance within the universe. The large sunspot, seen November 2014, and the resulting solar activity, was intended to raise the vibrational parameters of this universe, including our galaxy. By April 2016, we were told that the massive changes were beginning. This includes shifts in Earth's atmospheric gases, vibration, and orbit. The magnetic shift would come at a future date, the result of exceptional energy releases from the sun. By September 2017, the mentor comfirmed that small changes in the charged particles of our atmosphere had begun and that it would procede as the atmospheric conditions continue to build.

An increase in oxygen over time will also help in the species change, humans eventually becoming octarian, having the mental ability to see a more panoramic view of all things. There will be new animal species arriving, while others become extinct due to the changing atmospheric gases, which changes the pattern for how life forms are expressed. Man will continue to mismanage the atmospheric conditions, destabilizing vortexes, causing confusion among many. It has been indicated that too much noise is causing a change in the direction of atmospheric electrons, creating a negative atmosphere, and that the technology that many countries are using to alter the atmosphere are most responsible for the changes.

An increase of gamma rays

Around 2010, scientists had announced they discovered gamma waves coming toward Earth, originating from our galactic center. We later read about it in a newletter. Gamma rays are a type of electromagnetic radiation produced by either fusion, that which powers the sun, or by fission, the splitting of a heavy nucleus, like uranium, into smaller elements, such as xenon and strontium. Earth's electromagnetic field, which acts as a deflector, is disrupted when solar wind directly hits the earth, allowing both galactic and solar gamma radiation to pour down on Earth.

15 Aug 2017

Q: We were told to encapsulate ourselves, is this due to the gamma rays coming in?
Now you know. Protection a must to continue on the other side.

Q: Is it known how long we should encapsulate ourselves?
Two weeks; until the planets begin to align with each other. Consequential initiation of aptitude.

Q: Is the earth also entering a density of neutrons?
A brief particle disruption, the *electrons* will balance the incoming—eventually. The gamma particles disrupt the balance of the field; particles interrupt the balancing of the fields. Neuronetical influence begins.

Q: How will the neuronetical influence be manifested?
Through the protrusion of the plasmatic field by a temporary neutron bombardment, opening the effect of gamma particles.

Our understanding: On February 24, 2019, Spaceweather.com reported their high-altitude balloon launches, conducted by students of their Earth to Sky Calculus program for monitoring gamma rays, have shown a steady increase of gamma rays and x-rays over central California for the last four years. Correlating with the gamma ray increase, is the data being collected from the Sodankyla Geophysical Observatory in Oulu, Finland, who report a steady increase in neutrons coming into Earth. The present solar minimum is not feeding Earth's electromagnetic field and, as it loses strength, allows these cosmic rays to come in, magnifying our exposure to the radiation. NASA is now projecting that the next solar cycle, 25, may be the weakest in 200 years. The radiation has an effect on our

DNA, as will be described in **chapter 4**; the variations dependent upon how much we are exposed.

A change in vibrational parameters

Constellations are vibrating. Soon all to be in unison, then the one that is not will move.

Kent states, "Earth will come in line with the universe."

We are here to perform the end, but, yet, the beginning.

Last consequence for those not onboard. Universal reparations take place—prelation is cause of concern—isotonic change.

Q: What will the isotonic change create?
Longerian plasmic movement to reception of newest species.

Q: What kind of universal reparations are to take place?
Consequence from decision-making over [the] past. Severe movement some locations—irrelevant to where—vibrational parameters.

The diameter, referring to a conceptual being—the radiuses of planets are equal to the circumference of the planetarial distance, which is the parameters of the galaxy or Milky Way—create the ionic dispersion that will equal the distance of the parameters: vibrational distributional circumference.

[An] ancient descential being holds the perplexing equation of atmospheric vibrational quintessence.

Our understanding: We believe this is in reference to the ending of one cycle and the beginning of another; a correlated event of great magnitude to bring man's level of comprehension to more closely match that of the universe. The earth has not been in vibrational unison with the rest of the universe. Soon the vibration of the exterior planetary bodies will cause Earth to start vibrating at a greater magnitude, shifting the earth upward in vibration, creating the new spectrum for a higher level of learning. Remember, levels of vibration directly correlate to levels of understanding.

We are being warned that the time is nearing and people need to get onboard their spiritual journey before these universal events start taking place within the plasmic field, which is going to change the DNA of those who continue on. The destination: A new heaven, a new Earth and a new species we will be.

The influence of comets and asteroids

Kent describes a vision in March of 2007: "I see a comet; it just went by. And I see an eclipse, a full eclipse." Three weeks later, he had another vision, obviously describing the same event, "I can see a comet. The eclipse and the comet are related and will cause the waters to rise."

In July of 2008, comet Elenin was coursing its way back toward Earth, bringing into question the relevance of the previous visions. Again, Kent had a vision, "I see a comet heading this way. It is really pushing a wave out in front of it. It will come to this Earth and then skip the surface of the atmosphere. The wave it pushes in front of it is really going to affect things. I don't know when. It's not going to hit, but it's going to affect a lot of things."

> **Q: What can we expect with the approaching comet?**
> Beginning of a series; not just one. Series of comets, as referred by titles.

Q: Does each comet create subtle, unnoticeable changes in vibration until a tipping point by which the changes become obvious to us?
Like the winds that go through pine trees, you don't notice the amount of pine needles on the ground until it is quite thick. It would be as this is.

Q: What visual changes can we expect?
Atmospheric conditions, movement of water, so slowly the horizon movement.

On June 2, 2013, a large asteroid had just passed Earth:

Q: What can you tell us about the large asteroid that has just passed our atmosphere?
A parade of many, each one having cause and effect on your system.

The moon: a biosphere

Q: How did the earth's moon get there?
Part of structure created from expanding matter within universal galactic field: biosphere.

Q: Why is it there?
Gravitational influence, stability of orbit for this planet, shield when needed. Ping is the sound, ping.

Q: Why does it ping?
Biosphere; heavy plate creating gravitational field.

Q: Is it hollow?
Partial—includes matter of dense material—partial.

Q: Why is it partially hollow?
Biosphere area. Create field for orbit. Dense matter outside sphere: planetary substance from system.

Our understanding: Evidently, Earth's moon has a number of functions. Made from matter within the galaxy and universe, its' heavy outer plate influences gravity, stabilizes the orbit of Earth, acts as a shield for Earth, and is a base of outside observers of Earth.

Shifting of the moon and center field poles

There was much discussion about the predictions relating to the book by John Hagee, *Four Blood Moons*, regarding the period of time spanning from April 15, 2014, through September 28, 2015, in which four blood moons would occur. His work is based on significant events occurring in Jewish history over the course of seven back-to-back blood moons, setting the stage for his future predictions. These full lunar eclipses are named as such from the lack of blue light, scattered by Earth's atmosphere, allowing the remaining light that reflects off the moon to produce a red hue. The moon can also appear red from dust, haze or smoke in the sky and is often called a harvest moon.

> **Q: What significance do the four blood moons have?**
> A shifting in the degree change between the moon and the earth. A proclamation herald[s] the end-coming—quantcipitous occasion and event—polarian aspect a part of. Cursality of the human event, sipaporious by nature. Reverse the suffering of Earth creatures—except humans. Raglatarian, the poorest aspects shall arise to higher level of the event. Watch while unity disintegrates only to recapture its value after reconstituting itself after chaos.

> **Q: What further understanding can you give us regarding the polarian aspect?**
> Movement of the opposite poles: off-balance.

Q: Would this be the electromagnetic pole of the earth?
The center fields.

Q: Would this be the center field poles of our solar system?
No.

Q: Can you give further clarification?
Read; you forgot to. Serration of the field.

Q: Will the moon shift further away from the earth?
No, closer pole, creating aquarian effect on surface of Earth. Watch—signs tensify—ready for cause.

Q: Can we expect the moon to move closer with the 2015, spring equinox?
A correctional *after* equinox—consequence of outside influence.

Q: What would the outside influence be from?
Earth, outside of this sphere: Nibiru. Consequence of behavior.

Q: Consequence of which behavior?
Perceptual understanding. Perceptual understanding begins process for completion, awakens the inner Self through chaos.

All need time to complete the awakening prior to the movement. The astrosphere: the zenith of the solstice, will create the opening for the change.

A spherical degeneration to cause effectual understanding of All That Is. Clairvoyance will become widespread.

Hearing tones relates to an ability to hear the vibration of a specific area on Earth. The following discussions were prompted by Kent, Renee and a friend all hearing tones, then not hearing them for several months, before they started again in March of 2013.

Q: Why have we not heard tones for months and then all of us have started hearing them again in the last two weeks?

Reset gradient radiation. Unnatural beings in charge. Shift [in] diametrical field poles underway. Reset orientation mode. Notation drive caught within spherical change. Disruption of pattern condensation or density, changed by human intervention, a precept to cause and effect within the field's magnetosphere. Carnivorous effect, eating away at planet's core: belied judgment of human consumption of planet's power base.

Q: Is the shift in diametrical field poles man-made or natural?

Causation throughout the eons within the time-space continuum. Far beyond the human relevance of this sphere—species beyond—humans know this.

Q: Are there field poles between spheres?

Correct.

Q: Are the interspherical field poles electromagnetic?

Not to interfere with each other: repel pulsation, pushing away.

Q: Is this accomplished through electromagnetics?

A field.

In June 2013, many tornadoes had hit Oklahoma and gained our attention, prompting our asking about it:

Q: Why is Oklahoma having so many tornadoes?
Shift in pattern: diametrical change [of] magnetic field—caused by man. Machine has changed circular pattern of gases in the upper levels, stratosphere, causing a shift with intensified currents and diametrical pattern changes or shifts. Human causation from natural patterns will have adverse effects later—a build-up. A build-up of electromagnetic field manipulation enhances cause and effect off natural grid pattern. Various programs, several countries, cultures. Orgortaneous projects by many, creating a flaw in the natural cycle of dispensation: energy shift.

Q: Will the electromagnetic pole shift and interplanetary poles reverse at the same time?
A closure of interface, capturing the essence of this sphere.

Our understanding: There are many culminating aspects of the ending cycle, including the shifting of degrees between the moon and Earth. A movement of the opposite poles of the center fields will occur, most likely reversing. The center field poles have a repulsion effect that maintains distance between planets. The shifting position of the moon occurs as a consequence of Nibiru, which, in turn, causes an effect on the water on Earth's surface. Sipaporious is referencing the Hopi sipapu, a small hole in the floor of their ceremonial kiva, a present-day reminder of how their ancestors reemerged from underground after the great flood. It seems we are being told this will occur again, the curse of humans causing great suffering, but raising humanity to a higher level after the event.

Nibiru also has a consequence on our perceptual behavior and appears to be completing the human cycle of perceptual learning, which ended December 21, 2012. Our perceptual understanding, most often not aligned to truth, begins the process for completion, awakening the inner Self through the coming chaos as events disintegrate on Earth, revealing the elusive truth. Unity will disintegrate for a time but is rebuilt after the chaos and after truth is revealed. This enables humanity to begin to understand All That Is, setting the stage for a widespread clairvoyant ability. We all need time to awaken prior to the planetary movements, awakening to the truth of the world we live in. The alignment of planets at the height of the solstice creates the opening for change, most likely the solstice of December 22, 2012. But we are neither astronomers or astrologers.

Humans are the unnatural beings in charge: we were planted here and did not organically evolve. The pattern of the density has been disrupted, caused by human activity, and will have a cause and effect upon the magnetosphere. Human technology has created a change in the movement of gases in the stratosphere, resulting in a building up of the electromagnetic field that will create an energy shift, backfiring in some future event, a result of tampering with the natural laws. The positioning of the planet needs resetting in either the degree of inclination, and/or the curvature of the orbit. The notation drive seems to be some sort of system of symbols, possibly mathematic, that guides the movement of the earth and is caught up in the earth changes created by man. "Man has been eating away at Earth's core power base" is an assumed reference to man's mining of uranium and/or iridium. We have been told that uranium forms Earth's power base; iridium anchors the magnetic field, which interacts with Earth's iron-rich core. See **chapter 11** of *The Augmentation of Man: A Study in Renaissance*, "Do not continue to tamper with Earth's energy structure," and "An iridium hit may be necessary."

A shift of the axis

This is taken from a meditation on January 12, 2007, in which our journey had just begun:

> Here is your map. Tilt to the right five degrees, then
> fifteen degrees: two-fold; two levels. Do not search,
> it will be shown: to the right.

Kent explains his vision, "I was taken to an all-white room, with a large white desk. The desk was much longer than wide. On the desk lay a world map. Everything on the map started shifting to the right. They said it was going to be two-fold. First, a five-degree shift to the right. It paused for a short time, then a fifteen-degree shift to the right. I was told the pause was approximately one year, our time. The second shift will begin the new dimension."

9 March 2009

> The second shift is going to begin real soon. This
> will lead to an increase in earthquakes and volcanic
> activity. The animals are beginning to adapt
> themselves to the magnetic field change, but humans
> are lagging. The honey bee population will begin to
> reverse itself. People will begin to feel a false
> euphoric. The alignment is beginning. Opulence
> seems to be the word.

12 Jan 2012

> Spin will begin to slow. A lightheadedness will
> quicken; will come and go. A centrifugal oddity.
> Magnetic flux seizing the moment; elongated field.
> North moves slowly until resistance, then quick snap.

Q: The snap representing what?
The sphere movement to right...The north shall perish into the south, a reflection of what is to come, a green nautilus of intent. Procrastination is the

causation of another event. Causation a just matter.

Volcanic activity is heating the earth

Shift causing magnetudinal lines to bend. Volcanic activity is heating the earth, much activity. Why won't man tell the truth? Everything is based on *perception*. Perception of truth should be adhered to. Earth's heating all universe.

Primordial agreement: concentrated values are dissipating; conceptualism is not occurring among the human race. Virilacious is the coming of concentrated heat from within the earth's core. Prelatious is the word of magnitudinal concepts.

Q: What is causing the increased heat coming from Earth's core?
A fluctuating magnetic field: a degree of change.

Q: Does it increase atomic movement, thereby creating heat?
Frictional movement: subcutaneous osculation. Fracturial events within the subdural region of Earth.

Q: And this will cause increased volcanic activity?
Correct.

In April 2018, Kent started, "I saw a vision: the sky was all red. The clouds were all red. I could see the hills in the background. It was like a rust color. It was the sky, not the ground. We were standing looking across the desert."

Astute. Astute to the facts of the coming. Volcanic activity is going to heat up the sky. Plagaration of material will be justified in sequence.

Q: What is plagaration of material?
Justification of interdiameter of the plagaceous space. Open to understand events to come. Seignoirsis will begin at a serratious event of major magnitude. Authentic atmosphere to begin very soon [and] augment the colors. Your prohibition of this value will signify the movement of a new species. Prescription of aptitudes are ready.

Q: Is the plagaceous space in our atmosphere?
Correct. A variance in degrees of numerical change. A spreading of the field. A plasmic field event.

A cool-down is coming of the earth's core.

Our understanding: Combining both research and the above readings: Increased solar activity creates a dispersion of charged particles into Earth's atmosphere, bending the magnetic field lines and creating a fluctuation in the electromagnetic field. The magnetic field interacts with Earth's iron core. This creates a vibrational imbalance within the core, creating heat from friction between two curved layers beneath Earth's crust, accelerating volcanic activity. The words subdural and subcutaneous are both being used as metaphors here, drawing parallels between membrane layers under the skull and under the skin, and layers under the crust of the earth.

The increased volcanic activity will also heat the atmosphere, creating a red sky and red clouds, followed by a later cooling of the core. This is a step in a sequence of events, of which will grab our attention after an event of great magnitude. A numerical change within the plagaceous space of the atmosphere will begin soon, spreading within the plasmic field, creating a more colorful sky. A course of action has been decided to assist in our understanding of these events.

Crustal movement balancing the extreme ends

Sequence of events will influx to the temporate rhythm of Earth Mother.

Earth begins to shudder her virus. Occipital to begin.

Q: Can you elaborate?
Adjustment: eight sectors.

Q: What do the eight sectors represent?
Earth Mother movement: quantum collapse, of various outcomes, to begin. Octillate its beginnings: castronation of nations built upon this sphere.

5 Dec 2013

Q: What changes are occurring within the earth sphere at this time?
Synergen pushing up tectonic plates: pressure, upward movement. Increase in release, holes.

Significant crustal movement balancing the extreme ends. Curvature of isometer to change mathematical principle.

Ancient Lemuria is beginning to rumble, the sea will belch its ancient discovery [and] secret; a precursor to the shift of the plates, as before. The time frame is abstract, but absolute.

Our understanding: The sequence of events is beginning. We can expect much movement of the earth as her crust starts to shift, balancing her extreme ends and creating a new mathematical principle. The tectonic plates will be pushed up, causing crustal releases and sink holes. "Mountains will crumble. Drop, valleys will drop." This will bring about a collapse of many things, with various outcomes. Be observant of the beginning stages: a time when nations are being deprived of their power. Ancient Lemuria is beginning to stir, the sea producing her secret; a precursor to the shift of the tectonic plates, as happened before. Do not search for a time frame. It will absolutely happen, but it is dependent on the natural rhythm of Mother Earth.

Rotation reversal

> Native influence at hand to reverse course within planetary field: causation under way.

> **Q: What is this in reference to?**
> Spin.

> **Q: Why will this occur?**
> Correctional aptitude: the planet stops spinning, reverses. A new nomenclature of thought.

There are reports of ancient populations having oral histories that, in the distant past, the sun either did not shine for several days, or did not set for several days. Even Joshua of the *Bible* speaks of the "sun stood still and the moon stopped…The sun stopped in the middle of the sky and delayed going down about a full day." There are also ancient writings and petroglyphs that indicate the sun rose in the west at one time.

The stars will begin to tell the story to unfold

NOTES

Chapter 4

> ──────── ••• ────────

Transformation of Human DNA

Creation was designed to evolve. It involves the evolution of our souls to higher and higher levels of understanding all of God's creation. Through our evolution, we gain a more expansive understanding of energy flows, interactions, math, physics, astronomy, languages, and any other topic or thought that could be contemplated. As we expand in our understanding, we receive vibrational attunements, raising the vibration of the atomic field that we occupy. We have chosen to come to this experiential learning field called Gaia, Earth, for all the vibrational learning she has to offer. We have to master this level before we can move to higher and more intellectual levels.

Humanity, however, is confined in its intellectual ability—when compared to the intellectual capacity of other outside beings—by the limited genetic expression of the human body. Additionally, we lost the connection with our outside teachers due to our past arrogance, resulting in a downward spiral from a lack of wisdom to guide our course. We have altered nature, changing the vibrational background environment through various human activities. We are stripping essential minerals out of the ground that hold the electromagnetic field in place and supplies energy to our Mother Earth. Technology has manipulated the atmosphere to a negative electron balance. We have powerful tools in our hands, yet limited understanding of the path it could take us. Additionally, we are constantly at war with each other. All this and more has left Earth and her inhabitants in a very precarious situation.

Humanity must realize a higher genetic expression to bring our full intellectual abilities forward before we self-destruct. We need the help of our star brothers and sisters to bring wisdom back into our decision-making, while teaching us a virtuous understanding of All That Is. Life is about to change…

Understanding of coming events transforms DNA

Important to teach understanding prevalence of coming events. Quantcipital behavior preludes events process that activates human transformation of DNA: [a] significant event.

The coming changes are not a negative. It is so the new humanity can adapt easier to this new world. The changes are for a new humanity, it's geared for a new race. The old thought process will not survive without violence and the ego getting in the way.

Q: What do we need to be aware of at this time? (17 Aug 2014)
Atmospheric conditions: measuring the grid variances by watching parameters. Non-communicative abilities by humans increasing, open parameters to next step. Slow dictation of variances, angulated to complete concept.

Q: Non-communicative abilities by humans open parameters to which next step?
A communicative process directing all entities to a conceptual movement.

All of your seed DNA will become relevant only when the time-watch happens.

Q: What is the time-watch?
The relevancy of when everything takes place—the earth change—at once. Not the developing field before it, when the actual change begins.

Q: Does this apply to the DNA of all those moving into the next cycle?
No movement yet; a small handful will move.

Q: What can be expected?
Very soon.

Q: Are we going to be entering a higher level of learning?
Not humanity in general-sense.   Only a few.
Humanity seeking other avenues; appropriations
dwindling.

Our understanding: The current environment for much of the earth
is one of political divide and civil unrest. There are many agendas,
much manipulation of information and a great number of people
polarizing to the extremes. Instead of open dialogue, we are pushing
against each other; a wrestling match in which no one will win. The
number of those who will be moving on to the next cycle is
dwindling. Will the lack of communication eventually bring us to
the table of discourse?

Each event is a step in the process, creating the opportunity for
reflection and learning. From our new understanding, or lack of it,
we make our next decision, creating the next lesson. The field
around us is changing: the atmospheric gases, subatomic structure,
and the grid that provides the pattern for how life forms are
expressed. The abundance of events playing out before us are
changing the DNA through various means and various sources,
going unnoticed by humanity. The relevance of the DNA change
will become obvious once all the changes have been completed,
creating a paradigm shift all at once. We will then retrace the
steps—the sequential linear process—to reflect upon each event that
brought us to a new point in time and a new reality.

The sun's activity and genetic change

By July of 2012, the sun had reached the height of a solar maximum
and we had begun to notice the frequency of solar flares, the sun
belching its charged gases into the atmosphere in a game of hit and
miss with the earth. The solar wind it produces, when aimed at

Earth, blows her electromagnetic field around, displacing it. The charged solar particles, or plasma, as well as solar and galactic gamma rays, are moved by the solar wind along the magnetic field lines. The solar wind can leave a hole in the electromagnetic shield, allowing these charged particles to shower down on Earth. Gamma radiation can change our DNA through mutation. Too much gamma ray exposure can be damaging to our DNA and result in cancer.

> Don't be afraid. Ostuarian bridge—the bridge to human repose—human race hurries to become something they are not. The magnitude of which a mountain holds is based upon what you bring to the mountain.

Q: How would the root of ostuarian be spelled?

Kent, "I'm seeing e, like estuary, but it is not pronounced estuary. It is pronounced ostuarian."

> A comprehensive understanding of your language is at hand.

Q: Does an estuarian bridge combine energy flows?
Correct. The distance between flows designates a variation.

Q: What is the word estuarian in reference to?
It is a bridge to the other side—a comprehensive understanding of the solarsphere—an opening within.

Estuary is that part of the mouth of a river in which the river's current meets the sea's tide and a colliding of currents occurs. Visualize the movement of water as the river meets the ocean tide, then draw a parallel to the movements of energy streams in the same fashion. It is the flow of energy directing the human race to the greater ocean of universal consciousness. It is a bridge to the other side: the new cycle. A complete understanding of the sun's role in this will help to create an opening within.

Q: Beside heat and light, what other functions does the sun have?
You're not ready for this information: you don't have the understanding. Symbolic for creating life; it is but a small particle compared to the Light of the Creator at the creation point. The suns are placed where they would do the most good for the particles of life: purposeful locations—an organizational structure.

Q: What impact do solar flares have on life on this sphere?
Change in atmospheric gases, creating a gamma species; a crossover of the conscious being.

Q: Can you explain how a gamma species differs from the species here now?
You will see.

Q: How will the DNA change and manifest itself?
Prognosis of date given: an existence of mankind will proceed [the] linear extension of the helix cycle within Universal Law of Existence. All-natural material will exist on a plane of heliosis. Cultural cycles deviate upon the existence of Self-rule within the parameters of that organic circle. Austromolization of being acceptable on all levels of existence, except one: utilization inherent within the species directly causing disproportional influence upon the species itself. Numerical existence appropriated through universal mathematics—a conceptual agreement within that species—attainable through migrational delineation of species.

Q: What is meant by "all-natural material will exist on a plane of heliosis"?
Organic substance will be profoundly used to substantiate the cause and effect. Overwhelming evidence of species misuse is directing this cause and effect. A numerically-challenged species.

Q: Is our misuse of this planet causing this cause and effect?
A numerical challenge for change.

Kent later clarified that the human race is numerically challenged.

Overwhelming odds against replenishment of this sphere: acceptable limitations high in progress.

Q: For humanity to shift mathematically, would this also be achieved by the internalization of all lessons presented?
Correct; astute observance is in tune with universal parameters for this sphere, given the isometric configuration of universal law.

Our understanding: The prediction is that the next human DNA cycle will include a magnification of various parts of the genetic math codes, reflected in the sum-total of genetic amplification that coincides with the Universal Laws of Existence. All organic material will be subject to solarization, the solar activity being one of many tools used for our genetic change, as outlined below. Human cultural cycles vary depending upon whether the higher self is in charge, within parameters of that natural cycle. Extremes within beings are acceptable on all levels of existence, except one: the use of extremes that results in a disproportionate influence on the species itself. Universal mathematics are used to upgrade the DNA numerically, a conceptual agreement within that species, attained by outlining the mathematical movement of genetic expression from where it is now, to a higher expression in the future.

These mathematical changes to the human genome will set the parameters for humanity's direction.

Human DNA is numerically challenged. We are unable to move significantly forward to higher intellectual levels without intervention. The current dysfunctional state of humanity is evidence of this and is directing the cause for change to bring our DNA to a higher expression. There are overwhelming odds against the plan to supply what is lacking on this sphere, but acceptable limitations exist within the higher movement. The shift in our levels of understanding, through internalization of all lessons presented at this time, is aligned with the mathematically balanced parameters of universal law.

A gamma species

In this chapter, we learn how the gamma rays will affect our DNA. The questions were prompted by a 2013 article in a newsletter we had received describing how scientists had discovered a huge blast of charged particles coming from the galactic center; the energy five times that of a supernova.

Q: What is the phenomenon of the charged particles coming from our galactic center?
Hear the wind: a change in who you are. Magnitudinal increase in your true self: some good, some bad. Lay out the lines, magnetudinal lines; move the coordinates. Give way to a new beginning. Isotopes will yield the cause bringing all together as a force; the new beginning. Many will hurt, push against the force: [a] change in human cause.

Q: What changes will these charged particles cause?
The movement of all species related to structural changes at the subatomic level: DNA articulation within the field surrounding its structure. The

opening of the freedocks—which is a conceptual understanding of the particulate matter contained within the DNA helix of those subatomic nanomatter—within the constraints of all DNA on this sphere, flowing within the ionic pattern of all living matter organic. Change is beginning here.

Q: Will this also contribute to an acceleration of health and illness?
Changing matter configuration within the complex. Many will not accept the change and will dissipate into subatomic gases: matter reformation. A flow of neural energy will cease.

Q: How does opening of the freedocks relate to the flow of ions?
Freedocks is a variable port movement: creates opening to events of the other side. A Creative influence is possible when the opening occurs. Constance of value is adhered to a free-flow of energy [and] takes place when opening occurs. A consequence of behavioral changes can accelerate to cause of event proceedings. A freedock event can occur at any time, when given the natural occurrence dictated by outside sources.

Q: Will there be a thinning of the veil at this time?
Understanding its value in reference.

Q: How do the gamma rays affect our DNA?
Transverse a parameter of self-being, given the task of Self-indulgence, it awakens the being to self-perceptions of [the] true being. A concourse to understanding of Self—parameters narrowing—there's a causeway.

Q: Ultimately, what effect will gamma rays have on those who are exposed?
Change of species beginning. Acquiesce to your cause while here. A comprehensive value will be attained.

Q: Is direct exposure to gamma rays harmful to DNA, while indirect exposure causes a positive DNA change?
A little at a time. Possibilities are infinite on exposure amount.

Q: Is direct and prolonged exposure detrimental?
Direct exposure is harsh on the embodiment of the DNA molecule. A pervasive aspect of the change to come. Collapse of the sublime; an irreversible force.

Q: Is the sublime referring to genetic behavior or expression?
It is sublime.

Our understanding: In our limited research, we have come to understand that the cosmic rays collide with other particles in space and Earth's atmosphere, creating a fracturing of the cosmic particles and radiation into x-rays, gamma rays, protons, and neutrons, among others, as they reach the earth. We will only mention these particles, as these are the focus of the lessons we received.

In **chapter 3**, "A cosmic momentum is developing," we are told of a distant neutron explosion, a supernova, sending out a stream of cosmic rays, and Earth is in its way. Also, in **chapter 3**, "Solar activity influences ionosphere and magnetic field," is a reference to neutrons in the expression n^5. Could this indicate that the neutron field will be exponentially increased by a factor of five due to a supernova? The neutron field is designed to accentuate our understanding of who we are and where we are going through the opening of the freedocks. The freedocks act as a port—with variables—for all species to move to the other side through a new genetic expression. The freedocks reside within the minute particles of our DNA and are influenced by the patterns of charged particles in our atmosphere that dictate the behavioral expression of matter on this sphere. Quite simply, changes in the atmospheric gases change how DNA is expressed. Consequences from behavioral changes can create an acceleration of events to unfold, allowing the freedocks to open at any time, influenced by the natural events occurring outside our sphere. Once opened, an influence from the Creative beings is possible, allowing a free-flow of informational energy from other entities by way of telepathic communication.

By January 2016, the cosmic rays, identified by detection of gamma rays, had triggered the monitoring of pilots, airline stewards and astronauts for radiation exposure. The higher the altitude, the higher the exposure. The amount of gamma ray exposure creates a sliding scale of infinite possibilities in respect to its effect on the DNA; direct exposure being very harsh.

Through holes in the electromagnetic field, the rays shower down on Earth, coursing back and forth through the boundaries of our physical bodies. The gamma rays ultimately will lead to the collapsing of our grandiose thoughts. The combined events and effects will narrow the parameters, creating a higher and more direct path to understanding the higher self. Given the task to satisfy the higher self, we are awakened to perceive our own true Self. The changes have begun; our job is to accept the change.

Atmospheric changes and genetics

There is much talk about climate change, where there exists a clash between those that feel it is due to a natural cycle and those who feel it is human-created, with varying degrees of thought in between. On the human-created side, claims of a warming planet are primarily blamed on an increase in greenhouse gases, the focus on carbon, with methane now rising to the conversation. As of 2019, we now have a new crop of congresspeople who hold that we must make massive changes within the next ten years or face catastrophic effects. The following communication took place in June of 2007:

Q: Is there going to be a genetic change in human kind?
Yes, there is. And Prometheus asked the same question in his time. The change in genetics will be a resistance to the pollution or problems man has created. And the genetic change will be a tolerance of a warmer planet. The earth will cleanse itself of all the things that have been done to it so, once again, it will be clean. But, the atmosphere of the earth will change and the genetic change will take effect; and the resistance to tolerate the atmospheric changes.

Q: Is this due to the human-created carbon emissions?

Kent was not meditating at this point. Tuning in briefly, he felt the volcanic ash is pushed higher into the atmosphere, causing more of an effect; while vehicle carbon emissions produced a minimal effect in comparison. He closed his eyes and sank into a deeper trance:

You need *some* carbon.

Q: Can a distinction be made between warming from volcanic activity versus human carbon emissions?
The same paradigm. Your global warming is due to atmospheric gas transfer from volcanic Earth structure to upper level gases within this time frame. A perilogical quanticept due to impervious gas exchange. Quanticeptual understanding to take place within the interceptual program. A rarity within its own context of gaseous exchange, empirical by nature, quanticeptual by aspect.

Q: What effect do our carbon emissions have?
Change in atmospheric conditions.

Q: Specifically, what type of change?
A man function—new world—functionality cause a
species change.

Our understanding: The volcanic emissions and human-created
carbon emissions belong to the same paradigm. The volcanic
releases are being projected higher into our atmosphere creating the
global warming at this point in time. Through a logical, multi-
faceted awareness, we see that we are unable to influence this type
of gas exchange. The full understanding will take place during a
planned interception of our thoughts. This is a rarity, as the
scientific method is unnecessary; the gas exchange is a naturally
observable phenomenon, the full awareness obtained by looking at
all the various angles.

Ultimately, the gaseous makeup of our atmosphere is going to
contribute to a change in mathematical codes and the grid, which
changes the pattern for life form expression, leading to a species
change. We are told, "The resonance of magnetics is the technology
that will be unveiled."

Changes in atmospheric gases produce a new species

Quasi-atmospheric changes adapt new species
changes. You are rudimentary thought.

**Q: Will our bodies be changed to house the
twelve-helix DNA, as some channeled books say?**
We deal in atmospheric changes, which condition the
gases [and] chemistry of your bodies. No helix, not.

You are being observed for progress: tracked. Assumptions will not be made. Positive change, virtuous: transformation dignified. You will know.

Q: Is this change in atmospheric gas going to impact our DNA?
Correct.

Q: How do the changes in our atmosphere impact our behavior?
Behavior modification due to alignment of values associated with Self. Atmospheric gases contribute to any cause.

Q: How will our bodies change?
Electrical discharge, chemical profusion. Sceupharocal beings help accept protrudence of Self.

Q: Will there be a carbon change within the human body?
Molecular dissention within the field of human entity. Molecular dispersion within human magnetic field causes genetic consultation inside DNA—dispersion within the molecular field change. Equatious end event: a risen species. Activation upon cycle release and review.

Q: Does this coincide with the shift of the electromagnetic field of the earth?
Relative to exchange [of] ions within the sphere. Conceptual agreement maintained; parameters held.

Our understanding: The change in Earth's gaseous atmosphere and electromagnetic field brings about many changes for humanity, creating a new, more intellectual species. This is achieved through an expanded behavioral expression of DNA, changing the electrical synapses of our nervous system and the chemical makeup of our bodies, producing a higher-functioning species. The exchange of ions within the human electromagnetic field causes a new consultation within our DNA, aligned to conceptual agreements that have been made by entities directing the change within the new parameters of genetic expression.

DNA is attuned to Earth and universal law

The following paragraph is taken from *The Augmentation of Man: A Study in Renaissance*, **chapter 7**, "Layered vibrational changes," and elaborated on in the following:

> The changes are related to magnitudinal dispersions of this sphere and incoming waves from outside, affecting DNA molecular structure, tied to the planet's vibrational structure. You are tied to this sphere by choice. Vibrational equivalency will happen on other spheres. Correctional dispersion of layered vibrational changes takes place wherever you choose to be assigned.

> Your experiences equate to a magnetudinal direction of your life pole and directional spin within your sub-molecular structure of your DNA tree, the helix turn of direction and length. It is stretched to accommodate activation of molecular elements within that structure to receive vibrational waves from within the planet's core movement. A song metaphorically designed to be received by all living matter to this sphere. A dedication of aptitude designed to be here. This applies to all orbital spheres within your galactic field and beyond your reach and understanding.

Q: What is the relevance of a directional spin of our DNA?
Species to this atmosphere, to this place where you are. The makeup of who you are as a species. A small part of the whole.

Q: Will our bodies eventually become lighter, more buoyant?
The mind will be all that exists; bodies are irrelevant.

Those that are left, the change will reproduce offspring which will have a pervasive effect on the human race. Their DNA redialing will take effect from the exposure of the parent. Significant contributions will be made by outside sources to ensure a significant step forward in the development of the human species. Rain patterns will be changed: significant increase in intellectual capacity and understanding of universal phenomena. Egotistical behavior will not be tolerated, it does not fit in with the universal concepts of intellectual singleness of mind and the corazonian aspects of a single thread thought among many.

Q: How do rain pattern changes relate to DNA changes?
Rain patterns are consequential diagnostic tools for development of various DNA change. DNA reacts to vibrational trudence of each pattern, given the variances of many that are available; a tuning fork in its application. Being of various atmospheric conditions, each has its own vibration. A tuning consequence can be achieved through use of specific ring vibration.

Q: Would the ring vibration be circular energy?
Counter-clockwise movement of energies, creating a

ring-like effect. Not truly a ring; semi-circulating DNA strand attuning to that vibrational ring.

The behavioral patterns of man must be brought forth to the true identity. Those that have the correct resonance of mind will know the change and survive the coming. A biochemical change pattern increases on those that have the ability to understand, has no effect on those of sub-level intelligence who are not able to hereditate the opened areas of the mind. Therefore, 22 1/2% of the population is able to reach the open level of understanding and *could* survive the change.

Can you perceive the evolvement of man, with the limited knowledge that you have, in medical terms, considering the exposure ratios of various toxicological substances? What could be the evolvement rate without DNA restructuring, as found in the human source today?

Q: I don't see it. A lot of it is perception, too?
Perception! Correct. Evolvement is a must for the survival of any species, but at a cost.

Q: Will animals also evolve?
Animals are pleasure for mankind, as perceptual viewing and pleasure. They are not meant to evolve into a higher species. Ponder what I have given you to a perspective analysis of understanding the rain patterns and DNA sequential changes of pattern and numerical event.

Kent, "They showed me that there will be some tribes of people that will survive because they understand how the earth works and that everything is related."

Q: Man's manipulation of our own DNA is thought by some groups to be offensive to the Creator.

Technical understanding in concept only; relinquishing the parts of understanding to universal laws and conceptual behaviors. Misuse will pervade the technological advantage, which could be used by this race-entity, moving faster than understanding can prevail. Missteps are encouraged by this concept, setbacks to influence the entities that inhabit this plane. Not ready for the concept of universal laws relating to the God seed, the DNA of the beginning. Missteps may cause great harm—not ready—knowledge in a child's hand.

Our understanding: The changes for mankind relate to the totality of events taking place on this sphere: from human-created events, to the natural events occurring, both from within and external to Earth. All is set to affect the DNA structure, which is tied to the vibrational structure of the earth. All spherical changes require our coming into vibrational alignment with the new planetary resonance. This is occurring throughout the universes and wherever we choose to be assigned. Our life experiences coincide with the learning requirements of the higher self, which relates to the DNA expression for a particular species. All have to be in the same vibrational spectrum. The DNA is uncoiled to allow the activation of elements within the helix—the placement of protein markers that turn on specific genes—to be able to receive vibrational waves from Earth, allowing us to attune to her and all the learning she has to offer. Earth's vibration is moving up, the learning field is being raised, and human DNA is being upgraded, all pushing humanity forward in its capacity to understand higher conceptual ideas.

The atmospheric conditions create specific vibrational patterns that the DNA attunes to. Raindrops produce a ring of vibration, seen when the drops hit a body of water. The counter-clockwise rotation of vibrational energies it creates produce a ring-like effect that the

DNA strand responds to, evidently changing the bends and turns of the helix. The combined totality of events that influence the human DNA restructuring will be passed on to the next generation. This must be done to ensure survival of the species. However, not all are ready for this quantum leap. The biochemical changes only have an effect on those that have the ability to understand and have the correct resonance of mind. The DNA would otherwise not likely move forward organically due to the toxicological exposures we have been subjected to in our own chemical poisoning.

There is some work currently being done by our scientists to upgrade the human DNA, but understanding of Universal Laws and Concepts is lacking and will create the conditions for missteps, causing setbacks. We simply are not ready, at this point, for the conceptual understanding of the origin of the God seed.

The seed of Enoch

Behold the flourish, the fusion of equation to a paradoxal opening of the new humanity. A shift of magnitude not experienced before. The universe will repay in kind for the new ones.

The seed of Noch will prevail; a trusted understanding with a paradox that will arise. Prepare your influence. Calmness will be the causation of justice. Prevail your outcome to the understanding to the changes to come. Prognostication is not an outcome; it is the causation of what must come.

A concourse to follow the path of inception—a new formation of the human entity—a change in the DNA, increase production of the neuronetical influence. Here to establish a key, one of many, to open the new paradox.

Q: Who was Noch?

Kent explains, "Like a seed of Enoch."

> Many seeds around the world came from him. The planting of a derivative of hope for [the] future. A being of consequence: consequential, the new start, the strength of.

> Enoch: a purveyor of sequential knowledge. He kept intact the ancient language of the star ones—the embodiment for/of the equation for a higher human existence—the language of Atore': language of the star beings.

Q: Was he human?
> Star seeded: higher replication of DNA, multiple increases in neuronetical function. Behavior astute to a higher functional being, attuned to the universal frequency.

Q: Were his seeds genetic seeds?
> From the father: transferred, duplicated, and increased.

Our understanding: Watch while a combining of mathematical equations leads to an expanded influence on human genetic expression, resulting in what seems like contradictory results. The genetic coalescing will increase the neurological function and the ability of the human brain to process information at a much higher level.

It is interesting that this message also talks about the genetic remnants of Enoch, who had passed his genes on to his children, which multiplied in each successive generation. We are assuming this is Enoch, the great-grandfather of Noah of the Bible. His father must have been of the "gods," those from other places outside of

Earth; the Watchers who had a direct connection to this planet and its inhabitants at that time. He possessed a higher DNA expression and a more advanced neurological function, attuned to the universal vibrational frequency. He was able to speak the ancient language of the star beings. An ancient ancestor of many people around the globe at this time, they possess his genetic remnants, planting a seed of hope for the future.

What would the genetic effect be on the children of a couple who *both* have the DNA remnants from Enoch? Perhaps this is the fusion of the mathematical equation the mentor is speaking of that will accentuate the human genetic expression. Certainly, this would create a paradox in that the parents alone do not have the expanded genetic expression, but the children would. How could this exceptional child be born to "normal" human parents? Is it possible that the genes in the parents are recessive, as they came from only one parent, while the same genes become dominant if they come from both parents? Although we have not asked our guides about this scenario, it might explain why the parents don't have this gene expression, yet their children do.

Autism is a key to the new world

Coming from a nursing background, Renee wanted to ask what was causing the rise in autism:

Q: Why is autism on the rise?

Kent, describing a vision, "Aluminum just flew at me."

Q: What is the relevance of aluminum?
Part of process; introduction to begin change, moments ago.

The young ones can dictate the answer. Autism is a key to the new world; a higher level to understanding. Increase of young ones showing change: autism increase in young ones. They are the valued ones—various levels of change—a developing of a final species.

Q: How will the autistic communicate?
Well-developed psychic communication as progress continues. Feared by many; they don't understand.

Q: Will behavioral characteristics also evolve?
Higher level of being: clearer communication development [and] affirmation of Self.

Q: There are those that are diagnosed as lower level functional autistics, is this a misdiagnosis?
Understand[ing] of value: various levels of progress to the completion of the final being. Communication [is] not relevant to understanding beyond known concept. Various levels; a progress in order.

Q: Is there another disease that we are inaccurately calling autism?
You will learn. A pompousness still exists in human nature when it comes to vaccine.

Q: What can be said about our vaccines?
Pertuitous. Don't mix. Antiquitous results.

Q: Can you explain?
Out-dated.

Q: May I ask for a definition of pertuitous?
Purposeful.

Q: How does it relate to vaccines?
Forming a vaccine for a particular outcome; given the results of experimental cause.

Kent explains, "The vaccines are antiquated, like old-school, like living in the past."

Q: How would we protect our young from communicable diseases more effectively?
Undiscovered by your science. You will relate as you enter spatial plateaus corresponding with entities of another race.

Our understanding: We are being told that aluminum is the reason for the rise in autism. However, autism is an upgrade, done in steps, and is expressed at various levels along the development of a final species. Aluminum is a part of the process. As we will see later in this chapter, in "An introspective look at disease," it depends on what the aluminum is combined with. What are *all* the ways we are being exposed to aluminum? You will need to open your parameters for this one. The final human genetic expression is projected to enable telepathic communication and will allow a clearer understanding of the higher self.

Getting back to vaccines, the guide states that vaccines should not be mixed. From a medical standpoint, a vaccine is meant to stimulate an immune response to a particular disease. It makes sense that if we are giving children multiples of vaccines at one time, that we could be creating an exaggerated immune response. How might this contribute to future autoimmune disorders? Although antiquated, it is what we have for now and we will receive new information in the future from outside sources. Perhaps we should be giving only one vaccine at a time until we have something better. It is certainly food for thought.

The endigot, blue ray and magniferious children

We had heard the phrase "New Human Project" from a friend and turned to our mentors for clarification:

Q: Can you tell us about the New Human Project?
A conceptual understanding: DNA relevance. A nexus reformation of the neuronet cognitive: influential opening of the cerebral cortex, three degrees lateral to the occipital lobe. Stimulus package, opening to come. A flash of light stimulate[s] cerebral cortex area.

An advance creation of the new universal consciousness. The laws of universal consciousness will prevail the enlightened ones, a consequence of their beings. Consequential beings, as we are known as. The young blue ray shall correct those that have not. The vibrational output will increase by magnitude of seven. Others will envy and ridicule and create unpopular knowledge. Self-sustained are desires in helping direct human consciousness. Prepare the antiquities of the law, a universal concept.

Kent added, "We are headed toward a conceptual future, if, *if* we let it and learn. If not, it will be perceptive ignorance, which there is no room for in the universe."

Prepare for oscillation. Oscillation is set forth, [a] prelude to the event. Cautious understanding is admitable here. Vibrational atonement is accepted, aligned with the correct path and the correct tone. Tones are from the blue ray of understanding, a hidden quadrant of perceptual beings [that are] able to create genetical beings.

Q: Are the young blue ray and the indigo children one and the same?
One proceeds the other.

Q: Do the indigo children precede the blue ray?
Yes. The blue ray are coming soon. This is the last of the indigo being born. A conceptual agreement from the beginning.

Q: When did they start arriving?
Began in your years 1960. A mixture: not all indigo. Blue ray beginning: not all blue ray.

Q: What percent of the population are indigo and what percent of the population will be blue ray?
Thirty-percent indigo. Sixty-percent blue ray.

Q: What can you tell us about the young blue rays?
Integral part of change. Star entity's conceptual agreement to come here. Unitarian aspects to cause: bring forward ambition for unifier.

Q: Does the unitarian aspects relate to the blue ray of understanding?
Correct; given the parameters for each cause and effect laid upon the cause.

Q: What is the purpose of the indigo?
Proceed [and] open the path for the [new] ones to come. Two generations of indigo, [then] the blue ray will begin.

Q: How would we identify an indigo?
They are already here. Intelligence of being, a winding up of value.

Q: Are they more intellectual and intuitive?
Yes, correct. Many will not understand them; their intellectual being a must for the conceptual understanding to begin.

Q: Do they each have higher levels of DNA expression?
Called intelligence of universal language: in-di-get.
In-di-get.

Q: How would we spell in-di-get?
E-n.

Renee responded, "E-n? We are spelling the indigo children wrong! It is not i-n. It is e-n-d-i-g-o-t, endigot."

Q: Do the endigot possess the intelligence of the universal language?
A learned culture of variance: [a] higher learn. Pronastation of learning: incorporate into culture. Blue ray is a substantial movement of said culture.

Q: Does the blue ray refer to a blue energy?
Source, blue-ray Source; consequential to understanding—communicative.

Q: Is there an area in the brain of the blue ray that coordinates with this communicative energy?
Energy of need.

"What is magniferious?" Kent asked, responding to a word he was hearing in his head.

Magniferious children after the blue ray; [as] called by others. Give value now to your life. Do not procrastinate further in your understanding, dullatarious concepts of being.

The question below was in response to hearing people talk about rainbow and crystal children, of which we knew nothing about:

Q: Is there any such thing as rainbow or crystal children?
Man-caused names. Not universal.

Q: Would these human terms be referring to endigot children?
Universal condition of parameter; use in fluctuation of language. Consequential needs by adjustment within the panoramic field.

The following question was in response to personal guidance we had received, in which the mentor spoke of "those that are making the way":

Q: Who are those that were referenced as "those that are making the way"?
The young ones, the new ones, ones to be learned.

Q: How will we teach these children?
Know free-will value they have chosen. Remember, your temporary humanity is a gift to your understanding. They are willing to learn [and] accept higher level understanding; a move to extreme vibrational attunement. The task: raising their level, creating a running path for them to expand upon quicker than your learning path. Important task to be completed.

Renee had been told by an acquaintance that there existed a contract with outside entities to enable them to collect human eggs and sperm in order that they may use it to replicate themselves, as they have become sterile. The question had to be asked:

Q: Do outside entities have a contract to use human eggs and sperm to replicate themselves?
No! Understanding for species augmentation, for other entities, sustain the human population after

contractual events to save universal vibratory conditions.

Q: Are they holding human eggs and sperm somewhere?
Correct.

Q: Where would that be?
Occupational forces: cryogenic matter; we have attached influence to correct DNA sequence, produce higher conscious level of entity to inhabit this sphere.

Q: Who is in charge of this?
Counsel of Universal Reproductive Matters. A counsel of conceptual beings devoted to reproducing entities of a higher state of vibrational attunement— of a universal federation.

Our understanding: While atmospheric changes create an indirect pathway to genetic change, there are multiple other programs that create a direct DNA change. It is being done in stages. There seem to be beings who normally are incarnating on other planets, who have volunteered to come here to move humanity forward in its evolution through their own genetic upgrades, producing a higher intellectual capacity. The first generation, starting around 1960, are the endigot. The endigot will soon be replaced by the incoming blue ray children; another step up in genetic expression. The third phase will be the magniferious children, an even higher degree of intellect than the preceding. Not all children will be affected: thirty percent of the children are endigot, sixty percent will be blue ray, and probably more magniferious; a winding up and eventual conversion of the population to a higher degree of intellectual capacity and genetic expression, done in stages.

The eggs and sperm, in an effort to genetically upgrade the human genome, are frozen in a cryogenic chamber and are being used to advance the understanding of other entities in the subject of augmenting a species—the human species. The eggs and sperm are also being used to introduce the new children of a higher conscious level to sustain the population after the changes in order to preserve the vibrational balance of the universe.

A change in brain patterns

We're lining things up now. The equinox will cross the paths of those with understanding, creating a new perception of matter. It's going to be a change in the occipital area, creating a new understanding of new communicable ideas.

The occipital area will increase its neuro ability to translate a much higher and vast amount of language that will be coming from other higher biological entities. This flow of information will transform the human nature of mankind. A conceptual behavior will be created to conceptual dispersion, transecular convergence of the auditory system that has manifested from a higher Source. Energy magnification will abound, creating a paradox to electrical-magnetic field—consequential alignment of universal electron bombardment. Horizontal dispersion of the magnetic field to move the earth in a parallel direction of the movement. Consignment of ideas will abound.

Universal magnification will reach the threshold of the antiquities once misused. The precepts of understanding you must learn, analogous to understanding energy Source. Study, understanding and correct behavior as abundance is sustained. Release your ideas, prepare for new concepts.

Our understanding: A change to the occipital area of the brain, at the back of the head, will create an expanded ability of the nerves of the brain, allowing a communicative transfer of new ideas through telepathic communication. The flow of information will transform human nature. The transformation of human behavior will be created through a dispersion of conceptual understanding from a higher Source entity through a hidden convergence in the auditory system. It is important to understand Source energy: what it is and how it works. Studying, gaining understanding, correcting behavior, and releasing old thoughts will make way for new concepts.

A magnified energy will be released creating a circumstance that seems contradictory to the electromagnetic field; a consequence of aligning to the universal electron bombardment. This magnification will mark the beginning where, in ancient times, it was once misused. The dispersion of the magnetic field along a horizontal line will move the earth in a parallel direction.

Resetting DNA back to zero-point

Kent was sick with a severe cold, chest congestion and wheezing. He sat on the sofa with his eyes closed. Renee had started upstairs, when Kent suddenly announced that someone had just sat down beside him, prompting Renee to return to Kent's side.

Q: Who's here?
A friend.

Q: What can we do to speed Kent's recovery?
A similar to DNA change of the viruses or bacteria: change of molecular structure. Regeneration occurring. Adaptation a must for survival. Potentiate[s] the virus.

Q: We were told that we would have *less* disease after the changes. How does a more virulent virus fit in with this?
Adaptation of most species back to zero-point.

Q: So, we will become stronger also?
Correct. Zero-point: one species, all species.

Our understanding: It seems that there is a resetting of DNA, in most species, back to an original point, where a regeneration is occurring, creating a renewed strength in all species, including viruses.

An introspective look at disease

Renee, a registered nurse, obviously had many questions regarding the origin of various diseases. The following questions are about a few diseases that plague humanity, where we still lack clarity.

Q: What determines which area of the body is targeted in autoimmune diseases?
The weaker. It targets the weakest organ.

Q: What is causing the increase in Alzheimers?
Aluminum cans and aluminum containers, foil.

Q: Why does aluminum cause a genetic upgrade in autism, but a mental decline in alzheimers?
What it attaches to. Aluminum is not the *only* thing; it is just a part of it.

Q: Is it the type of aluminum?
What it is mixed with.

Q: Could you explain why children are born with cancer?
Environmental effect; not natural learning. Disease:

man's contribution to vibrational dispersion effects. Change in molecular structure of natural background of environment, releasing unwanted parameter designed within the atomic structure. Variations that have been effectually concentrated beyond natural conditions within the planetary nomenclature.

Man's human culture design of cause and effect: parameters to self-judgment without conditions to repercussions of decision-making. A consequence of non-linear structure: no conditions set within the universal conditions of laws and concepts, as dictated through time variances as brought forth. No relevance given to these concepts, now payment becomes due for irrelevant thinking and self-egotistical behavior, not of high vibrational influence for conceptual intelligence. Put[ting] self above all Creational concepts has disastrous consequential effects upon any world plateau. Natural cause and effect will return without human interference to balance this sphere. Repercussions will be many from misuse of vibrational influence upon the atomic structure of this planet. The spherical nature will be widely influenced as correction continues—begins and continues—a nirvana effect.

Q: Are all man's activities that alter nature those that also alter the vibrational background?
All related. Connections never cease.

Our understanding: The mentor is saying that childhood cancer is not initiated through a learning cause but is the direct result of man altering the natural vibrational background environment, causing an unwanted parameter within the planet's vibrational script. Man is oblivious to the creation of these unnatural conditions of his own making: there seems to be no direct correlation, as relating to the timing. But Universal Laws and Concepts eventually produce consequences relating to our decisions. Humanity has not given relevance to the laws of nature in our own lower egotistical desires. We are not looking at the whole picture. When we put ourselves above all Creational concepts, manipulating the natural environment, we create disastrous effects for ourselves. There will be many repercussions from our unnatural tampering with the atomic structure of Earth and her environment. A cause and effect will balance this sphere, returning the pristine nature of the natural world once again and ending this cycle of altering the atomic structure that results in pain and suffering.

Nutrition, genetics and spiritual magnification

Within the human DNA helix are many, many instructions for gene expression. In order for a particular gene to be expressed, it must have a protein marker attached to that particular "rung" of the DNA ladder. Yet there is an enormous amount of DNA lacking a protein marker, that is not activated. In **chapter 1**, "Humanity was a short-term experiment," we learned that scientists at the University of Oxford determined that 8.2 percent of human DNA had not changed over the eons and, therefore, was deemed to be absolutely necessary to life and that any other genetic change that occurred indicates that DNA was non-essential. This became the basis for the junk DNA theory. We were told by our guides that human DNA was originally altered to the least amount of expression and that there is going to be a transformation of the human DNA in the near future.

> **Q: How does the eating of animal flesh affect us physically and spiritually?**
> Magnification of life essence, a stamp. Not all able to handle small amounts infusion particles: over-use capsizes diametrical field geometry. All living particles infuse to a pattern life force to be utilized in learning interdimensional being. Purer particles desirable for infusion. Eat spinach, asparagus.

Q: What does the consumption of spinach and asparagus do?
Protein marker accentuation in preparation of coming enhancement of markers: coalescing vitamins and minerals to enhance the movement or activation. The protein markers to come: readiness for self.

Q: Is it best to eat them raw or partially cooked?
No more than partially-cooked [or] lose value. A complete cycle of nutrition needed to enhance value of what is to take place.

Q: What is the complete cycle of nutrition?
Spiritual: foods that increase the spiritual complex; a natural movement for Self-cohesion. Spiritual manifestation of the Self-complex; liquefication of atomic particles within the structure.

Q: What is the length of a complete cycle of nutrition?
Length-dependent of self-evaluation, each individual, in enhancement of bodily functions. Many variations; no set or determined time frame of self-evaluation. Completeness is not exact, only a representation of what you *can* accomplish.

Architectural dispersion is taking place to reform the structural sub-impertinences for the rebuilding and expansion of the human entity.

In a meditation many years later, Kent opened the communication with a single phrase that was heard:

Fiber-ten.

Q: Who is this information for?
All. Consequential analysis is a must. Interferal to the concepts.

Q: Does the fiber-ten relate to our diets?
Correct. Astute analysis of perceived material. Aculate the conceptual nature of what you see. This is a must for procedural understanding.

Q: Are we to denature the fiber-ten sequence?
Sequential beginning: analytical exposure of material. Correctional behavior within: the must sequence.

Q: What does it relate to?
Relative to conceptual learning. Know the parameters of the fiber.

Kent, "I heard we would live longer. It will increase our life span. I keep getting the word *ancient*. We have to make ourselves healthy to receive this information."

The meditation was paused as Renee searched ancient grains on her phone, which produced a site that recommended ten ancient grains for health. As we read about sorghum, we noticed that it was more often used as animal feed. Kent picked back up on the communication:

> Those that know the value of sorghum have done that to influence those to not touch it. They played on the ego of mankind.

Kent, "I keep hearing 'sorghum pie.'"

> Durra variety: It came from the stars. The food of the gods. Given the right amount, increase[s] longevity. One fourth of a teaspoon each day.

Spelled d-u-r-r-a. In a ground form, ground up. Six days a week, a pause in between. Much water.

Q: Is it cooked with much water or taken with much water?
Back then, taken. Water was precious then. Austromolosis is formed in the stomach, gut: more healthy sensation, longevity.

Q: How are we to take the other grains?
You will be given [more].

Kent, "Is there a green sorghum, one that has more of a green stem? I'm seeing the stem."

Hybrid is a little different color.

Q: I'm wondering if the stem on the hybrid is more olive color?
The durra is green.

Kent, describing a vision, "I'm looking at a field of ancient grains. All, almost all of them are hybrids."

This is just one of ten.

Q: Do we eat the white or the red sorghum?

Kent explains, "We have to do the research. One is not from the stars. I see the red dwindling near the ground and the white standing tall."

Research 3,000 B.C. in Egypt. Original were purple or red. Pheromone: lactavius, a creative substance high in potassium; a magnified version.

Kent, "The plant has potassium, but the plant lets off a pheromone.

I was asking about one of the fiber-ten plants and I heard 'weed block.'"

Renee added, "It must block the weeds around it."

> **Q: This pheromone, lactavius, is this substance high in potassium?**
> Substance high in potassium; magnified version.

Later, after beginning to eat many ancient grains, including sorghum, we checked in with our Ancient mentor with new questions about the sorghum:

> **Q: Am I preparing the sorghum correctly?**
> Mix in with grains.

> **Q: Do we need to drink a lot of water with it?**
> One glass with grains.

> **Q: Why such a small amount of sorghum?**
> Mixed with grains. Increase [to] half teaspoon.

> **Q: What beneficial effect does it have, not found in my research?**
> Heart palpitations. Migration of sexual desire on human. A coronarial effect: heart.

> **Q: Can you further explain this effect?**
> Desire fluctuation—stronger heartbeat interpretation—actuate the cause event.

> **Q: Are we still talking about strengthening the heart?**
> Yes. Interpretation needed.

Kent added, "I saw you sprinkling the sorghum over the wet grains after you're done cooking them, then putting it away."

Our understanding: In our limited research thus far, we discovered that sorghum has to be grown under certain atmospheric conditions so as not to produce a toxic chemical, mainly from too much heat. So, we have ground the sorghum and not cooked it, but added it to the other grains after they are done cooking. After eating, we follow with drinking a glass of water. We were initially told to take one-fourth a teaspoon sorghum with the other grains daily for six days, then one day off before starting again. A few weeks later, we were instructed to increase the sorghum to half a teaspoon at the same daily rate. After consuming the grains for about six weeks at the rate of six times a week, then one day off, we were instructed to cut it back to half a teaspoon, three to four times a week.

We discovered many of the ancient grains to be of great benefit in the management of many diseases, including heart disease and diabetes. Additionally, it was discovered that wheat in the U.S. has been genetically altered to produce significantly higher amounts of gluten than it once had, possibly the cause of the recent gluten intolerance and sensitivity surge. Studies have also found modern wheat to be lacking in many minerals that it contained previously. Lastly, our milling process has also changed the nutritional advantages it once had. Ancient preparation of the wheat included soaking the grains to sprout them prior to use. We are being encouraged to do our own research, examining all the constituent parts of the grains, as the study will produce a more profound conceptual understanding, connecting the dots. We urge you to do the same. We also want to state that this should never replace physician advice or prescription medication.

Step two does not come before step one

NOTES

Chapter 5

‹—— ••• ——›

The Spiritual-Physical Interface

We are on a vibrational journey. Everything relates to vibration, from the atomic environment in which we reside, to our thoughts and relative levels of understanding. This physical experiential field provides "bonus" opportunities to further our study of vibration. It is through our senses and the exploration of the three-dimensional space around us—and the interactions and events that take place in that space—that provide events for our contemplation and growth in understanding vibration. We need to understand how and why our spiritual being interfaces with this physical reality. Our incarnations are scripted plays, where we assign ourselves to various roles, interacting with others in their various roles, learning and growing from our reactions and counter-reactions with each other and our environment. Karma weaves its way through our decision-making, dictated by the higher self, to present the various lessons along a vibrational spectrum that reaches from one polar side to the other, to deliver a more complete understanding of all sides. As we turn inward in our reflections, listening for further guidance, we expand our vibrational understanding. The new understanding creates a vibrational influence on the organic matter within the field that we occupy. It is a field in which all things interface and interact with each other in a symphony of vibration.

Our physical existence relating to organic matter

> A purveyance of understanding is essential to the universal consciousness. Your essence will be in alignment and harmony with the peace that is present in all of the universe. That includes Mother Earth. Building a house of universal understanding needs nails, hammers, saw. Tools are others around us. With them, you can build a house. Without them, you cannot.

Create your own path, your perceptive understanding on your own value. Astute behavior to the oculant understanding: surveyance of one's purpose. Ostracize your understanding to self-worth, a prelude to Self-value, augmentation of the Creative forces, the resonance of being; but not a view of the value of true Self.

The tie that binds all living matter organic, the plant, can give one a conceptual understanding of Self-worth; a theoretical level of organic matter that pervades the understanding of *all* life connection. Hostility of nomenclature not important; concept of all connected living matter, which gives the concern to each, [is]. Survival is on a plane of universal vibrational connectiveness. True value of Self is in direct relationship to value of purpose—not immediate.

Fluctuation of time variance equates to quantum values attained through various paths of Self-analysis; a sequential thought to directional behavior. Pursue your path to theoretical concepts on a level of simplistic understanding. Teach the value of living organic matter in relation to human self-worth—your value is misplaced. A conceptual understanding of who you are varies with understanding of who you will be.

A shift of the electrical-magnetic field must be perceived as part of your understanding of organic behavior. Pursue this understanding in your research—importance to come.

Our understanding: The expansion of universal consciousness is entirely dependent upon the communication connections for the sharing of knowledge. Our journey here is a large part of our expanding consciousness through the reflection upon events that we create. Our lives are entangled for a reason: we are assisting each other in the learning process. As we share understanding, as we make choices, as we react and counter-react, as we learn through our own events and through events of others, we are observing, learning, expanding. Be clear in your purpose for being here, following the drive within and being observant of all that takes place in the field around you, turning inward for a deeper conceptualization of what has occurred. Step away from the egoic perception of self-worth, to realize the value of the growing understanding of the higher self. Listen to the inner voice, the Creative guidance, expanding your understanding as you rise in vibration. A clear understanding of purpose, observing all that takes place around you in the physical world, is of utmost importance to the higher self and life eternal. A shift in the electromagnetic field will help us with this. Time should not be a factor when it comes to learning: take the time to discover the more expansive truth. We are informed that we will never see the *entirety* of what exists in the higher self while we are in this physical form.

The life force

Life force is a continuous flow of energy released by Creator and Light Beings to *naturally* inhabitable planets to give life to all things. Life force is universal and applies to all life. It creates the soul and gives it the essence. It is our direct connection to God, our Creator, and makes us who we are.

Q: What location does the life force energy stream originate from?
Beyond your recognition. A perceptual habitat of being, in your words.

Q: Do all life force energy streams originate from the same location?
This is not for you to know with your level of understanding at this time. A correctional influence

is pervading an intellectual being.

Q: Does this life force energy stream travel through space within the plasmic field?
Correct; to its destination of intercept—advances in plasmic energy.

Q: What kind of advances?
Redundancy exchange of the life force field—a reoccurrence at a faster pace—exceptional rehabilitation of the energy field.

The life force energy advances at a quickening pace with each exchange of ions within the plasmic field, a result of a restoration of the field to a superior function and operability.

Q: Does each cycle start with a rehabilitation of the energy field?
No, a complete diagnostic interpretation of field resistance is in order.

Q: Is this in reference to human resistance of the field?
No, acquisition of the field.

A complete analysis and interpretation of the opposing factors within the plasmic field has to be conducted from time to time to gain control of the energy field.

Q: Would the next destination of intercept include the mass density of this body?
No, density of planet involved. Human race is immaterial to consequence of this event: irrelevant by natural concept.

Q: If life force energy advances to next point of intercept, the planet, how does life force energy move to our physical body?
All inhabited—naturally inhabited—planets.

Kent, visualizing, "I'm seeing a stream."

Q: If it's generated to the planet, how does it come to our physical body?
Give credence to its value: it's a stream. Not all planets, only those that are naturally inhabited.

Q: If there is no life on a planet, there would be no life force energy?
No life force stream.

Kent, describing his vision, "I saw a single stream coming into this solar system and other naturally inhabited planets and the stream goes through us." The life force stream is not directed at us as humans; it is projected from Creator and Light Beings to inhabited planets, passing through our bodies in the process.

Q: If the life force energy passes through the plasma field, does it travel through the neuronet?
In relation to. Independent, but related to complete the cycle of life within the universal pattern. Parallel flows within each stream—monteculiar domain—flow participates within each molecule.

Q: Can you explain what monteculiar domain is?
Molecular singularity of one within one. A mathematical inconvenience to most mathematical minds, or scientists. A flow of one within one: diametrical perceptual participation of more than one within one, a unitarian concept of multiple layers. A perceptual anomaly as viewed within your realm.

Q: What sustains the flow of the life force energy?
All That Is: constant energy flow from All That Is.

Kent further explains, "Life force is a geometric pattern. It is not a soul; it is a particle pattern. And, as each pattern is taken out of the differential—I'm hearing *quadraplex*—a soul is created and given to those particles and then it is moved into a body, a box, a fetus."

Q: If life force is a geometrical particle pattern to which a soul is created, is the soul interfaced with these particles?
Conjunctive in aspect for cause: related to, but not part of.

Q: What is a quadraplex?
Multi-lingual denomination of numbers used to capture. The soul comes in after the life force particles come together.

Our understanding: The life force stream is independent of the neuronet but related to the complete cycle of life: the purpose of our physical existence, interfaced with our expanding consciousness. The two flows are a part of a larger flow of energy through the molecules of space and matter within the monticuliar domain. The entirety of this picture may be difficult for our scientists to understand, as the mathematics to prove it evade us at this time. It is a different way of perceiving a concept of multiple layers within one concept. Once the life force particles come together, the soul is brought in and the two are bonded to each other.

The interface of physical life with spiritual learning

The acceptance to move in a quantciprocal orbit shares the afflation of the electrical particles that are present in all matter. Sequences that are involved in the making of essence that forms geometrical life patterns extending to life force of light; consequence can become fortunate to subatomic influence of the essential life force. Neuron release presents particles of light crystals projected into a connective tissue: the life force of all atoms connected.

The Light force is the plasma. The life force is the geometrical pattern of Creator: Light particle. The plasmic Light makes up the geometrical patterns, which connects everything to the universe. The geometric patterns are released when creation was first created—there all the time. The particles are released when a new planet is created with new species. The geometric pattern is there all the time; it is the numerical value of the universe, the math code of the universe.

All said to a cognitive value to Self-worth relating to all organic matter, understand this: Your existence is only for the matter to obtain the higher essence which emanates on a diffused pattern from the main neuronetical energy field, the Creator. We direct the patterns of life, entities higher than those of your knowledge, cipherious in nature, directors under the Creator, directors of neuronetical field alignment and adjustment relating to cognizant beings.

Our understanding: Humans—beings of lower understanding—receive the understanding from mentors of a higher knowledge, in a relationship that shares the driving inner force of communicative knowledge present within the electrical particles in all matter. Geometrical life patterns stretch out in various directions into the life force, resulting in a favorable subatomic influence to the life force that is essential for all life in the making of essence. Universal neurons project particles of light crystals into the life force of all connected atoms.

The Light force, the Light, travels over charged ions that make up plasma. The Light is the communication energy that carries intelligence. It is the universal consciousness and it connects everything in the universe. These geometric patterns were created with the big bang, are there all the time, and contains the math code of the universe. All That Is, is all understanding, which equals all vibration and the combined total of all math codes for creation. All That Is changes with the flow of intelligent Light as it meets its goals of ever-expanding universal consciousness.

The life force, a light particle with a geometric pattern, is released by Creator and Light Beings. Our existence is to develop a higher character of the soul through growth in understanding provided through the nervous network of intelligent communication, which also raises the vibration of the organic matter in which we reside. We edit our thoughts, correcting our understanding, resulting in a purification of the soul.

Kent then describes his vision, "Matter has essence of the Creator. Thought entities—and humans are thought entities—are controlled by the essence of matter that surrounds them. Example: You are in a forest: this is beautiful, this is God. Standing in a city full of skyscrapers, you absorb the essence of emotion around you—no organic matter influence. The neuronet plasmic limitations: the neuronet controls everything in the universes. We don't create the thought; the thought comes from the universal connective thought. We receive and then we create and learn. Creative peoples are more receptive to hearing the thought and then create and invent. It is like we are all neurons of the universal neuronet. Every person has the ability to open their essence to the thoughts of the universe and it has to do with the organic matter that surrounds you. It is through this thought process that everything is brought forward in the future."

The making of essence

Time [is] controlled by Creator: the increasing pulse of the neuronet. All energies controlled by a neuronetical field pole, like your brain. Light crystals equal flow of energy. All energy has a pattern—not all [the] same, as many think. Don't think of electrical energy pattern as the same as an energy pattern with this concept. An energy pattern has geometric shapes, unlike electrical energy.

Unlike electricity, these energies have geometric shapes which make up the light crystals.

Q: What is the connection between geometrical life patterns and particles of light crystals?
Forming a bond.

Kent describes, "I keep getting cold fusion. In other words, it doesn't create heat; but it produces energy."

The two come together to make the essence. Spiritual essence determines what physical form: organic life form. Making of essence forms geometrical life patterns: light crystals projected into a connective tissue. These are universal life signatures obtained in stratospheric conditions, which life forms are presented. It determines what life is going to be on that planet. Each planet is different and depends on the stratospheric conditions of that planet.

The universal neurons release the particles of light crystals and are projected into the connective tissue—the atoms of all life forces, the life force of all atoms connected—[and] come together with geometrical life patterns. Then vibration is brought forth; then aligns to universal vibration. This determines physical form of all life forms. Life signature and vibrational signature are different. Patterns establish what forms will look like: creates to physical life forms.

Universal neurons release light crystal particles that are projected into the life force field of connecting atoms and bond with geometrical life patterns. Vibration specific to that sphere is brought in and coordinated with the universal vibration. This occurs within the atmosphere around a given planet and creates a pattern for how all life forms will be expressed on that particular planet.

Understanding the value of your bodies, relating to all organic matter: your physical existence is only for the organic matter to be raised in its essence, which comes from the Creator—[a] diffused pattern from the main neuronet energy field. It is the combination of geometric life patterns [and] light particle crystals released from the neurons that, when enter stratosphere and interact, determine life forms.

Difference between life signature and vibrational signature. The propensity of light ions to penetrate the cell's structure globally conducts the life force. The life force within emanates from Creator. It is the energy force, Source of All That Is, the life essence. The soul's box contains nanoparticles of which the life force is reflected into. It is the memory.

Our understanding: The making of essence forms a geometrical life pattern, which has a mathematical code. It extends into life force of light and influences the life force essential to all life at the subatomic level. Life signature is the distinctive set of characteristics for life on a given planet. Vibrational signatures refer to the distinctive characteristics of that vibration. Your vibrational signature is made from the unique characteristics of vibration at the soul level. Life signature determines what distinctive characteristics that influence what you look and behave like in an incarnation, the humanness. The life force emanates from Creator (and Light Beings) and is the energy force permeating the cells of all life throughout the livable spheres. The life force is projected into the soul, which contains nanoparticles that store your memories of events in the physical life and beyond—a memory stick.

Geometric life patterns

During Kent's meditation, July of 2010, Renee pulled out Drunvalo Melchizedek's book, *The Ancient Secret of the Flower of Life,* and asked the mentor about the geometric pattern on the cover:

It is a life form of a single planet.

Kent injected, "Possibly our own. But it's not a universal life pattern."

> **Q: What can you tell us about this pattern?**
> Pertains to this universe only, not outside. There are eight patterns in this universe. This is your galactic pattern, this section of the galaxy. Not the universe; this section of the universe. The universal life pattern is simple, yet complex, and resembles the neuronetical structure.
>
> **Q: Is there such a thing as sacred geometry?**
> Life geometry. No such thing as sacred. Geometry of life; a pattern of life. Man-made word—sacred— all universe understands this for being. Narrow parameters for life geometry: a crescendo of events come together to create the pattern on each sphere.
>
> **Q: Is this the template for how life forms are expressed?**
> Correct, as given through *all* the creation. A change

is coming to this system. Atmospheric platitudes are created for development of this race. Preemptive arbiture is created for the new understanding. Simplicity is virtuous in cause—a Creative understanding.

Q: Do the geometrical life patterns have anything to do with the merkaba?
No. These are universal life signatures obtained in stratospheric conditions of all planetary objects through which life forms are presented.

Q: What can you tell us about the merkaba that people talk about?
Merkaba dead—no longer needed. Auspication penned. Magniflux sustained. Proceed the interloculence, maintain auspication.

Q: What was the merkaba used for?
Coordinating sight energies for balance. Use antiquated in this existence.

Our understanding: If you change any part of the formation of essence—the vibration, the geometry, or the atmospheric gases—you change the pattern for how life forms are expressed. The earth will have a new vibration, a new mathematical expression and a new balance of atmospheric gases, changing the behavior of life forms here on Earth.

There are entities and technologies developed within the universe for a particular purpose. Once the purpose has been fulfilled, that entity or technology is no longer needed and its' energy is recycled. The merkaba is no longer in use, as it is antiquated for the current times.

Ethereal bodies

Ethereal bodies irrelevant to the existing human kind. Do not partake yourselves in non-essential illusions outside your course to attain a higher self in place for the ethereal being, which is to come.

Q: Why are ethereal bodies irrelevant to the existing human kind?
Inconsequential being.

Q: Do we, as human beings, have an ethereal body?
Not on this plane. Prognostic purification will exist.

Q: Will there be a change in the prognosis?
Complete, virtuous by nature.

At the human level, we have not yet developed an ethereal body. We are predicted to have a purification of our thought process to hold a more complete and virtuous understanding in the future.

Life and death

Q: Prior to physical incarnation, does one choose physical attributes, such as gender, physical stature, etc.?
Time.

Q: What kind of influence do we have on gene expression prior to conception?
Gene makeup is formulated during the formation of the atomic structure of the human. Gene expression is consequential and tied to those that are formulated from the beginning. Consequential evidence is when expression and DNA collide within subatomic

formation of the entity. Does not completely form. Left out: expression of being. Nutrition of being is part of the formation that creates the whole.

Q: Are there any unplanned events or deaths or does everything occur as planned prior to our birth?
This is not for you to know. The truth at this point is not at an understanding at your level. The truth cannot be attained through books.

Kent explains, "It's like on a one-to-one with the higher ups. You have to talk with somebody in the higher level of consciousness on a one-to-one level to understand what that is."

Too many surmise.

Q: Are we judged after physical death or do we judge ourselves?
Your thoughts are correct: you are your own judge. A learning process: mysteries will only be solved by analysis of Self-events. You are the Self-diagnostic; a tuning of soul's resonance. None are left without the experience from a point of simplicity to a convexing diagnostic behavior.

Q: Does it make a difference whether we bury or burn the body after death?
No, the soul goes to the reflection area. The body is just to house the soul for learning, the reflective part of learning, to house the soul while you are here; irrelevant to cause.

Our understanding: The genetic expression is formed at the time of conception. Nutrition plays a role in the development of the physical body. We only choose the timing of our incarnation and the family we will be born into and have no influence on other physical characteristics. Genetic expression must coincide with the life form pattern for a given planet, as discussed previously. We do, however, choose our desired experiences and receive a vibrational attunement from others prior to birth to open the pathway to those experiences. Life experiences relate to the attraction of like vibrations: the vibration you are attuned to at birth attracts the experiences and people into your life for learning purposes. Once all the various angles have been viewed and comprehension is attained, we receive a vibrational attunement from spiritual beings to the new level of understanding. Our behavior and decision-making then change. The new vibration attracts a new level of events and people into one's life for the next higher step in learning. This continues to progress throughout our lives. If you are doing a lot of movement, you will see friends come and go as you progressively are attuned to higher vibrational levels, where your vibration is no longer in harmony with those who have not moved. See **chapter 3** of *The Augmentation of Man: A Study in Renaissance*, "Reincarnation".

At physical death, and if significant learning has taken place, we progress through the tunnel and then to the reflection area. Our life experiences are replayed in a hologram. Then we go into an intense microscopic study of those events before we can move on to new learning. See **chapter 3** of *The Augmentation of Man: A Study in Renaissance*, "Death and spiritual rebirth". We are the judge of whether our learning goals of the higher self have been met. None are left out of the act of analysis and interpretation of one's life events. It does not matter whether we bury or burn the body at physical death; it was only there to house the soul for learning purposes and the soul has moved on.

Karmic lessons: learning both sides

Kent sat down to meditate and almost immediately went into a class. He came out of meditation to explain:

"They were giving me a lesson. I saw us teaching in front of a class, talking in front of a group.

I was drawing on a chalkboard. A major decision is enclosed in a circle. For ease of understanding, we are only going to make three to four quantum directions from that major decision. The spokes of a wheel within that circle represent the decisions.

When society itself decides on a direction, it's because they have something to learn. Russia had something to learn, China had something to learn and other countries around the world had something to learn. Whether the government is controlling or people are controlling, all societies need to go through that because it gives you both sides of the learning process.

American society has had constant material wealth. Not having gone through the other side of being controlled, we really haven't learned. It's not up to us to criticize what the government is doing or not doing; we need to learn the lessons that we are going through. Countries that have material wealth versus those that have nothing: those that are wealthy can't learn what it is really like to be poor until *society* leads them down that path.

In this classroom, I asked how many people in this room felt like they are well-off and how many felt like they are not well-off? They were divided: the well-off sitting on one side, the not-well-off sitting on the other side. The not well-off group were compared to the not well-off in another place: Africa."

"The ones in Africa live out on the desert lands or out in the open. Their situation seems different than those that live in the village and seems even more different than someone who lives in a big city like Chicago. But the learning is the same. They become either the predator or the prey, whether they live in the open lands of Africa or in a big city. They are either being preyed upon by people or by animals. When you bring these two seemingly different groups together, both are basically the same. Even though we put different words on what preys on them, there is no difference.

So, everyone across the line is in various learning stages. But, how far are they willing to go to learn? Are they stuck where they are and won't move along that line to learn? Are they just going to criticize and criticize and stay there, frozen in their tracks? Or, are they opening their eyes and saying, 'Oh, okay, this is what I see as coming, this is what I have to learn?' Then they can begin to help their own humankind to learn this process, to learn what's coming and to learn how to cope with things that are going to happen. They are not going to change the flow of the energy stream that began from that initial decision until they get to the end of that energy flow, where another major decision has to be made, based on the analysis of the event. Then there will be more quantum paths to choose from.

People get frozen in their ability to learn due to their perceptions. It can also be other people or peers keeping them in a state of non-learning. If you learned, you make different decisions. If you didn't learn, you make the same decisions."

It is when we have come to see all angles, we receive a vibrational attunement, and we make different decisions—the behavior modification.

Various plays, various roles

Your children not new to you: movement within various roles. Octagonal movement in sectional devariances within the time structure of any DNA period where events are procured upon. Various, varied experiences within the paradoxal field for evaluated learning. Each learned event causes process to the next level of interrelated movement within the proxarmial family; each boosting the other entity's vibrational movement, a concerto within each familiar circle.

Cordessential: Quintessential beings that are attached by a cord through eternity and keep coming back with each other. Many have this; it's the soul level. Don't be biased on your perceptions. Open your parameters to understanding.

Again, quantessential being's aptitude of perfection will quantify perceptions of understanding as to the relevance of the quasi-essentialness of beings upon this Earth.

All as is, all as was and all will be, will be the beginning.

Our understanding: Our children are not new to us in this life. We have had different roles with each other in different lives. This allows us to study various events and subjects from different angles within each life. The goal is to be able to see and understand from all eight sides. Each side represents an angle we can see from, and each has a mathematical equivalency that brings our own understanding into mathematical balance: the angular learning.

We will have experiences from both sides of the spectrum: health and sickness; happiness and sadness, etc. Karma is the ability to experience all sides for balance in understanding. It is not a punishment and reward system; it was designed to give us a more complete understanding and is scripted from the higher self. Each event that we have experienced and learned from gains us access to the next level of interrelated experiences for our continued movement. We have various lives, playing various roles, extending out from the same soul group, which are attached to each other by a cord.

Dealing with energy vampires

Q: In the book, *The Celestine Vision*, is there any truth to humans stealing energy from other humans?
Correct; has value since the beginning of the race. A nourishing effect for some, sanguistical in nature.

Q: Does this correct itself when we learn to access the universal energy?
Able to stave off the collectors, when aware.

Q: Do the collectors use this to enhance self-worth?
And longevity; creates a pod of energy for later longevity use.

Q: Longevity as in physical life?
And spirit Self. Significant manipulation of energy pattern at the expense of another.

Q: What energetic effect does it have on the others?
Resulting in decreased neurologic activity. Sequential numerical events control the neurosynaptic field of each individual. Mathematical serengnosis takes place within the energy field of the synaptic release: a number combination unlocks all activity.

Q: Can you clarify?
Einstein able to patternize the numbers of the neurosynaptic energy within, allowing the tapping of universal information of a high mathematical skill.

Q: So, the first step in dealing with the collectors is to be aware of what they are doing?
Correct. Vibrational awareness a must. Walk away.

Our understanding: There are those who we come in contact with that are absolutely draining to our reservoir of energy. They are literally collecting energy from us, to be used later in a physical sense, as well as a spiritual sense. They manipulate energy patterns at the expense of others. The victims are suppressed, where the perpetrator creates the sequential events that have a mathematical effect on the gap between the nerves within the victim, shutting them down neurologically. The victim is able to mathematically unlock the consequence, releasing the neurological activity to again gain access to universal information on a higher level. The first step is in recognizing what the "collector" is doing, then walk away, disempowering them.

Life's path

The purification is within. When you give yourself to the Creator, you are editing what is within that gives purification. Life's book is not written in works; it is written across the heart in understanding.

When you look to the north, it is those that have gone and will not return. When you look to the west, you watch the father setting. When you look to the south, it is the words of the wind. When you look to the east, it is the newborn. Look for your spirit. The newborn picks up a new stick; the newborn becomes a new father growing.

Bring songs to Earth Mother, give her what is yours and she will give you what is hers. Credence is given to value.

The love of the Creator is reflected on the connective

love you have with each other. What you give is who you are. What you are is what you chose to be. What you are is manifested in the love of the Creator. Therefore, the truth is manifested within and life's path is written upon this truth. Do not be a benign being. Bring forth the truth of understanding from the knowledge you know in your vibrational resonance.

May the words of God speak through your lips. May your body be strengthened by the strands of God. May the Creator give you the understanding of truth that you may call upon others, that you may give them the path. Your willingness to understand what is within creates the learning that comes [from] outside yourself. Preserve yourself to the humbleness of the Creator. You are a reflection of your soul's resonance.

A drop of water upon a lake is only but a beginning to understand the value of all the water in the lake. Are you willing to create that first drop? To sacrifice the flow of essence to understand the Creator? The understanding has a ripple effect, much like the water in a pond. It will continue if you are willing to receive and give your essence to the Creator, as water is added to the lake in a continuous flow.

The only value is our true Self, in all we have ever been, and all we will ever be. Learn.

Vibrational understandings cannot be set in one lifetime

NOTES

Chapter 6

A Conscious Connection

Humanity is moving into a new cycle of massive learning. It will not be without help from others outside our sphere, both physical and non-physical beings, in a teacher and a student relationship. We must first let go of belief systems that do not hold a universal truth and open our minds to new possibilities. We must also humble ourselves before those prepared to offer the new and profound understanding. Learning how the communication works is a part of the process. The quieting of our minds and listening for the voice within enables a communion with the higher self that is able to feed the knowledge from previous learning, stored in the soul. It is then possible to start a communion with the higher guides for new learning, with some exceptions.

Spiritual guidance

Q: Did we choose this path prior to being born here, this life?
From the day of birth, the voices are speaking to the child before man intercedes. They still have a choice. All have choices to their destiny. Some choose right. Guidance is early.

Kent injects, "I chose this (path); they chose the time."

Q: Do we have spiritual guides with us all the time?
No, as needed.

Q: Does the same apply to all humans?
No, as needed. Placate yourselves to human understanding.

Q: Where will the majority of communication be coming from for most humans who meditate?
Outside self. Preparations: beginning configuration.

Q: Would this be from their assigned guides?
Relevant to Self-existence: communication only a process to Self-clarification.

Q: Is there a difference between the energy level of a human who channels higher beings vs. the energy level of humans that channel lower-level beings?
Distinct difference. Consequential being a priority over humanity, given the difference in vibrational aptitude. One has to *earn* the understanding of a consequential being: ordinance of universal laws that dictate the parameters of the beings associated with universal thought and understanding. Contemplex realities are the thought patterns of each individual culture.

Q: As levels of understanding are acquiesced, is one able to channel higher levels of vibrational entities?
Acquisition is open for these parameters.

Q: So, one cannot simply *wish* to communicate with a higher being, they first must qualify their level of understanding?
Correct. Understanding the concepts of a connected species is attainable through progressive process to a consequential being of higher vibrational aptitude, *universally accepted* as a consequential entity of higher vibration within the sphere of thought pattern.

Q: How do we decifer if the communication we are receiving is correct?
Ask for those you trust. Many variations; some incorrect. Patience, Council declares the time frame, not individuals: pre-planned. Much work to do. Teach what's been given you. Not all has been spoken of. Trust your inner Self: listen. Hurried is ineffective.

In the next conversation, the guide is referring the question back to an Ancient to have the far-reaching effects of a Creative understanding projected for entities upon Earth. The question is unrelated to the preceding topic, but we will include it so that the answer is not so confusing.

Q: When the system reverses polarities, is this in reference to a larger system?
Another's fact: binding.

Q: Can more clarity be given?
Another's direction, given the circumstance of human behavior. An aptitudinal Creative understanding is a must for deep ethereal projections of entity prognosis of this sphere.

In another meditation, Kent began, "We are going to be given a new guide, but they haven't decided yet."

Q: What is the purpose for the change in guides?
A new understanding: higher level. Ready; given a higher level.

Communication arrives from Self-needs, not wants. Coursational aptitude is a given. Process the information as given. Redundancy is a cause to Self-nurturing. Release Self and learn.

Guidance is virtuous to the understanding of what is happening now. Behemoth is only relative to the amount of understanding which you can comprehend. Understanding is virtuous to knowledge, which is only comparable to the degree of either. Do not be swayed by the amount of understanding which you are to receive. It is all comprehensive.

Our understanding: Guidance begins at birth and comes from outside ourselves to clarify an idea or concept. Guidance is in sequential steps. One cannot simply ask for a higher guide and expect that is what they will get. It completely depends upon the person's ability to understand the higher communication. To receive communication from a higher entity, one has to qualify themselves as a consequential being: to possess the ability to understand all the laws associated with the conceptual understanding of events. This is a universal law that dictates the boundaries concerning universal thought and understanding that we must operate within, given the network of thinking patterns within our, or any other, given culture. Communication of concepts between two different entities moves through steps of progressively higher states of enlightenment until a higher understanding of vibration is achieved within the realm of one's thought patterns, and *only* when one has been accepted as a consequential entity by other universal beings. At this point, one has been qualified as a consequential being to be able to understand the concepts that are given by a higher vibrational entity with greater understanding. We are only given information that we have the ability to comprehend at that moment. More information will be given in time. In the meantime, we will receive communication from entities with various levels of knowledge.

As one progresses in their level of vibrational understanding, progressively higher levels of guides are assigned to teach. It is required that we spend the time to contemplate, often repeatedly, what has been given and come to full understanding of the concept before more will be given. We need to release the human thought pattern and think in terms of achieving the full understanding, regardless of how much time and effort it takes to achieve it. Don't let the ego get in the way, it all comes in steps. Lay a strong foundation of basic understanding and then build upon it a little at a time. The amount of knowledge we will be given is only relative to what we actually comprehend.

Opening to the life messages within

Truth of utterance, directional equivalence of neurtactic purpose: unveil your perceptive being to create conceptual aptitudes within soul's resonance. Directional path to be attained yourself. Astuteness to meditational diameters yet to be learned. Proportional consequence evolves as meditational parameters widen—to be learned. Open biobonic messages that have yet to be attained through conceptual meditation of Self-concurrence. Truth occupies all. Love beyond seeing, your variance in conception, not yet attained by humans.

Professor of Directional Proportional Changes within the Sceupharic World or Universe.

Kent explains, "They are anxious for our accomplishing deeper meditation and extreme deeper truth. Others will come to seek the same. Meditation now is surface…He asked if I could feel my feet. I said no, they feel numb. He said, 'this is what it feels like when the total energy force is within.' The only thing of value is my brain. The rest of me, under my brain, is really of immaterial value. My brain, when developed, can see, speak, and hear without the superfluous body."

The above professor's title is mentioned for the sole purpose of allowing the reader to see the expansiveness of the entities that exist and what their assigned duties are.

Our understanding: Truth be known, we are being guided by a procedural system within a universal nervous network with the desired goal of continuously expanding conscious levels. Remove the veil that exists between the physical self and the higher self to gain the concepts of understanding at the soul level. We must be guided from within. It is important to learn to discern our thoughts and introspections surrounding the entirety of each event. As we open our minds to new possibilities, a greater ability to compare the various aspects of each event follows. Working together with the higher self, allow the life messages to come through to deliver the conceptual contemplations that bring forth the truth of an event. To love All That Is allows one to accept all that are different from one's current physical expression to share in their understanding with us in our ever-expanding conscious evolution. This includes the love and acceptance of the higher self.

Meditation and communication

We were receiving guidance in our teachings in the following reading. Kent describes a vision, "I see posters and spiritual things representing all the different masters who taught disciplines of self-meditation."

> Teaching serenity of mind and the discipline of the meditative state. To focus outside of self in order to gain entrance of Self.

> Understand the deeper concepts of universal connectedness. Gain wisdom of understanding through meditation to release the burdens of self-worth. Fasting will be included to those who want to reach a higher visionary level. Meditation and reflection, meditation and reflection. To reflect the knowledge that one has attained.

Q: Will we be teaching?

Yes, on who they are, the ones that are searching for their means to the value of their being. Correctional vortexical energy at hand for each who enters. Must learn deep concentration of being. Value is in Self-attunement, or adjusting from the isolationist behavior that lies within their soul [and] guidance from those who speak the truth; has given inceptions forbearance.

Q: What is the method by which we teach and learn deep meditation?

Consoling the soul, complete relaxation—the muscles, skeletal, surface—lethargic.

Q: Which type of brain wave activity is necessary for our communication?

Open completely.

Q: Will we be teaching people how to align themselves to heal themselves?

Yes. Not heal. Healing of the mind. Aligning understanding. The aligning—the value of the different situations of the body, physical—aligning the soul of its value of the event going on in the physical plane. Not healing in the sense of physical healing. Healing the soul to understand the learning of the physical event. Releasing the mind concept of perceived physical event going into the conceptual understanding of why and acceptance.

Our understanding: It is important to be introspective and contemplative with each event that presents itself to the physical body, aligning with the soul and its accumulated knowledge. The objective is to attain the conceptual understanding of why a physical event has happened, releasing the perceptions and accepting the truth of the event. This can be attained through a deep meditative state with three people sitting together, triangulating to create a counterclockwise rotation of energy. Triangulation excites the movement of atoms to create conditions for receiving information from the higher self. We must have a reconnection with the higher self first. Outside communication from guides will follow.

The guide is saying that fasting can help create a higher visionary level. This is not recommended for those who have medical problems, especially those who have blood sugar instabilities or those prone to seizures. Always check with your health care provider before attempting any fasting.

The DNA and communication connection

Q: Do all humans have the ability to communicate within their DNA?
No.

Q: What percent of the population has the ability in their DNA?
Up to five percent have it, but very few able to use it.

Q: Only five percent?
Yes.

Q: Are more able to communicate with the higher self?
A higher percentage.

Q: What percent can?
Twenty-two and a half percent.

Q: Is there a correlation with the percent of those who are able to move into the next cycle?
Yes. Now you get it.

Renee, "Interesting."

Forbearance to these conclusions.

Communication precautions

Precaution is advised to those trying to receive.

Q: Would that apply to those trying to receive before they are ready?
Yes, not ready to receive. Acquiesce their judgement. Singular movement creates cause of defect, noostortic to truth or cause.

Q: Would singular movement be one that is not supported by an appropriate teacher on the other side?
Correct; not supported. A movement singular to cause. Apprehensious movement appropriate to being with no cause.

All *human* life forms consist of a plasmic electrical life pattern. Expanding understanding creates new geometrical patterns within the life form. Once severely damaged, unable to expand; ulopic pattern continues to exist. Expansion ceases, cannot continue. All life forms existence precept to expansion for longevity of species of a particular pattern. Invasive procedures early within pattern formation can deflect a pattern dysfunction. Tapping into neuronetical release creates this dispersion of electrical malfunction.

Kent clarifies, "It's like plugging into a 220-outlet—a higher level—before ready for it."

Q: What kind of event would create this dispersion?
Event of a migrate magnitude to the organic body, which the plasmic spirit or energy resides, influenced from outer sceupharocal energies at one point. Unable to recreate balance of energies from event. A continuous causation [is] carried forward without willingness to comprehend or reliable evaluation upon Self-conflicts that are perceived within the plasmic energy flow of one's Self-being. Not willing to change, comfortable within Self-conflict. Creates vibrational field which is uncontrolled; conflict as their balance—false balance—enjoying conflicting results.

Lucerian event: All experience this type of event, but are able to participate in separation, when needed, to eventually understand, then partake in its true value in the sense of learning. Some desire not to separate—gives a thrust of energy—a form of narcotic events on emotional level. In charge, 'I'm in charge.' With the knowledge is event changer—precarious undertaking at best—feeds on emotional events. Creates a cycloneuretic field increase within the self-field; a narcotic-type event for self.

Our understanding: It is important that we go through all the steps of learning at the basic level, gaining the true understanding and forming a solid foundation, before moving to higher levels of learning or abilities. For example, trying to channel before the teacher has arrived (because the student is not ready) creates a singular movement that can create a defect in their understanding due to lack of additional clarification by a teacher. Remember, one has to gain basic spiritual understanding before a connection with the higher self can be achieved. Connection with the higher self must be attained before one can communicate with higher beings. This type of communication is processed through the higher self.

The ego must be removed in order to do so. All are steps in a process. On the other hand, someone who is too fearful to move forward in their understanding probably lacks the cause to do so, the fear overriding their need for a higher level of learning.

All human life consists of a life pattern within the plasmic field of charged atoms. An electrical current flow exists within those charged atoms. The pattern reflects our understanding. As we expand our conscious level, new geometric patterns are formed within the life form pattern. Tapping into a higher level of information before one is ready can cause a malfunction within the electrical pathways, creating a distortion in the geometric life pattern. It also changes the electrical pathways within the cells of the organic body. Once severely damaged, one is unable to expand their understanding because the distorted pattern continues to exist.

One may also not want to evaluate or comprehend the inner conflict, perceived from the chaotic plasmic flow of energy within. They are unwilling to change, comfortable within their own self-conflict. Conflict becomes their false-sense of balance and is vibrationally projected out into the field around their physical body. Tapping into the Light of higher information, higher than what one is able to comprehend, can result in a distortion of one's electrical circuitry and geometric pattern. Stepping back and separating one's self can create an opportunity to fill in the gaps in understanding through the study of the basics, eventually gaining the value of the true learning. Some do not want to self-correct because the higher-level information gives them a boost of energy on an emotional level and a feeling of being in charge. The knowledge is a game-changer, creating uncertainty at best, feeding on emotional events that they continuously create within their field. It's addictive and conditions have to exist to make them *want* to change. Universal law dictates that all life forms must continue expanding within the geometric pattern formation in order for that species to continue to exist. All are given free-will to change or face the consequences of their decisions.

Communication and mental health

The following paragraph is taken from **chapter 4** in *The Augmentation of Man: A Study in Renaissance,* "Quillerium flap ignites communication," in order to clarify the remaining information. The quillerium flap contains an opening in the aura in front of the abdomen that allows a communicative energy to enter our field, and then our body for interpretation. It opens when we are in a trance state and when our vibrational level rises. We must also learn how to close this opening so that our bodies are not subjected to the continuous stream of communicative energy, which can injure the neurological system.

> **Q: How do we initiate the communication process?**
> It has to do to the level of vibration when you meditate: your level of vibration is increased. Even though you are to the point of Self-consciousness, you're unconcious of it. At that point, the quillerium opening is accessed. You have the ability to turn it on or off...Through meditation and increasing your vibration levels to the point of accessing the opening and able to control its access. Uncontrolled access leads to changed brain patterns. Your words are mental health problems. Increased communications increases your salivary glands, like you're watering at the mouth.

Kent clarifies, "There are those who are receiving the communication and it overloads their brain. It has to do with this quillerium opening. They can't control the information coming in. They lose the ability to close the quillerium flap, so they are constantly hearing communication. The only way to stop it is they have to learn the ability to close it. It does something to the brain pattern."

Q: When we are teaching people meditation to receive information, how do we teach them how to control it?
You have to teach them to control it: it becomes uncontrollable. Visualizing through meditation, using their own vibration to try to close it, and they first have to understand what is causing it to want to no longer receive communication.

Q: Does it cut off the communication forever?
Yes. The communication is like a narcotic; it is difficult for many to want to close it.

Kent explains, "Somebody is hearing the communication all the time and then it becomes muffled because they are given medications. When the communication becomes muffled, they feel like they have lost something, like losing a close friend, and they want it back. They go off their medication because the communication is like a narcotic; it's like having a companion."

Q: What about schizophrenia? That seems to be passed down through genetics?
The ability to open this *is* genetic. It's in the DNA to open this communication. Not everybody has it. Remember when we told you about too much energy flowing to the brain can burn it out? This is what this is. Many have the ability to access the communication and energy field, but very few have the ability to access it *and* control it without doing harm. Remember, we told you what would happen if the energy level were too high and you were to access it? Severe brain damage. The neuronet cannot handle this type of communication all at once. This is why we told you to learn and understand the process and to access the energies, which carry the communication, *as you are able to*. Not everyone should do this.

Kent added, "People don't even know that the communication was open and they lose their ability to close it because their brain waves get mixed up."

Kent describes a vision, "I see clouds churning."

> Now you understand; you're getting it. This is why we said only twenty-two and a half percent will survive.

> **Q: What other factors play into schizophrenia besides uncontrolled communication access?**
> Uncontrolled brain waves, thought patterns: conjunctive alignment to neuronetical being. Abstain from adjunctive connections within thought patterns: a release of genetical being.

> **Q: How does one release the genetic being?**
> Not fully formed: abstract definition of who they are.

> **Q: What is the causative factor for chemical imbalances in the brain?**
> Displacement of cause.

Our understanding: We are being advised to release the complicated understanding of our genetic representation of who we *think* we are and to avoid lower level communications.

We are not doctors, and this channeling should not replace any treatment plans set forth by a health care professional. It is only given here to add a level of spiritual understanding. Attempts at spiritual communication is absolutely discouraged for those with personal or familial histories of schizophrenia.

Accessing the neuronet for communication

Neuronectular understanding: study. All within Self;
Creative guidance from outside.

**Q: Do all humans have the ability to access the
neuronet?**
No. Their accomplishments are many, but not to
access truth, or the ability to access what is, given the
redundancy of what they have [and] their ability
for—cannot access the stream. Agulation of value
given to those of spherical value. Ellipse in time
frame.

**Q: To access the neuronet, one has to be ready for
the truth?**
Correct. Abstain[ing] from truth not acceptable for
accessing caldarium in response to access value, a
cause in misperceptive human behavior. Furoration
a must. No value in human behavior. Furoration is
a concept of being astute to understanding right from
wrong.

Q: What is a caldarium?
Place inhabited by a previous race, sympathetic to
peaceful understanding. War-like synopsis
misunderstood.

**Q: Is there a reason why some people have the
DNA to access the neuronet, while others do not?**
Coordinated access to those born many times over
from ancient learnings. Most humankind young. A
few ancient beings. Do you understand this?

Renee, "Yes."

Cosmology will interface this truth in your realm.

Our understanding: Most humans are young in comparison to other non-human beings and there are few humans that are ancient. Those born many times over carry with them the ancient learnings, qualifying the activation of their DNA. They are also given coordinated access to the neuronet. The future study of the universe will deliver this truth regarding those older souls.

The reference to caldarium above implies that it was a place where the Romans went, not only to enjoy the public baths, but also in search of truth. Adjacent libraries and reading rooms support this statement and the Ancient communicates that it was sympathetic to peaceful understanding. It is assumed that it was also a place of social discourse. Perhaps there has been a hypothesis that this was also a place where wars were discussed, but we have not found any data to date to support this, even though the Ancient states it has been misunderstood.

Communication with humans difficult

Lackadaisiness are the beings of this sphere.

Extreme apprehension among peoples: turmoil within, not ready to share. Humans difficult to understand. Secrecy abounds within each individual, makes difficult communication to allow understanding. Neuronetical influence not a factor; self-judgment is.

The world will function from inner thoughts and communication from above yourself. The world will not function from self-thought. Learn how to listen to inner-communication, your own inner-communication. Teach consequences of not listening to the inner-communication.

We have a difficult time with your language. Your meanings are inconsequential to thought, your language. Value is sustained to our mental overhaul, relating to the meaning concerning this life pattern.

Humankind has it wrong. Difficult, stubborn people, as related to human race. Entities that subscribe to this sphere of self-indulgent creatures has sustained value lesser than the universe dictates. You humans are difficult to work with, too independent to Self-guidance.

Nomenclature: study, know its value. Precipitous understanding [is a] consequence of ideology.

Human language is absurd for understanding, a creative misconception of meaning through egotistical behavior of the author. Ancient language more descriptive, direct. Copulation oscillation through time created false language directive. Presumptuous is best for this language.

Our understanding: The sole purpose of language is to communicate an understanding. Human language—especially English—makes it difficult to deliver higher states of conceptual learning. Our value will be when we, as humans, can catch up in our thinking capacity to a level equivalent to how the universe thinks. We are also difficult to work with, as humans are resistant to change. We love to indulge in the pleasures of this life, distracting us from our true purpose and our own guidance from the higher self. Humans are fearful and have much turmoil within from self-judgement of this physical world, making it difficult to penetrate the lower thoughts with a new and more profound understanding. This creates a dysfunctional path. Instead of seeking a deeper truth, we surround ourselves with earthly pleasures, having no time or desire to seek the real understanding. To correct, we must steer away from the material wants and pleasures of the external world and start listening to the needs of the higher self, tuning within to hear the inner voice. Understand that a communicative language is one that accurately transfers a valuable understanding. Spend the time to decipher the communication.

Understand that ideologies make for narrow-mindedness, unable to conquer the insurmountable understanding. We must open our minds to new possibilities for contemplation. Language today is senseless; the ancient languages were more descriptive and direct for communication of conceptual ideas of higher understanding. Over time, language has taken the direction of a vacillating use of connecting words, creating a false narrative. That is why, in these channeled messages, the higher guides will use the ancient root words to create a direct and more descriptive communication of conceptual ideas.

A communal understanding

Q: Do charged atoms form strings as each entity initiates communication with another to transport the communication?
Yes.

Q: Do you choose the corresponding words in our language or does Kent's neurological system interpret the energy?
Our language difficult for him: concentrational effort. Interpretation not required, just communal release of Self-interpretation. Repository set within to maintain a static balance for our communication.

Release yourself to all that surrounds you at this time. Let the energy flow without direction on your part— becomes a natural cause. Release your energy. Contemplate this.

Q: Is there a universal language that you use more often?
Conceptual language of being, artifactual in nature.

Luciferious by those that do not understand the language. A negative response, consequence to ignorance outside themselves.

Communication is based on conceptual understanding: the value of language. Most beings are in an archaic mode to communication. You have reached a point—even though low level—is a higher point to communal understanding and reflection of corresponding language value.

Our understanding: The mentor's language is too difficult for Kent and requires much concentration. The release of the communication is between the guide and the higher self; the higher self does the interpretation. The intent to communicate begins with a vibration that forms strings out of charged atoms, connecting the two communicating entities telepathically. Think of fiberoptic cables for telecommunications. A storage area was created within Kent to enable him to be able to receive and store the information and maintains a continuous balance for communication between the two. The guide is telling him to let go and let the energy flow without trying to direct it.

The universal language delivers a valuable conceptual understanding. Unfortunately, people do not understand the universal language and respond to it in a negative manner, as if it were "coming from the devil." It is a consequence of our lack in understanding of those outside of our own existence.

More on the chi and the quillerium flap

This is a continuance of information found in *The Augmentation of Man: A Study in Renaissance*, **chapter 4**, beginning with "Quillerium flap ignites communication". The quillerium flap and the chi are structures that allow communicative energy into our body.

You are able to receive dictation from our thought processes. You are able to decipher the communication process through thought transfer in an auspicious manner. Hunger and thirst of knowledge has opened your quillerium flap.

Kent, pointing to area in front of his abdomen, "I can see an aura all around the body and there is an opening. They called it a quillerium flap."

Q: Is there any communication that takes place out through the top of the head?
The asking. Receiving through the chi, as call it. The abdominal crustacean of the subliminal subfracture of the energy line that constitutes a pathway to the neuronetical structure that is influenced by the electromagnetic field plasmic lines attached to the universal neuronetical field. A loop of sorts for communication. Subfracture cause equilibrium—balance.

Use your gut feeling. It is time you choose your destiny—learn. Nothing is absolute. Creative cognizance is a guide to a higher self understanding.

Q: Does the chi give the gut feeling?
Relevance to understanding its value, quanticeptual in nature; a natural product within the realm of humanity.

Q: Is the main structure for the chi also around the umbilicus?
True.

Q: The quillerium flap and the chi are involved in this type of continuous communication. Is the neuronet also involved?
Neuronetical in nature. Holds these events at trust.

A thought pattern is taking all these small vibrations and putting them together to make a word out of it. A thought is a mathematical particle of vibrations, mathematically bringing together of vibrational particles. There are billions of these vibration[al] particles to choose from. Each spirit has their own mathematical equation that you [they] are born with. The upwardness is a delusion.

Our understanding: The chi is a portal that allows the life force energy to enter through the area surrounding our umbilicus. It also allows a degree of emotion to enter and has an ability to perceive many things, giving the "gut feeling." The quillerium flap is an opening in each person's aura that, when stimulated by a higher vibrational level, allows communication energy to enter. The communication energy enters the body in various places, depending upon the person's unique anatomy, then travels by way of nerves through the chakras to decipher the emotion, language and visual aspects of the communication. Our communication exits out of the body through the crown chakra. The communication comes in through the aura in front of the umbilicus, the fifth chakra, creating a loop that connects to the universal neuronet. The universal neuronet behaves like, and interfaces with, our own nervous system.

The communication energy is a stream of vibrational thought patterns. The vibrational patterns, mathematical in nature, form particles or vibrational groupings of words. There are billions of vibrational particles that form words to choose from. Everything has vibration and a mathematical equivalency. The upwardness is a delusion; we are expanding in our understanding, not moving up in our understanding.

More on chakras and communication

In *The Augmentation of Man: A Study in Renaissance*, **chapter 4,** "The chakras" explains that chakras are for one purpose only: for communication with the Ancients and, through the Ancients, with the Creator. The fifth chakra, the chi, is a portal and allows various things to come in, including life force energy and some emotion. It gives the root feeling of the communication. The chi controls survival and sexual instinct. The fourth, or heart chakra, is used for emotional deciphering of a communication. The third, the throat chakra, is for determination of language. The second chakra, or third eye/pineal gland, interprets visual communication and sees the emotion that the heart feels. The cerebral cortex of the brain deciphers and connects the dots between the various sensual interpretations of the chakras to complete the understanding of the communication. Our thoughts, questions and prayers exit through the first chakra, the crown. The first and fifth chakras are the most important and create the loop of communication. There are only five original chakras. Man added the other two. Sexuality and survival are so strong, they must be chakras, right? Wrong. They are associated with physiology and instinct and are controlled by the chi.

Q: Are the chakras only activated for those who communicate with the Ancients?
No. All chakras are not activated to each individual; only as needed for clarification of a thought being. Chakras are individually-activated, above the human fray.

Q: Are the chakras activated by the one communicating?
Reciprocal in nature, in natural use; for reciprocal addresses within human culture.

Q: Are chakras only activated at time of need?
Correct. Its value sustained by quanticeptive precepts; perceptual assets.

Q: Is the activation of the chakras temporary?
Only by those in use.

Q: Do the chakras remain activated after the communication?
No, only upon need, given the asset value within its context. The need for continuous activation not required—only as needed.

Q: How does one open the crown chakra?
Distained behavior has sealed the process.

Q: Can it not be opened at this time?
After a function—new beginning. Wrong reduction of human behavior. Return to Creator, as before. Myopic behavior to cease on Self. Turn to a connection severed 2,000 of your year's past. Small amount remains open today: exceptional usage. The seeds for next world.

Q: Does religion have anything to do with the severed connection?
Correct. Correct; closed the loop, the opening to All That Is. Given direction, distorted the results.

On one occasion, we were talking about the consciousness of the heart. We had questions: Where does emotional vibration originate?

Kent tunes in, then summarizes, "When the communication energy enters the body, where is its first stop? Like any other thing, the first stop leaves the biggest imprint." He returned to his trance:

Emotional servitude of the heart, a cleansing for the truth. The brain is the generator of the heart vibration. The neuronet of the brain deciphers the communication vibration of the heart. Again, all vibration is made up of numerical code.

The pineal gland magnifies the heart.

Kent injected, "The pineal gland is the third eye because it sees what the heart feels."

Q: Does staring at the sun activate the pineal gland?
A vision plan cannot be activated or move forward by outside source: a gift at the soul level. Misnomer by humanity. Higher level understanding to those that have. Misguidance received upon others: *want to be*. Much knowledge, uninformed by those beings not of value.

Kent added, "Activating the pineal gland by looking at the sun is being propagated by man."

Q: The consciousness that is stored in the heart, is it only the current life experiences or does it hold the soul's consciousness?
You will not know the soul's consciousness: cannot comprehend total stagnetic value. It is of the consciousness of those that wear the heart—a value of this life only. You will proceed.

Q: Does fluoride affect the pineal gland, as some people believe?
No, the declaration of Self affects the gland.

Q: Is fluoride beneficial for the strength of the teeth?
A waste product.

Q: What affect does fluoride have on the physical body?
Non-sensical relationship, given the proaxiomer of the material.

Our understanding: The chakras are only activated upon communication with another entity and only the chakras necessary to clarify the communication. If it is necessary to activate the pineal gland to give a visual for understanding, then the second chakra is activated. Others may also be activated, but it is not always necessary to activate all five chakras for a communication of an idea. They are activated and sustained between someone with less understanding and a higher vibrational entity for teaching purposes. Once the communication is over, the chakras are turned off, so to speak. The crown chakra was sealed off eons ago due to religious ideology and self-indulgence, the disdained behavior that closed the communication loop. It will be reopened in the future when humanity, in its desperation, reaches out for Creator and finally lets go of materialism. Why religious ideology? Because it replaced our direct connection to Creator with man, whose concepts and understanding are far less than perfect.

We will not have access to the totality of the soul's consciousness. Nor could we understand, in our human existence, the value of the conscious stages and the information that it holds. The heart stores the consciousness of this life only and works with the pineal gland, which is able to visualize what the heart feels.

While fluoride is a waste product, it is not what is responsible for shutting down the pineal gland. Staring at the sun does not activate the gland. Both are misnomers. It is the higher self that is responsible for the activation of the pineal gland. It is all done from within, enabling a higher level of understanding through visions.

Colors represent communication energies

When Kent begins to meditate and enter trance, he will wait for colors to develop before an actual communication begins. The colors help one to decipher a communication to some degree, as each color represents a kind of energy. What we have learned, is that receiving communication while seeing black or grey, behind closed eyes, yields unpredictable information that we tend not to trust, and we will note it on our written dictation.

Kent started, "I am in a white area."

> Warmth is the understanding of protection and the purpose of each individual color. White is protection and directional; a pure truth path. Truth to perfection, truth to understanding, and truth, universal perception. White does not give power, it cleanses to the truth.
>
> **Q: What is the significance of colors compared to energy?**
> They *are* energy.
>
> **Q: Can we have a lesson on the various colors or main colors and their associated energies?**
> Associated plasmic energy: lime-yellow. Purplish: cosmic energy and informational. Green: regulated neutronal.
>
> **Q: For clarification, is neutronal green?**
> Yes. Light blue: the gaps between energy levels, the space.
>
> **Q: What about deep purple-blue?**
> Informational, high level. White, or Light: concourse to truth, soul's resonance.

Q: What about the grey tones?
Consequential energy: possible outcomes—more than one—quantum; depending on the field shift.

Q: The grey tones are reflective of quantum outcomes?
Possibilities.

Q: Is medium blue directional?
Concentrated.

Q: The color yellow?
Pharoguyance.

Q: Red?
Austerity, a measure of.   Oculators: many sub-colors—not obvious.

Q: Which are the preferable colors for communication of truth?
Green is knowledge. Overlapping/intruding blue: giving discernment. Black is noble cause, not of correct value: wanting to add to knowledge without viction. Yellow is a consignment to being, creating a broader path to levying a higher self for value to the sounds one hears. A mathematical guide is at hand through a purplish effect, creating a higher communication of being. White: a pureness for understanding a communication, creating a simple, simplistic view of a difficult concept. It is not truly white, it's a being representation of what you consider white—carnarian attribute. Grey is a concourse to many understandings. True discernment is a value here, and the correctness of the being at hand.

Q: Colors are a sign-post to possible cause and effect?"
Yes.

Kent explains, "The blue is a higher Source of information, but he (the Ancient) is able to transfer information from a higher Source to a different level."

We have found that the colors white, light blue and purple develop when communicating with entities of higher understanding. Green can also be associated with health and healing. Swirling lime-yellow spheres can develop for some people just before communication begins. This reflects our experiences and may vary, depending on the energy of the communication.

Crystals and communication

We had met a woman who claimed to have a Mayan crystal skull, given to her by natives of South America. We had questions, which opened into a lesson on crystals:

> **Q: Can you tell us about the Mayan crystal skulls?**
> Vibrational information, that's what they are. Tap into the universal infusion quatrain. The information has been exhausted from the skull. Now all eyes must turn to Egypt. That is the next opening.
>
> **Q: What can we expect?**
> Ancient crypt. Informational knowledge open[s] to the perveyance of analytical studies: your attunement continues.
>
> **Q: Can we have a lesson on crystals?**
> They are a window of time to time, even though time does not exist. Information and communication on a vibrational level.

Q: Are they alive and how do they work?
They are storehouses, storage: live storage units.
Quiaxle distribution of information knowledge:
linear neuroelectrical function of energy. Quiaxle
distribution: Neptune's Angle, a distribution point.
Energy source: records of human existence kept
beneath the sand. Hexagonal distribution to magnify
an energy source along the crystal linear length, a
neuronautical field captured and stored in each
crystal. Growth of cellular structure based upon
vibrational energy received, compounded by the
density within the linear structure. Each crystal is
only a piece of the information storage. Some have
immature storage; they shouldn't be taken.

"They were showing me a linear line in which crystals grow off of,
like a neuronet all over the earth," Kent explained while having a
vision.

They grow according to the amount of energy
coming from the area. If the crystal is broken off and
becomes damaged, the information is also damaged,
or missing, like having a scratch in the record.

Kent further describes his vision, "Our extracting the crystals is
causing problems; we're taking the energy. Each crystal has a piece
of the information. There is a place in the earth where there is a
huge cluster of these crystals under the sands. Another under water,
like under the ocean. There are at least three clusters in the world.
They create a triangle of energy and hold the world intact.
Especially the big ones, which hold more energy. They are cellular
structures of informational energy. Each cell carries information.
The bigger the crystal, the more the information. Once broken off,
they can't be put back. This structure around the earth is really
amazing. It looks like a white light. It's not, but it looks like it."

Our understanding: Crystals can store information, distributing the knowledge in a linear nerve-like energy release from the center, out in six directions. The mentor is describing crystal beds buried beneath the sand in various places around the world, storing the history of human existence. As the crystals develop, the dense linear structure receives the vibrational energy from unfolding events and grow accordingly, the vibration recorded within the crystals. It is extremely important that we not disturb the large crystal beds.

In this next meditation, Kent describes, "A sphere or ball shape with six triangles within another triangle."

> The triangles create the source. Each point of the crystal are clusters of these triangles. Between each point is the crystalline line.

Kent adds, "People are not going to like this: others can hold the crystals."

> It is information and knowledge. Anyone can hold the crystals because it contains information. Has nothing to do with a person's energy; it just magnifies energy. It is an information and communication tool; it magnifies your own energy to receive information.

Q: Do you bond with the crystals?
No! Man is making up their own rules. Your ability as a receiver only makes the crystal of value. If you do not have the ability to receive, it is just a crystal. It magnifies the person's energy they already have.

> In certain areas of the world, there is energy emanating from these areas and, when you place crystals in these areas, it can bend the energy coming out of the earth in these areas and affect the weather. Analogous to one bending a light ray to disperse the

pattern of energy particles.

Kent, on another occasion, was having a difficult time receiving communication. "I'm having a hard time getting in. This crystal is cold and it is making my hand cold!"

New stone, need to look for a new stone.

Q: Why would a change in crystals be necessary when used for meditation?
Energy.

Q: Has the energy been exhausted out of the stone that you have been using?
Has to be purified and recharged: salt, water, sun.

Kent explained his vision, "I'm seeing putting the crystal in natural salt and water in a glass dish, placed in the sun."

Our understanding: The crystals, in addition to information storage, are able to magnify one's existing energy in order to receive information. We will use crystals when Kent is in trance, particularly when he is having difficulty receiving communication. It does not give a person the ability to receive spiritual communication, they must already have the ability, it just magnifies what is already there. The crystals usually become quite warm in the hand during a communication.

Sex is a communicative project

Kent, breaking away from his trance, "I just got when you have sex with someone, you bond your souls. When you are having sex, and when you look into each other's eyes, you can see into the soul's box temporarily, which creates the bond. It only happens during orgasm. It leaves a temporary imprint on the mind, but it still lasts some time." He returned to his trance:

Q: Why is the orgasm the trigger?
It's the imprint.

Q: Like a neurological imprint?
Yes. It's a very long temporary imprint.

Q: And when couples don't have sexual relations any longer, do they have an unbonding?
The unraveling. The imprint can be very long-lasting, if it is imaged correctly. This is part of the human response system to the neuronetical reliance upon each other—creates a communicative device imprint. Humans are experimental in their nature, in their being. A creative understanding of the neuroflex adheres to this cause. The bonding is important in each life to cause sustainable energy upon the individual at hand. Causation and effect is in force here.

Q: What happens with those individuals not in a relationship?
Toxic by effect. Give[s] credence to understanding their Self-worth, unavailable at this time. The neuroflex gives birth to a newer understanding of the communicative process. All is not well without a life-long, at this time frame, partner. Sexual contact is a communicative project—proposal to understanding of Self. Share this.

Our understanding: The mentor states that looking into each other's eyes at the point of orgasm can allow viewing of the partner's soul, leaving a neurological imprint and creating a long-term bond. It also gives a new understanding of the communicative process between souls. The bonding between couples creates a sustainable energy upon each individual, providing the conditions for understanding the value of the higher self.

Deception in communication

Working with higher beings does not make one immune from other entities trying to deflect one's path. We had been given advice from an unknown guide, later to find out that it was incorrect. Even so, it is a learning experience and fine-tuned our ability to decipher who we are communicating with. The following question followed one such event:

Q: Can you help us understand the motivation for this entity?
Consequence [of] diffraction to the neuronetical field dispensation of informational energy. Not who you know. Correlean effect. Intunable sequence. Works with others to dilapidate influential aperture. Closes off informational field, a due process of consequence influenced by derision of other entities. Laphyrasarian extension with cause on informational influence. Realignment within the sceupharocal presentage a must to continue aperture opening.

Q: Could you explain correlean effect?
Not known to you at this time. Universal correlation within planetary sphere.

Q: What prevents an entity from communicating with us, in spite of our request to speak to those of truth?
Freedom to speak. Discernment is the issue at hand. Know your colors. All want to speak; few discern their words. A correct equivalation is due when communication is valid. The word is equivocate. A consignment to the truth is continually fluctuating by those of lower knowledge.

Our understanding: This entity was not known to us and works with others to deflect the Light to influence another's understanding by closing off the information field, a consequence of their mockery. Think of the common neighborhood bully. The person at the receiving end is unable to receive an attunement as a result of incorrect information, fraudulently given, robbing others of the true understanding. When this happens, we must realign to presenting entities of higher consciousness in order to continue the flow of the Light, which carries the knowledge.

Just because we set the intention of speaking to higher entities, does not mean that is what we will get. All want to speak, but few of us really discern their words. The transfer of truth is constantly fluctuating among those of lower knowledge. In the end, it is up to us to determine the quality of the information. We must also understand that it is never the entirety of information on the subject. Even with higher level entities, understanding is piecemealed, where we have to digest each bite of information to understand it, then return for the next bite. Universal law prohibits the complete download of information on a given topic to ensure the basics are understood before more is given.

Hallucinatory drugs and consciousness

Q: What can be said about the use of ayahuasca for spiritual learning? Is there proper assimilation of understanding when ayahuasca is used?
No, arbitrary discussion. Only value with native shaman. Inconsequential beings use this herb for clarity—not achieved. Aspergar use of consequential beings. Reflection of absurd behavior gives trudence to the natural being: obsessive behavior.

Q: Does the native shaman give guidance to the understanding?
Yes, correct. There are few of them, a prophetic interpretation of reality; intellectual absolute.

You do not need hallucinatory drugs to attain the information of the transformation. Others use them due to their infractive value. A self-judgement and inoculation *from* the truth. They are tappers of the information, not the communicators of understanding. You do not need this.

Our understanding: The natives have mastered the use of ayahuasca for ceremonial and spiritual purposes. It should be used only under the guidance of a native shaman—and there are few—to give a perfect interpretation issued by a spiritual guide. But others, according to our mentor, are taking it for its infractive value: to breech the laws. They enjoy tapping into the information, but are not able to communicate the true understanding. We are able to obtain the true understanding without the use of drugs through direct communication with a spiritual guide during a meditative or trance state. Therefore, drugs are not necessary for true enlightenment.

Kent explains, "When we take drugs or alcohol and then when we dream, it takes out and dulls the consequences of these possible paths in the dream so we don't learn. With drugs or alcohol, it doesn't show the true consequences of these paths."

Be careful of who you listen to

> **Q: There is a belief here among some humans that we already know everything and it is our job here to remember...**

The mentor interrupted before Renee had finished the question:

> Incorrect. You are learning, human in spiritual realm. You are not astute enough to know All That Is. Plagiarizing the value of the knowledge ones does not make one more Creative in thought [or] asterical in nature. Human race is below vibrational aspects of knowing All That Is. You cannot recall what you

do not know, as a culture of any type. Arrogance is processed to the height in humans.

The Ancient seemed to be very annoyed with the arrogance of this statement, especially given that humans are at the lowest level of understanding universally. Simply repeating what one has heard or read does not equate us with the universal beings of higher understanding.

Communicating with the higher self

We finish with a communication from Kent's higher self, an achievement of his reconnection:

> I am your upper Self: pinnacle of seeking. Go with the others, seek the wisdom. Do not hold back. Seek your own understanding, not a derivative of other's. Seek the path; others are waiting. My upper Self is my Source, my high Source, the Source that will lead us to wisdom and understanding beyond the lessons.

Your derivative of understanding is directly proportional to what you will receive

NOTES

Chapter 7

Development of the Higher Self

We live in pivotal times. December 21, 2012, marked the close of a grand cycle of perceptual learning within a physical third dimensional space and a focus on the rediscovery of our true Self. The higher self is a part of our soul that resides in the fourth dimension and guides our learning process. We are soon to enter the next cycle of conceptual learning. This requires that we come to completion of our perceptual learning; to uncover the truth about who we are and the world we live in. For many, this also means getting to know the higher self and to begin a process of accessing the stored information within the soul to bring a new level of understanding to our physical self.

To discover the higher self is a process; one that requires the ability to tear down the self-imposed barriers to our objectiveness in order to open the mind to see a more complete truth. It requires that we let go of false perceptions of the past: the titles, self-worth, the material world, and allowing others to define who we are. Planetary alignments begin to create a vibrational atmosphere that will enable those who are ready to finally reconnect with their higher self. Initiated ourselves, it requires our going within to align with and get to know who we really are without the distractions of this temporary physical field. It is the melting away of thinking of ourselves as separate from the whole of creation; enabling the "I" to become the "we." As we come to respect and love *all* beings, we understand that even those we view as negative can serve to expand our understanding. Becoming one with the plasmic field of Light, we allow a constant flow of intellectual energy unto ourselves, becoming one with All That Is, in a continuous expansion of conscious understanding.

Self-conflict

This lesson was embedded in an event where Renee had disclosed to a friend a prediction for an Earth event. The friend respectfully commented that she did not feel it would happen. Reacting within, as if it were a blow to her integrity, Renee fiercely tried to conceal her reaction from the friend. A short time later, the two joined Kent in a meditation together. The spiritual guide was not fooled by Renee's efforts to conceal her reaction. Once again, the physical self is uncapitalized; the higher self is capitalized.

> One is lugubrious.

> **Q: What is the significance?**
> Vibrational circulation of perceptual confrontation within, self-assertion of judgments. A continuous conflict within human entities. A contagious consequence of self-infliction.

Instantly realizing the guide was referring to her, Renee announced, "These patterns are difficult to break, even when you are aware of them."

> Consequential addiction to self-annihilation of personality character to offset an understanding beyond self—a dysfunctional reset of the human entity. Clearance of self-value creates a new forbearance [and] quantum paths. The wisdom of fortalis exists within each mysipical quadrant of Self-evaluation. Force, a force; there is a disturbance in the force.

> **Q: What is the wisdom of fortalis?**
> An equivalency to natural law.

The addiction to character assassination offsets an understanding beyond the physical self, a dysfunction of humans. Once we clear the misperception of self-worth, quantum paths can open.

We stopped to talk about Renee's reaction to the friend's comment and how it may have been vibrationally perceived by the guide, then returned to the meditation:

Q: What are the four quadrants of Self-evaluation?
Perceptual, archaeological, occipital [and] consensual.

Q: Can you further explain the four quadrants?
One, the realization of Self-worth; two, Self-thought [and] understanding; three, concordance of value for directional movement within Self-atmosphere; four, cornerstone thought for all humanity with wisdom and understanding.

Narrow parameters these are for beginning of Self-understanding and association; only the beginning of a quantrasuitrical movement to understanding.

The four quadrants of understanding the higher self involves: first, the realization of the worth of the higher self; second, the listening within to the thoughts and understanding coming from the ancient higher self; third, the directional movement in conceptual learning guided by the higher self; and, fourth, the wisdom and understanding forming the foundation of thought for all of humanity.

Want versus need

Communication arrives from Self needs, not wants. Coursational aptitude is a given. Process the information as given. Redundancy is a cause to Self-nurturing. Release Self and learn.

Q: Where will the majority of communication be coming from for most humans who meditate?
Outside self. preparations, beginning configuration.

Q: Would this be from their assigned guides?
Relevant to Self-existence: communication only a process to Self-clarification.

We must first learn to quiet the mind and listen to the inner voice, releasing the higher self to give clarity to who we are and why we are here. Spiritual guidance will then follow.

In the following reading, Renee questions why, during the many trips to Santa Fe, New Mexico, Kent was unable to communicate with the spiritual guides while there.

Q: Why does Kent have such a difficult time meditating and communicating in the area of Santa Fe, New Mexico?
Cause and effect are there. It will not survive: greed.

Q: Is it the energy of greed?
Greed sustains the energy of conceptual non-being. No value to Self-worth; only tied to material acquiescence of value. No roots for those who was, Puebloans of many; cause of who they are is deceased. Serrated knife has pierced their past, separating who they are. Those outside will become one, those inside will become none. The royalty of self becomes destructive.

The ring of ancient past will be seen, signifying the beginning of the next phase of the humankind. Many lives lost; many lives gained. Perception you must understand. It is not as you see. Reach beyond this concept. Santa Fe is not your realm to understanding. Materialism is ineffective of the past.

Show them the ways of the ancients.

Santa Fe no longer represents the spirituality that existed in the ancient past within the Puebloan societies. The spirituality is dead due to the value placed on the acquisition of material wealth, where the royalty of the physical self creates the conditions for self-destruction. The ring of ancient past possibly is referring to cycles, returning to the values of the ancient peoples of the past to start the next learning cycle. We need to understand the perception behind the value we place on things and reach beyond the material world in our understanding. What is the only thing we take with us when we leave this world? It is the understanding. This is where the true value lies. The following lesson continues to define need versus want:

> The maturity of needs will come into being. Wants will be extinguished by the understanding of Self-being. Desires will cause character assassination to one's self, a reality to a pervasive behavior conjured up as irrational ego. The need for self-identity will be corrected according to Self-value in relation to the definition of a consequential being.

> Learnings [are] now based on the perception of time involvement according to perception of self thoughts. Learning is an extension far beyond the perception of need or wants. It is the value of understanding the connection of all things that are based on a single alignment to the worths of *all* living organisms. Self-value is now based on a single entity, not congruent with All That Is, connected. No understanding yet.

> Learning is not a perception, but of opening the mind's expanse to the ordinance of all concepts unlimited within the universal understanding. True learning has no parameters of being. Limitations are

a perception to self-indulgence to learning. Communication is based on one's perception of ideas, a self-taught limitation based upon understanding of time limits and matter intensity.

Lessons to karmic energy: lessen the value of past and increase the value of future understanding of events. The energy is retrieved under the expanse of a fusion of higher understanding and a defusion of lower level concepts; an accelleration to further [the] meaning of life itself. High expansion energy fusion: Karmic energy; a dispersion of the life-energy field. It is a key for—answer—to all that exists in relation to All That Is. The now, the now to be. Study this.

Arcturian theory.

Our understanding: Now is the time to let go of the past—the material world, the ego associated with the lower physical self and self-indulgences—which only obstruct the true learning. The value is not in our individual self, but in the connectedness of a continually expanding unified conscious field. To be a part of this universal consciousness, one must realize that, above all else, the development of the higher self is of utmost importance. Materialism is an obstruction to the advancement of the higher self. The perception of time limits and difficulty of the subject matter cause procrastination. But lessons can be found in *all* events. We are reminded that karma is the experiencing of both sides for our balanced understanding and not the punishment or reward for past decisions. Karma is the learning path directed by the higher self. Therefore, we need to let go of what occurred in the past and focus on our future learning and the events arising out of the life-energy field that create the opportunities for our growth in understanding. Letting go of past perceptions and self-imposed limitations will allow an ever-expanding understanding of value to develop.

The illusion of self-worth

The relevance of listening to your inner Self and how: The world will function from inner thoughts and communication from above yourself. The world will not function from self-thought. Learn how to listen to inner-communication: your own inner-communication. Teach consequences of not listening to the inner communication.

Trust in who you are and what you are, and people should trust in who they are—not what they want to be. Equational vibrations: people are living off the vibrations of others; titles: seer, intuitive, psychic, shaman.

Incongruent as to seeking true Self: manifesting justice of behavior through the perception of others. Reliance of Self is a by-product. Importance of self dooms one to unrealistic value; the consequence of not understanding a perceptual vibration of the inner Self. Titles are variations of self-worth, unrealistic to Self-value. Coordinated flow of energy is unfolding; self-worth will diminish because of not understanding true Self-value. Release titles and perceptual abilities to create true gifts of value associated with connective tissue of universal plasmic cord.

Incongruent behavior of self-worth projects the value of self-confidence. A nexus of understanding is coming. Preparation is the understanding of conceptual behavior. Titles cannot save you from consequences. Form triads to complete the energy Source.

Q: Can you explain how this works?
Feeds energy for Self-understanding. Does not rely on others to chart your course. Triad increases energy for Self-thought, discussion of outcome. Go within Self. Seek guidance within the triad, not from title sources. Many charlatans pose as knowledgeable and no understanding of Self-worth. Seek help to find Self-guidance path only. Not information on *who* you are, only on path to *begin* understanding—where you fit in the puzzle.

Know what can give you the journey—only beginning direction. Nefarious shamans: holders of untruth. Learn to listen; a coming of late. Not much time. Path obstructed by self-taught guidance counselor; many absorb what other's perception of who they are. Contractual agreements not fulfilled with many here, relying on others to sacrifice their truth. A nocturnal effect over their soul—not Light. Ostracization is at hand for many who give false value to others. Actual events will vary. Form triads—a true meaning within—not outside the Source.

Q: Does the nocturnal effect mean keeping others in the dark?
Truth not given to true value: useful ignorance. Perceptive promises to many; useful ignorance for cause.

Q: How can people prepare?
Releasing their value: not ready to let go of material perceptions. Must stand at the edge of precipice before realizing or absorbing truth.

Charlatans giving others information—not to find themselves—but need information to help *them* find themselves. Triads will give those guidance for those who cannot on their own, but not with those seeking titles.

For subconscious subtitles, all have a title of self-worth. Titles seem to be important to the value of the human kind.

Our understanding: The mentor is not speaking of the true shamans, rather, the self-taught people who call themselves a shaman in an effort to find a false sense of self-worth. These people, according to the guide, are telling others what their path and value is, disrupting the natural course of Self-discovery and their *true* path. Yet the self-professed shaman has not gone within themselves to find *their* own higher self and correct path. Our real value cannot be found outside ourselves; it is only found within and only relates to the discovery of our true Self and our continuously evolving understanding.

For those who have difficulty listening to the inner communication, the positioning of three people in a triangular formation during meditation helps excite and redirect the energy pattern to facilitate the inner communication. It does not, however, work for those who are seeking recognition.

Expanding your parameters

Q: Is life force energy applied to all organic life, but not applied to the soul?
The soul is a temporary relief of Self, the true variance of living matter.

Q: Why is the soul a temporary relief of Self?
It is written: you cannot attain the higher self without it. Souls are in consonant of Self.

Q: How does the true variance of living matter relate to "soul is a temporary relief of Self"?
All living matter has variances. In humanity, it's the soul. In other living matter, it's a higher Creative force that protrudes the matter. This matter proceeds the event of Self on a quick redaction of a young organic molecule. This is what creates your changing atoms, which you experienced in a molecular change of water. Activation molecular change: when water is adaptive to free molecular movement, acting upon surrounding gases.

Kent describes a vision, "It's like a human. Say you are an individual atomic molecule that makes up water, and you're in a 10 x 10 cell full of water. Your movement is totally restricted. When you are let out of that cell into the atmosphere as a gas, which way will you go? You have so many different variables, which you can take then."

Because the gases within your individual cell become used up and you become restricted in your movement.

Kent explains, "It's like the water within your cell becomes compressed and densified so your movement is very restricted. Assuming you are a molecule, a hydrogen or oxygen atom, and you become very restricted in your movement because the cell is densely compacted with water and there are very little new gases coming into this cell to replace what is there. You are still a water molecule, but with less and less variances."

Q: Does this relate to the changing atmospheric gases to enable *our* expansion?
For those on the same variational plane. Acquiesce to this. Humanity is locked within self-annihilation, unable to create variances of higher sphere.

Kent elaborates, "It's like water in an aquafer underground. You have no variances, or your variances are very limited. If you keep it contained, it remains liquid. If you open it, it evaporates into its variances, into differences in molecular structure through evaporation."

Our understanding: Matter has the capacity to change, having a set of mathematical parameters in which a sliding scale of behaviors may be produced. In humans, the soul has an energetic effect on young organic molecules. The higher Creative force protrudes other living matter, giving the variance in matter expression. For water, the variances would be a liquid, a solid in the form of ice, and the gaseous state of hydrogen and oxygen atoms.

Quantum theory states that just observing the behavior of a molecule changes the behavior of that very molecule; that the observer changes the observed reality. This theory arose out of highly controlled experiments at the Weizmann Institute of Science, where the behavior of a beam of electrons was changed when a person was observing the beam. The more the beam was observed, the greater the influence the observer had on the beam.

The mentor seems to be referring to the Japanese author Masaru Emoto, who claimed that water molecules respond to human vibration and who later produced photographs of ice crystals taken from frozen glasses of water after being exposed to various pictures, words and music. The photos show the variances in the frozen water crystals in response to the vibration produced by the pictures, words and music.

The activation of molecular change occurs when water is able to freely move about, interacting with surrounding gases. Variabilities are limited when molecular movement is confined.

If we set parameters for ourselves, we are restricting ourselves to the point we cannot move in our understanding. Open your parameters to let a free-flow of thoughts, opening the quantum field.

The true Self-worth

Obtruse discussion brings knowledge to understanding. Know the variances of self and the platitudes of others' self-worth and understanding of self-conflict. Conceptualism is a degree, a variance, of/to reality: your concept of mechanical, the detailed intricacies you provide to bring knowledge to Self. Use this pattern to understand the worth and value of your own process.

Your release will prevail as you attain your higher self. The power of calm will be attained: let it all go. Love is the perfection of yourselves. Everything around you is irrelevant; the relevance is your perception of its value. Let go of the values that you place on things.

Credence to the understanding of Self: Ostracize Self from self-worth. *Give credence to truth.* Levator: levitation of being is constructed without prior knowledge of self-worth. Give this even though they will not understand immediately. Laborious is the road to Self-understanding. Credence of value to truth comes hard.

Your bodies are not [of] value. It's only for communication [and] of transportation. Do not be concerned. As soon as you put on value, [you] are not here to stay. Man has tampered with the incorrect; given the obnoxious behavior of one's self. The creation of understanding becomes more difficult. The pleasures of the human species take priority over learning and understanding. Cause and effect is the case here. There are those that desire to learn, but very few. In those areas they do not have much; a wanting is created. Noticiousness is a cause for understanding. You must give meditative communication a cause; effect will reiterate itself. Suprecious is understanding.

Use your gut feeling. It is time you choose your destiny: learn. Nothing is absolute. Creative cognizance is a guide to a higher Self-understanding.

The forbearance of natural law will take place, a prelude to the paradigm of existence. Uphold your Self-worth. Not to the egotistical aspects, but to the natural or true Self. Universal laws constitute the parameters of All That Exists. Give credence to the understanding of All That Exists outside your sphere. Palakian concepts are due for your learning. Ostracize the attitude or aptitude of others in your environmental field. Movement will begin soon, a prelude to galactical movement within the universal laws and understanding of why. Explore the unknown to your perceptions given through anxieties lost. All as is and was. Correctional aptitude a must for this human existence.

Our understanding: Credit is due the awesomeness of the universal understanding. We are being nudged forward in our learning through changes imposed within the palakian field that exists around specific spheres. The palakian field holds and influences all life force, as first spoken of in *The Augmentation of Man: A Study in Renaissance*, **chapter 3**, "Death and spiritual rebirth". The palakian field surrounds specific spheres to move the cause of change for those areas, most likely younger cultures that need moving forward in understanding. It is associated with the magnetosphere of that particular planet. The movement of ions creates the magnetism. Ions are charged atoms. Intelligent Light travels on strings of ions, or plasma cords.

The mentor announces that our movement will begin soon, prior to the galactic movement, as everything is moving up in its vibration. We need to put aside our fears and explore the truth about our perceptions. A correction in humanity's understanding is necessary for the survival of the race.

> Trudence best performs the concept of true Self-identity. True Self-identity: trudence. Truth is a consequence of understanding. Acquiesce to the truth.

> A silique to understanding the first precepts that are to come; a coordinated effort by all who desire as a pre-tense that is coordinated by the love of the Creator. An harmonious effect to the vibrational attunement of those that are in alignment with a conceptual understanding of what is to come and what is to be, a puerdurial understanding within of Self: a knowledge of Self.

> An octavian understanding of precepts qualifies for perfecting the soul: see all sides.

> The veil that you see will be a reflection of your true Self. Sound bites of human nature will show the path of destruction: a cautious understanding of what is to come.

Kent later clarifies, "This veil reflects their true Self. Many will see themselves and they won't like it."

Our understanding: We have to contemplate the idea that if we were to recall events from past lives, what might we have done in a previous life that we now find difficult to accept? How does the recollection of our human nature show the path of destruction? We need to keep an open mind with this answer. A vibrational attunement occurs in those who are aligned with the understanding of what is to come and wish to take part in knowing, with certainty, the higher self. Silique seems to be used in a metaphoric sense, like opening a pod or husk to discover the contents that it holds. The new understanding that evolves—the ability to see from all sides—is what qualifies for perfecting the soul.

Not everyone is ready

The following was given as personal guidance after encounters with others who tried to influence our priorities, downplaying the lessons and telling us, "all you have to do is love." There is a lesson in the guidance in that love goes beyond our understanding as humans, which we generally tie to an emotional and conditional aspect. It does not incorporate the love and respect of all of creation as an interacting and communicating system in the promotion of higher consciousness. It is for this reason that the true definition of love incorporates both the ever-evolving expansion of universal consciousness, as well as all the connecting entities that work to that objective. Not everyone is ready to see that connection, still caught in the emotional snares of "it makes me feel good."

> Some of the others cannot learn; they are cast in their own shadow. Too long have they been there, insecure outside their own realm. Do not be negligent to them. This is their lot they have cast in the shadow of their past regressions and [are] reliving their insecurities to truth. They are abstract in their volume thinking. It is their shadow of Self-truth. Do not be pulled in. The Light is beyond the shadow of Self. They have yet to learn this. They are hiding in their perception of love, which is indefinable on this plane.
>
> You must continue your path and reach those who are reaching out to learn and understand or attempt to. A perceptive concurrence to argumentative value is irrelevant to actual concepts you learn. There are

no persuasive accents to this event. Now teach those that only desire to find their understanding that has a quantum connection upon their part of the universal flow of vibrational energy.

The love concept is not, does not, redundiate upon the past concepts—far beyond your relative understanding as humans. Can only be conceived at a higher level of understanding within the universal concepts. Their irrelevant behavior: 'It makes me feel good.' Contrarian argumentative stance; [the understanding] cannot be achieved because of the relevance they perceive within their shadow realm.

Continue your journey as requested by our ancient body as we continue to teach you. Do not look back upon your understanding. All is desired that flows as your conceptual being unfolds. Give credence only to those that desire a continued understanding in the field of knowledge, flowing on the plasmatic field.

Now rest your mind and spirit. Prepare for the coming events and your movement to new learning: higher value.

Our understanding: The love and reverence for all beings who encompass a communicating web of knowledge and wisdom comprises the universal definition of love. Even those who are negative and the ignorant impart a greater understanding to our knowledge base. Our soul desire is only to connect to the flow of information within the plasma field and to continuously assimilate the understanding and vibrational attunements, and to pass the knowledge on to those who are searching. This is the true definition of becoming a unified One.

Awakening

The whole purpose of language is the communication of understanding. However, we often use words to which the actual meaning evades us. The words can be attached to a false perception that creates a false narrative. It is important that we be very clear in the meaning of our words. When we realize the true definition of the word, a shift in our perception occurs, bringing a new depth of knowingness. *Awakening* is one of those words. As a reminder, the higher self is expressed as Self; the lower physical self as self.

> **Q: Can you give us clarity to the meaning of awakening?**
> Avoidance of Self-conflict in nature: [a] natural drift within nature's plasmic field. Self no longer exists: the true plan of spirits. Conceptual being; knowing All That Is; guidance presenting Self as non-existent. Essence pervades all within embodiment of spiritual essence, without self. Moving to higher communication with conceptual beings. Self not included in any concept. A flow to and through plasmanic field. To awaken is to dissolve self.
>
> Bleaching force. Cognitive value from bleaching force, given the value of Self.
>
> **Q: Can you explain *bleaching force*?**
> Bleaching self out of existence.

Bleaching out the oneness of self, the *me*, and becoming One with all.

> **Q: Does awakening also mean to develop a level of understanding and wisdom?**
> To be able to use.

Q: A premature awakening was previously mentioned, what is it?
Awaken without understanding: lack of wisdom. Perceptual understanding missing. Conceptual beginnings deceased to perception. Reversed course—no platitudes for movement or directional behavior—prepietous to concepts of truth as derived on conceptual being.

Q: What should humans be working on?
Self-comprehension of life force: Self beyond *who* you are.

We once encountered a man who had a previous near-death experience. Our overflowing excitement to question him further about what lies on the other side soon turned to disappointment. His answer was simply, "We are all One and there is nothing more than this life." Over time we came to understand that, in his near-death experience, he had an awakening. But the awakening took place prior to his full understanding of the perceptual learning cycle. This left him at the beginning of the conceptual understanding of all is One, yet still stuck in the old paradigm of perception with no desire to move forward, thinking this life is all there is.

Opening the soul's box: a higher self connection

Q: When the soul is created, does it have a certain amount of innate knowledge?
Soul is the conscious value of All That Is. There is an essence that is beyond the soul that is part of the life force—it is beyond the soul—the essence of a living organism yet to achieve a soul. Beyond your understanding at this time, but you are moving to a level of understanding.

Kent inserted, "Essence-soul-physical body."

Q: Is there an encapsulation of part of the life force with the creation of a soul?
It is of an essential life pattern, the vibrational aptitude where all is started, the essence of All To Be.

Kent, "It's beyond creation, but not beyond the Creative vibrational force."

Q: Are souls born out of one location or multiple different locations?
All planes of existence.

Q: Is there more understanding that can be shed in this area?
Not for you at this time.

The mentor will not give more than we are capable of understanding at the time of the lesson.

Q: Can we have a lesson on the higher self?
Within.

Q: Is there a procedure for retrieving the higher self?
Self-diagnosis inadequate to feed the natural Self for cause: prelatious to an event. Forgiveness is very valuable for Self.

Q: Is this forgiveness in a future or past tense?
All tense, irrevocable of time. A consequence of being: neurological release of thought patterns digests the worth of each entity—a consequence of being. Change is coming soon.

Q: What kind of change?
Neurological indulgence within Self-parameters, influence upon human species given.

Q: The phrase "opening the souls' box" was used before. Is the souls' box within the physical body?
No. It's within the realm of who you are; a shadow of Self: associated with the being of Self. A consequence to understanding this meaning.

Q: Is there a difference between opening the souls' box and the reconnection with the higher self?
That is the higher self.

Q: How do we open the soul's box?
To open the souls' box is to know your value and the worthiness of Self that lasts within. The box is the mentor of your being. This is what causes you to be who you are and who you will become. Be fruitful in understanding who you are and your value will be set forth. All is in your minds' wind. The soul's box is the higher self. You are who you've always been and who you will be.

Wind is sometimes used to denote how communication of higher understanding travels through the atmosphere, as in "traveling on the wind." This atmospheric communication can be between the higher self and the physical self, or between the higher self and communicating entities.

You will make it to your future when you know your past, you understand your past—your change.

The completeness will come full circle now: you are who you were and you were who you are today. The relevance to this understanding is magnitude to the transformation. The truth of Self. Contemplate this. You are who you were and you are who you will be. Miscalculated connections are now being corrected.

Kent injected, "The question is, why do we want to become older? Or, why do we want to stay young? I keep getting, 'we are afraid of the future.'"

> All is relevant to your being, a conglomerate of evidence of who you are. Estuarian: estuarian evidence.

Like an estuary, the flow of the river as it meets the sea, so too, our integration with our higher self.

> **Q: What determines the timing of the integration with the higher self?**
> Always integration [is] Self-taught.
>
> **Q: Does this period of time allow this to happen because of planetary alignments?**
> Yes, the conjunction of Neptune will release energy within the system. Conjunctional arrived; Neptune not engaged. Asperian delivery of correction.
>
> **Q: What will create the conditions for Neptune to engage?**
> Change in scope: movement of planetary bodies, conditional void.
>
> **Q: Is it movement of planetary bodies outside of the conjunction?**
> Correct.

Our understanding: The life force creates the soul, or soul's box, which is the memory stick for all lives that an entity has lived, holding a conscious value of all lessons learned. The soul has an aptitude for higher learning. The higher self is the part of the soul that directs the higher learning process. The soul is our mentor, feeding the physical self understanding gained from the past, pertinent to current life experiences. When the souls' box is opened, we will know the value that we hold within: the knowledge and wisdom we have accumulated over the eons. It will release who we are and our plans for who we will become, on a conscious level. Our true value is aligning to the understanding of who we are and who we will become, creating the opportunity for refining our decision-making to make way for an efficient and productive learning path forward.

We are responsible for our own reconnection with the higher self. However, as the planetary alignments move into their positions, the conjunction with Neptune will allow a release of energy that will provide the most opportune time for it to occur; albeit will be a rough and unpleasant delivery.

Connecting with the higher self

Dreams can say a lot about what is going on at the spiritual level. Having had fearful dreams of bears and extremely large horses, Renee began to believe that these animals represented the larger higher self, whom she was fearful of reconnecting with. Assuming that it was a signal for her and Kent's reconnection with the higher self, she asked for confirmation from their mentor:

> **Q: Is it time to open our souls' box yet?**
> No, you have yet to learn transparency of universal nature—visualization yet to come.

> **Q: Why do dreams of trying to reconnect to higher self reflect fear?**
> All comes to the surface—all the past—who you really are, raising your worst fears, reliving who you are. Non-correctional: no value; we provide the value from here.

Q: Is this to say we need help with this event?
Must do self; all have issues of past.

Q: Are issues brought forward from past life events?
Each independent life within learning.

Q: With the reconnection, is there a flood of past memories from past lives?
Realization of important learning events, consequential to being.

Q: When the reconnection with the higher self begins, is it all at once or in stages?
Process of: all is in process by written rule. Ocularian process for universal understanding: you will see reenactment.

Completion of Self can be attained. Completion without renumeration of Self is attainable with various degrees of accuracy.

Q: How would you define the completion of Self?
Self-attainment on the neuronetic field of communication.

Q: Is this the reconnection with the higher self?
It is the higher self.

Q: Do we have unlimited Self-direction within the parameters of universal thought?
Correct.

Q: Is our spiritual intellectual ability greater than our physical intellectual ability?
Much, when exercised on a continuous basis.

The fear of the higher self is, in part, created from the fear of recalling past learning events; the memories of significant events going back through a multitude of lives that have been stored in the soul. We can complete the reconnection with the higher self, experiencing a reenactment of some events, in order to come to an understanding of the complete Self—with various degrees of accuracy. Correction of our understanding occurs through a higher Source entity, imparting thoughts that result in the epiphanies that bring a deeper, more conceptual, understanding that is also more mathematically correct.

To understand this in a simpler sense, Renee dreamed of being in an older house with an older woman and a girl. The house had three living rooms and the older woman was telling the girl to sneak down to look at the bottom level with the third living room. In the dream, Renee realized this was a house she had lived in before, as it looked familiar. The house remained the same, the only difference was the woman currently living in it had added her own new and personal touches. Later contemplation bore the realization that the dream was a representation of her own past, present and future in the three living rooms. The older woman was the higher self who was talking to the girl, instructing her to take a look at what her future holds.

The communicating higher self

On this occasion, Renee heard and transcribed Kent's full dictation during his trance. But, when she played back the digital recorder, the recording was different than what she had heard and documented. The middle of the dictation was interrupted, followed by a brief period of silence and then what sounded like a computer generation of Renee's voice saying "coming to una," recorded over Kent's voice. The recording then continued with Kent's dictation.

Kent's actual dictation heard and transcribed by Renee:

> Lindacious will move you as a being in the correct direction.

What was played back on the digital recorder:

> Lind… [Renee's digital voice: *coming to una*] …will move you as a being in the correct direction.

The recording then proceeded as it was originally dictated:

> Hold on to Self-cause. Movement within the lineal field increasing.

> Use your gut feeling: variables surmount. Use your instinct as it swells. Short time left. Feel your inner Self: the bulge will tell you the way and when. Must be very, very soon.

Renee brought up the event during Kent's meditation a few days later:

> **Q: The other day the recording had a voice like my own, saying "coming to una."**
> Unification of Self-thought.

> **Q: Did the recording pick up a thought from my higher self?**
> Correct. You are more than you are.

> **Q: What is the significance of "coming to una"?**
> Reliance on Self-understanding: procurement and confidence of the inner Self.

Both Kent's dictation and the dictation from Renee's higher self were picked up on the recorder; Renee's higher self overriding Kent's physical dictation.   Interestingly, they were both communicating a message about the higher self. In Renee's case, the higher self was speaking to the physical self in an effort to bring both into unification, to procure and have confidence in the inner Self. The dictation was telling us that being in alignment with the path of the higher self will move us in the right direction.

The following communication, a different event, started after Kent had been watching a movie—a love story—causing him to reflect on his own interpretation of true love. Renee was a bit confused at first and guided the questions. In this reading, Kent was channeling the wisdom of his higher self. He was not in his usual deep meditation, or trance state, he just "tuned in." The information did not come from another entity, it was a communication of his higher self to the physical self. This can only be accomplished as we reach a higher level of spiritual attainment. The answers in this section are not indented, as it is not coming from outside of Kent. It began with Kent reflecting on his love for Renee, then reflecting on universal love.

Puzzled, Renee questioned, "How does it relate to universal love?"

Kent explained, "It *is* universal love. The love you see reflects upon you. This is what the Creator meant by love one another as you love your Self. What you learn is love. One has a desire to capture it forever."

Kent, speaking to Renee, "You are the value of Light Being; the renaissance of my soul. I keep hearing, 'you are all that I am.' You have helped make me. The hearts of the eternal being are marked in time. Prelucence is the key to eternal love."

Renee asked, "Can you explain prelucence?"

Kent continued, "Transparency of our love. That is the value of our Creator. Absolute progression of Self depends on your understanding the virtues of a true unselfish love for another. A virtuous capacity can be attained through this eternal being. This creates the universal understanding, the basis of All That Is."

He continued, "I am the higher self, prelucence to the level of understanding beyond the self. A concordance of universal love."

Renee, speaking to Kent's higher self, "Thank you for helping *me* understand."

Kent's higher self replied, "Prepare your heart to expansion of understanding the true Self, the higher self, with the love of All That Is."

Renee asked, "Can a picture be painted of your higher self's connection with All That Is?"

Kent tuned back in, "Spark: a reflection of the Self, seeking eternal being."

Kent later added, "It looks like a small speck of light."

Renee questioned, "One must secure a certain level of understanding to secure eternal being?"

Kent answered, "Progressive task: not in one human life span."

When Kent was done, Renee half-jokingly asked, "You were talking to yourself, how does that feel?"

Kent explained, "It feels like I understand. There is no ego at all. It is all based on understanding and love of All That Is. The one true love of your life and you search together. All this does not happen in one life of learning. Open Self. When you don't understand, you create your own parameters. Completely open Self to understand what is beyond here."

Our understanding: The reconnection with the higher self is done as a process over many lifetimes. A basic level of understanding must first be attained. The addition of meditation, calming the mind and putting forward a conscious effort to unify with the higher self comes next. Stored understanding can be accessed as this integration begins. The third step is realizing the higher self is a part of the universal consciousness and that communication with higher understanding entities is done by way of a communion of the higher self and the communicating entity. This can only be accomplished when there has been a sufficient amount of integration with the higher self first.

More on the higher self

We continue with the lesson on the higher self from **chapter 3** of *The Augmentation of Man: A Study in Renaissance*, "The higher self." The higher self works in conjunction with the soul to direct the learning process through a vibrational scripting of movements to our path to gain an ever-expanding understanding of who we are and All That Is. The higher self works within the plasmic field, channeling knowledge and understanding unto itself.

> **Q: How is understanding corrected for someone who had mental problems in the physical life, once they cross over?**
> The enlightened state of subdural being. A learned process through enhanced disclosure of Self: a learning process.

> **Q: Can you give us a more expanded understanding of the term subdural being?**
> Quasi-learning experience within the spiritual realm. Quasi-learning field, given the realities of natural law; curtacious in cause.

The subdural area of the brain occupies the space between the dura mater and the arachnoid membrane. Perhaps this is drawing a parallel between the function of this area of the brain and a space within the spiritual realm, in which the two share similar properties in that both areas provide a brief learning field, aligned to natural law.

Q: Would the "enhanced disclosure of self" be the enhanced disclosure from higher self?

Some do not possess a higher self; it only comes through cause.

Q: What would create the cause?

Self-annunciation of inner Self-worth, a repetitive junction in one's atmospheric relationship with the upper beings, or entities as you would call them— unknown origin by your thought process. Atmospheric condition changing as we speak, controlled by ionospheric damperings.

Q: How is this accomplished?

Multi-function of happenings. Replenish your thought. Atmospheric conditions changing to reflect the neuroesolence of change.

Q: And this also changes the human atmospheric relationship with the upper beings?

Opens parameters for communication with those outside this sphere.

Q: Does the higher self make up the entirety of the soul, or is it a part of the soul?

Tied.

Q: In other words, the two are separate, but combined?

Complete.

Q: Does the entirety of the higher self and soul exist within the physical body during an incarnation?

Movement along the path of plasmic force as one unit; a thought in understanding. Quasar influence: a perceptual being is manifested.

Dissipation a must for those incomprehensible beings: a last furnace effect upon their life force.

Q: What ultimately happens to those beings who lack a higher self?
Gaseous nature of molecular structure.

Q: Are they recycled?
Correct. An abundance of natural material to take place.

Q: Is a quasar instrumental in the dissipation of these beings?
Yes, influential force will prevail.

Q: If an entity does not have a higher self, do they also not have a soul?
Limited soul's box: a reprehensible figure within the box. Coming to the end of the experiment; reprehensible beings will dissipate upon release.

Q: Was this category of beings designed as part of our learning process?
Nonsensical in nature are they: asperian creation.

Q: Why were they created?
Experimental beings: many here of various cultures.

Q: What was the cause of the experiment?
According to legend: being strength over others of non-consequential ability; gone wrong. [An] experiment.

Q: Were they to test the strength of those with a higher self?
Guidance for those needed.

Q: Can you elaborate?
Quinterrium to be given to those going into the next plane of existence; a polutionarian conceptual existence of All That Is.

Q: Does the word polutionarian refer to poles?
The poles release a conceptual agreement for cause: irrefutable contact with another culture.

Q: Is their existence to serve as a teaching tool for the others?
Yes, a coordinated effort to substantiate the learning process of Self-worth and annihilation of self: [to] learn understanding of both ends. Prelaperious is attaining the value of looping atmospheric changes into a vibrational complex to understanding its nature.

Q: Approximately what percentage of the human race makes up reprehensible beings?
Thirty-eight percent.

Q: Are there also non-human beings that make up reprehensible beings?
Not at this time; a coordinated closure of those.

Kent defines, "What I get is various outside entities put different races of people here as a part of their experiment. I'm guessing it has to do with genetics."

Our understanding: Those who lack a higher self, conditions that only exist now here on Earth as a result of an experiment, still provide a valuable learning experience for those who have a higher self. We have all encountered someone whom we find offensive in that they seem to lack any sort of moral compass. The changes in the surrounding atmosphere they cause produce in others a desire to understand the many different aspects within the reoccurring events they are creating. It produces an effect of wanting to understand the situation better before the next event loops back around. Even negative or incomplete entities can provide a more expanded understanding. In this case, it is learning both sides of the true value of the higher self, *and* the loss of a soul who does not learn the value. The value and worth, in a universal sense, is always about the learning gained. This conceptual understanding must be completed before we can enter the fifth Earth cycle, that of conceptual learning, where we regain contact with those outside of Earth. Once the understanding is realized, those lacking a higher self will cease to exist.

The changing atmospheric conditions will have a direct impact on humanity, paving the way for an improved communication system with those outside the earth. It will begin an enhanced guidance of the human entity, bringing man forward to a new level of comprehension.

The many selves

The following question was generated from hearing about the various selves, as in the physical self, the etheric Self and the spiritual Self. The answers received were quite unexpected:

Q: How many selves make up the human entity?
Approximation: 3 billion, 500 million. Causation to understanding defect.

Q: Does this number represent a single human entity?
Correct. Variance in underlings. This is missing: apartions—confusion to cellular level.

Q: Can we have a small sampling of the types of selves within the human entity?
Gaia type T pulsator; coagulation resolution, P-structure, correlate to interlock; servacious

connection, a formulation to structural content. Pulsators apply movement, pulsate to rhythm of biofield.

Q: Are each a single strand of energy?
Complex correlation of individual typeset: [an] interwoven complex [of] correlators opening on individual faces; a complex parameter within each whole. Neurology is apprehendible within panoramic field.

This certainly wasn't the answer we were expecting. That being said, our definition of hologram is insufficient to adequately describe its true complexity on the earth plane. The many selves associated with our incarnation incorporates a Gaia type T pulsator that applies movement to our physical body while pulsating to the rhythm of Earth's life field. It also includes the bringing together of all the intricate constituent parts, including genetics and the application of the senses. Tied to our neurological system, our senses provide the means to gather data from our panoramic field for further understanding, as relayed in the following:

> This is very much like a hologram; the perfect technology to feel, see, taste the essence that is not there.

Kent announced, "I'm asking if this Earth a hologram? I keep getting, 'It's symbolic of a hologram. Not a complete hologram.'"

Pain and the higher self

Pain, too, can have an effect on our spiritual growth and direction. Much of this has to do with our perception of self-worth in a physical sense (lower-case self), how aligned we are with the higher self (capitalized Self), and the purpose of our journey here.

Pain is the searcher of truth. A deviation to reality.

Q: Is pain the motivator to find truth?
Pain serves.

Q: How does that work?
True pain opens the reality of Self.

Q: When the reality of Self is accomplished, is the pain resolved?
No, it gets you there. Directional being's needs: the virtuous augmentation of Self. A wound, internal or external, gives direction of Self. Exceptional cause with an effect.

Q: Is this the same with those that have long, enduring pain, such as with the back?
No, a wound of magnitude. Temporary visual of Self.

Q: Is this associated with the fear of physical death?
No, reflection of reality beyond the passing of self. Passing of self not a true reality; temporious only of this range of existence.

Q: What is happening with intractable pain?
Here and now event caused. Non-true reality: temporal block.

Q: What is being blocked?
Past aggression to self-worth.

Q: Would that aggression to self-worth be from another person, or self-induced?
One reflects the other. A reflection of aptitude: levels of perceptual intake. Habit to circumstance.

Kent clarifies, "Making yourself a victim over periods of time. Some can adjust and others keep creating it."

Q: How can people with long-term pain heal?
Change attitude towards Self: inside healing first. Hurt lingering due to Self-conflict. Open thought pattern: more acceptance of truth. Change inside character: solution.

Q: How can I (Renee) heal my joint pain and stiffness?
Conflict within your life pattern movement, one you chose that coincides with human correction. The flow, the life stream, is having conflict with outside influence that is surrounding the nature and value of Self. Pull back within your flow, your purpose received from environmental conflict of thought patterns influencing the movements. Concentrate on your purpose. Other's influential patterns [are] blocking the value of your purpose. Consign others to their own value and purpose. They must reach their own concepts. Flow within yourself, the nature of who you are and who you will become.

Q: What about the pain of grieving?
Give grievance a cause for understanding, paradoxical in nature. The learning experience is exaggerated so you can comprehend its value and cause.

Our understanding: In the above lessons, a significant wound causing pain serves to magnify and give direction to the higher self, that part of the soul that gives direction to our learning path. Pain does not necessarily go away once the effect is realized, though. The internal conflict resulting from unresolved emotional pain is what the mentor is suggesting is causing most long-term pain. Traumatic life events can create the block, manifesting our own aggressive attack on our self-worth, resulting in the victimization of ourselves. The healing must come from within first. Accepting truth changes our character, resolving the inner conflict. In the case of Renee's joint pain—and this may not apply to everyone who has joint pain— there existed an inner conflict between following her life path and following a path that she perceived others expected her to follow. Once this was released and the true path was given precedence, the joint pain ceased. These lessons may not directly correlate to all who have pain, as each person has unique life experiences that serve as influencing factors to their situation. The general point being made here is that even pain and suffering is intricately connected to our spiritual path and how aligned we are to that path.

Self-direction

Consequential evidence is at hand on self-perception. Calmness: step back from where you've been, reassess your true value and meaning of who you are. What value do you place on yourself and your meaning of the life accomplishments? True Self-direction comes from your inner Self-perspective, not from other's wanting you to be. Perplexed behavior exists when not listening to Self-guidance, gut feeling. Set a true task of who you want to be— your value to the human race. Surplex is the consequences of irrational movements within behavioral concepts of what you should be as directed by others. Simple, but complex in the nature of Self-guidance: act in your own behalf. Create your support from those that relate to your true being. Exaggerate your cause and effort to accomplish your tasks. Acting comes first if you insist on the path you are on. Acting who you're not relates to a position of who you *think* you want to be, on the course you are on now.

What do you hold sacred in your life? The value of

what you hold; the circumferences of everything around? You hold your diameter, your center point. Look at your circumferences to determine your value. Not only things, but of the people living in your circumference: perception of value, circumference of value.

Q: Is there a correlation between spiritual evolvement and physical DNA or intellect?
Not DNA. Understanding the quanticeptive parameters within the quantum field of decision-making, argarious in nature: a Self-attaining. Reliance on others to Self-attainment [is] not acceptable.

Our understanding: Stay true to yourself and your true path. It is not appropriate to let others tell you who you are or let them chart your path for you. Use your gut feeling for navigation. Look around at all that surrounds you and if it supports your true path to greater learning and your value to the human race. Create your support system from those that understand your true being.

Correcting humanity's direction

Kent starts with describing a vision, "I'm seeing lots of rings."

Rings of life events: the learning experience, or non-secular learning. Atrocious is the act of now. Consequential beings is inevitable to event. Atrocious: cause to secular living.

Q: What is the desired effect?
Opening of the veil. Curiosity seekers a must. Prevalence of attitude performance will prevail upon this planet. Antiquitous behavior is surplexing those without cause, a consequence of who you are will emerge at the next crossing.

Q: Is antiquitous behavior that which is guided by the higher self collective?
Correct; of fortitude to understanding the wellness of All That Is. A correctional distillance of behavior to correct the value of within Self, a variancial aptitude of cause given to those of higher understanding and variance.

Q: Why are curiosity seekers a must?
Those that want to learn a must to open the veil. Austeriosis settles into those that proceed from within the veil.

Q: We heard the term over-soul. What is it?
One who takes over for another. A preponderance of evidence: a stagnation of a conscious collective, which is over-shadowed by a collective ensigneous value. Counter-productive to the significance of the contrary value: provided to the consciousness of the collective. A significant value of Self-awareness or consciousness as predicated by an ensigneous nature—a shell of the particulate.

Our understanding: We are living in a world that is asleep. Our attention has migrated from our Creator and our spiritual evolution to an indulgence in the material world; offensive to the higher beings. Curiosity must exist to be able to see beyond the veil of misperception. When this condition exists, a collective of souls, working on behalf of the greater good, act to correct this stagnation of the physical world by instilling a sense of desire for a more expansive understanding. The over-soul functions as being counter-productive to the stagnation of the conscious collective, over-shadowing and providing a significant Self-awareness to the group to push them forward in their spiritual evolution.

Movement to a higher vibration

Are you prepared?

Q: What was it in reference to?
Movement, unlike before. Movement of Self within the field will take place in conjunction with the earth.

Q: Is this at the time of the pole shift?
After. Movement is preserved for higher level vibration of which mankind is not ready; a fragrance of aptitude not yet discovered.

Q: Is this a shifting upward of our own vibration in conjunction with the earth?
Yes, a cognitive repulsion of the past vibration, uplifting to those that care for the survival of the species. The beginning and the end in conjunction with each other. Universal aptitude in relation to universal perspective.

Q: Will this only affect a percentage of humans?
Correct. Redundancy of natural law, purveyance will accomplish this task. Acquilliate is the word to come—a pattern of dissension.

Our understanding: A small group, compared to the whole of the nearly seven billion people who reside on Earth today, will shift upward in vibration after the interplanetary pole shift, which may include Earth's electromagnetic pole shift. This will produce a repulsion of the past vibration, propelling those upward who truly care for the survival of the human species. The end of the cycle of perceptual understanding begins the cycle of conceptual learning, which includes the universal understanding according to the universal perspective.

Aligning to the flow of energy

Align yourself with the electromagnetic flow: three days of alignment in a spot where the electromagnetic flow is intense, purging oneself. Purification in order to align oneself with the flow. Cannot align with horns and words of irrelevant value. Must be driven from within. A purification of food and water to open the congestion within that obstructs the inner flow of energy to align with the magnetic flow of the earth. Three days [of] self-purifying.

Q: Is this an exercise for us?
All. It is for all who seek to align themselves. It is the simplicity of self-prostration to the flow of energy, which is universal. A consequential pattern will emerge. But, are you willing to step within and maintain the parameters from self-indulgence, creating a new pattern of life that must be followed by inherent intent to keep the flow available? To attain the understanding and benefits that is derived from a completely unobstructed magnetic flow within and aligned to the soul's resonance? Simplicity is the key. Complexity creates the obstruction, creates unacceptable parameters of self-indulgence. Water: pure. Food: unleavened bread, fish meal.

Learn the three quadrants of behavior: One, love without passionate being; two, unconditional surrender to the flow of energy to dictate higher self; three, number three, sagarian in nature, giving up who you are to the natural flow of Earth Mother renovation, becoming one with her. Adopt her fortitude, her being with creation. A rock with magnitudinal understanding, she is. Aspire your

Self-contentions, which are valueless for the human
understanding of the curelacious events about to
unfold.   Cough   up   the   non-numerical
understandings; a Self-diagnosis of the planetary
field. May be beyond your understanding when you
don't try—a deeper meaning.

The inner consciousness collective: a universal
embodiment of All That Flows.   The universal
consciousness is a collective vibrational output of All
That Exists.   We are here to help...the new
world...attune to this and you will be ready. Let it
all go, no reservations as to the consciousness of
absolute value.

Our understanding: Among the non-indigenous, ceremony
becomes more about bells and irrelevant words than the true intent
of the ceremony. Ceremony need only be simple: acquiessing to the
flow of energy within the magnetic field. This is accomplished
through abstaining from self-indulgences and purifying one's self
with water, unleaved bread and fish meal, which perhaps is a
referrence to dried fish. This is done in an area with a high
electromagnetic field, which is sensed by some people. We are
given this exercise to enable us to align with the magnetic flow of
Earth, aligning to the flow of knowledge that the Mother has to offer.

We do not suggest this if one has a medical problem, such as blood
sugar instabilities, heart conditions, seizures, etc. Always check
with your physician before attempting this fasting-type of exercise.
It is meant to be used to align to the vibration and the flow of energy
from the true Self, the higher self, and becoming one with Mother
Earth. She will highlight the misperceptions within, to be later cast
aside.   Aligning to the flow of universal consciousness and
becoming one with all that exists results in the arrival of a collection
of entities that feed the higher self with continuously new and
profound contemplations.

We are given instructions for three of four behavioral changes to facilitate our reconnection with the higher self: First, love unconditionally; second, surrender to the flow of energy from the higher self; third, give up who we are at this time to become part of the natural flow of Earth's renovation.

Earth is a living, breathing organism, full of wisdom and understanding to share. The events that are unfolding are meant to cause us to cough up the misperceptions of the past to take in a new and deeper truth, held by our Mother. Align to the plasmic flow of energy, connecting to All That Is to indulge in the higher concepts that are held by the universal conscious collective.

Neutrality of nature brings cause for perceptual agreements to your being...humble your attitude toward Self

NOTES

Chapter 8

Humanity's Awakening

Each grand cycle encompasses a movement forward in learning. We have been learning through our exploration of space and events within the first four dimensions of a time-space continuum. It has also been learning about ourselves: who and what we are at the soul level, the soul currently residing in the fourth dimension of time. We can access the fourth dimension through both meditative and dream states, contemplating possible future events that help to clarify who we are and where we are going. The soul contains the nanotechnology that stores learning events of current and past lives. Completion of the first four dimensions opens the door to a higher vibration enabling our reconnection to the higher self, that part of the soul that directs our learning process. It allows our ability to begin accessing the stored understanding within the soul. The reconnection gives way to a recollection of major events of past lives, which may cause confusion for those caught unexpectedly, or for those whose belief system does not recognize reincarnation.

This period of time, in particular, is one of human-created chaos as our misperceptions rise to a crescendo, then collapse from lack of a foundation based on truth. This chaos and polarization are further magnified by various energies being used to destroy our misperceptions, clearing the way for our acceptance of a more comprehensive truth. It is also, through a series of events, taking us to a final destination of unity; albeit, not the way one would imagine. The totality of the events creates such disparity that we finally reach out to our Creator for help, thus facilitating our reconnection with the soul, en masse. It is an end of secularism and materialism and a return to God, our Creator, as the focus. This will also be a period of massive catastrophes as Earth rebalances from what man has done to her. The earth's shift and our own shift are related and hold certain unexpected events that are designed to awaken the masses.

A shift in consciousness

Kent announced he was hearing the question repeated, "are you prepared?" We sat down to meditate:

Q: Kent kept hearing "are you prepared?" What was it in reference to?
Movement, unlike before. Movement of Self within the field will take place in conjunction with the earth.

Q: Is this at the time of the pole shift?
After. Movement is preserved for higher level vibration of which mankind is not ready. A fragrance of aptitude not yet discovered.

Q: Is this a shifting upward of our own vibration in conjunction with the earth?
Yes. A cognitive repulsion of the past vibration, uplifting to those that care for the survival of the species. The beginning and the end, in conjunction with each other. Universal aptitude in relation to universal perspective.

Q: Does this affect all matter within the universal plane?
Correct.

Q: Will this only affect a percentage of humans?
Correct. Redundancy of natural law purveyance will accomplish this task. Acquilliate is the word to come: a pattern of dissension.

Newitarian one—then bringing new life. Have excelled beyond their capacity—now returning—a bold stroke within the universe to change which you cannot comprehend.

Difficult speaking with you on our part—concepts not high enough—this will change.

Molecular structure interface with conscriptical influence from molecular particles, subscribed in the particle infusion that is beginning among all species within this sector of the placonic shift within the plasmanic molecular field.

Difficult to describe to you, as your concepts are not inherent to these terms.

Q: Is the placonic shift a shift of Earths' plate?
Placement of land mass essential for new shift realities. Placement of plate shifts essential for new beginnings of consciousness relative to now.

Q: What can humanity do to help align with this shift?
Repression of self-guidance. Consecrational energy field up-ticking.

Q: Are we to allow this consecrational energy to guide us?
Correctional aptitude a must for direction of Self.

Watch the horizons—a time of change—your perception must shift. The shifting of the universal consciousness. Everything has a time within its path of recognition, a conscript of recognitions.

Our understanding: The shift is going to absolutely disrupt our entire being. It is a change in our physical reality, combined with a change in our conscious reality. It is both an end and a beginning, bringing humanity to see the truth as the universe sees it. Each event is a step in the process to deliver humanity to a desired destination of a greater understanding. Our perception must shift to a new paradigm and a fresh way of thinking. The next crop of children will bring forth a new reality to man's future.

Quantifying human consciousness in the chaos

[People] will be separated. Occipital patterns to change. Reverse the magnetic field of the body's vibrational tuning. Those that don't have the understanding, they will become like Cro-Magnon. Their dispair will increase, based on their lack of vibrational tuning. Their understanding will be deligent to the concepts [and] events that are coinciding with the universal exiting of the vibrational field. The attuned ones will prevail, separating themselves from the unfortunate circumstanced individuals. Your concepts will bring you through…Wake up.

Variances will be made to quantify the release of energy information. A quantifier has to be put in place. An elixir is being prepared for the general population of the human race.

Q: An elixir for what purpose?
To stupor the human entity; to deaden the thoughts of the non-potential. Quantifiers are set in place throughout this world or sphere.

Q: What are they quantifying?
The energy dissipation that is taking place within the field, derived from the human consciousness of subduction within quantum quantifiers that humans release when involved in an event of magnitudinal implications.

Nothing is as you see. Serve others as needed. Simplify the Creator above All That Is before you.

Simplify the analysis of the Creators' creation, his/her non-perplexible being.

Creative influence coming to those that understand, that have obtained universal knowledge; the beginning of All That Is again. Augmentation of natural Self; a uniform cognizance.

Perceptive behavior a congruent path to the other side. Look beyond what you see—a value of All That Is—congruency. Perpetrude of knowledge is not seen on this sphere. Teaching a must. Give the value to what is, a perceptive concurrence. A new horizon of perceptual learning is breaking; congruency is of value here.

Our understanding: From "The angulation of proclamation," **chapter 9**, *The Augmentation of Man: A Study in Renaissance*, the angulation of proclamation is an atmospheric structure that monitors the reaction to an event through quantifiers released relating to the quality of understanding an event. Angulations of various degrees protrude the protoplasmic energy field, measuring a movement in the energy field, and then dictates the next proclamation to be set forth. These structures exist throughout creation. In our section of the universe, it quantifies human understanding relating to an event having great implications for the human race. It also measures the vibrational impact the understanding has had on the memory within the cells of the brain. Remember, levels of vibration relate to levels of understanding. The angulation of proclamation measures the vibrational understanding, both before and after an event, then redirects the energy flow, relative to the amount of understanding gained, setting up the next event for further understanding. It is monitoring whether a culture is needing to repeat learning events because they have not learned, or progressing forward in their understanding, through the measurement of the energy quantifiers that are released by humans, or any other culture in the universe.

Those who are ready to continue on into the next cycle of conceptual learning will be separated from those who are not. Many people, not ready for the next cycle of higher learning, will be facing the end of this chapter and will have to incarnate elsewhere to continue at their current level of understanding, leaving less humans on Earth, but more creatures. This is due to the fact that Earth's vibration is moving upward relative to the higher learning she will be providing, and many people will not be a vibrational match and would not be able to comprehend the new lessons. They will have to go to another learning sphere to continue from where they are currently in their level of understanding. Those who are aligned will move forward, the ability to comprehend the concepts of the next learning cycle will bring them through.

Time to awaken

Enlightened culmination will happen when the vibrations surpass the height of the eclipse of the earth's crested rotation.

Beware of false: those who say they are enlightened. They come to deceive. Man is fortuitous of his behavior, of others around him; fortuitous and the exactness to the enlightenment of others. Be heralded: shout.

Propensity of behavior is obnoxious, the obscenity of a culmination. Bombardment of nations will supersede the culmination. The stupidity will enhance the process of culmination. Be intact with others: the encirclement of detrusious environments.

Be prepared to receive the shift. Happenings will occur. Wine will flow like blood in many places. People fighting, confused, some will say, 'Why me? I've been true to God.' They do not know the truth.

Negative energy, human, increase[s] [and] destabilize[s]. Government surprise—arterial infusion in the human event: control of all consciousness—creating a supportive path mindset is perception of reasoning. All hell to break loose.

The spirit shall be awakened within each one of their past—all lives. Native Americans lead the way. Constellations are vibrating. Soon all to be in unison, then the one that is not will move.

When Native Americans agree, unite, fourth dimensional change will be within. Man will perceive one another as an extension—[an] existence of their past from other places. A new reality will prevail. Pretentiousness will no longer arise. New values are conceptual to the realities of man's true being. The effervescence of perception to the truth will flow in the veins of man, creating a new concept in appreciation of who they are and where they come from.

The completeness will come full circle now: you are who you were and you were who you are today. The relevance to this understanding is magnitude to the transformation. Correctional behavior depends on the world's results. Now it is strictly meditations for guidance and the beginning of preparation for transformation. Transformation: spiritual and youthful heredity. All is as was, all will be.

Our understanding: All consciousness has been controlled. Even those who say they are enlightened have come to deceive. Any true understanding that we have seems to have occurred by chance. The behavior is seen by outside entities as obnoxious. The bombardment of radiation particles from the rise of cosmic rays working in conjunction with solar activity will bring the needed change to the human DNA, increasing our capacity to understand, replacing this declining trend. The downward spiral will enhance the culmination of our learning experience and we are being warned to not be influenced by those who are trying to suppress others, but, instead, loudly and publicly call out the truth. Now is the time for our preparation to move to a higher plane. Observe the sequence of events happening; each is a step in the learning process.

People will fight and turn to alcohol to numb themselves from the disintegration, asking God, "Why Me? I've been true to you". Even the believers have been ensnared in the deception. A government surprise will bring to light the total control of consciousness that has occurred, directly injecting the population with the understanding, while trying to create a supportive mindset in their reasoning. All hell to break loose.

When the Native Americans unite, the fourth dimensional change will occur within, allowing us to see our connection with others through the multiplicity of lives past, creating a new reality of who we are and where we have come from. They are the focal point of our spiritual shift. The constellations have been vibrating with a higher level of understanding. Soon Earth and her inhabitants will join in the higher vibration.

Our correctional behavior depends on the world's conclusions to the events before us. Our transformation will be spiritual as well as genetic and will take us back to a period of time in the ancient past where humanity valued the expansion of their understanding and knowledge, bringing us full circle.

We created the world we live in

Man is not inoculated from events because they have not learned Universal Laws and Concepts.

You are the consequence of your own actions. Prognosis has been made: a new beginning, new creation. The disease has abscessed and will be relieved.

Q: What is the event that is being repeated at this time that was previously mentioned?
Despicable event—once was—many lives lost. Outcome unperceptible. Let the money-gatherers form there. The natives will shudder under the new sign.

Q: Does this despicable event have anything to do with a nuclear event?
Possible outcome. Human race: unpredictable behavior. Cannot control outcome. Astronomical occurrence on horizon precipitate[s] the outcome of horizontal latitudinal adjustments pertaining to this planet sphere.

Imagine all the self-proclamations to come of many—and none are right. They all have the book of answers and none have opened the pages. A swirling indemnity to Gods' creation, never to be paid in fact. A promissory note that has been broken. A wally Immanuel bring them forward.

The heart of One is worth more than the axis of a thousand. Clean the diverseness of thousands; create a channel of One. The influence of the Creator is all that is needed.

Ostracize perpetual understanding, to be replaced by variant degrees of quasi-truths. Formality a must. The quivering rapture created by a listless man evokes indenturedness to the character of self-indulgence: pious in self-worth; exploding in radiance of little value.

I cannot conceive with more understanding that the misunderstanding has already happened. Man is a qualitative creature: his vastness is disproved over and over again. Our verbatim is unheeded. Know the consequence of fruitility of an interconsequential being. Earth will be brightened with new tranquility. We will guide from here: place of desires. Many will want to return but cannot.

Q: Where will the lower vibrational entities here on Earth incarnate to after the shift?
Their vibrational level seeks cause. Many vibrations within the galactic field, new places forming with various sceupharocal values. All this, [and] more, beyond your understanding as a human species, but arrogance prevails within your small amount of knowledge.

Many will cease to exist on a subatomic level, dispersing their atoms throughout molecular space to form new gases to incorporate what is existing; restructuring of molecular diagram of once was. All within universal structure are recycled into the whole of being to reform matter, as needed. No conscious value at that time of restructuring. Some, very few, will proceed to higher attainment level, adding to existing structure within Self—only value to universe consciousness.

Q: Are those that are being recycled ones who have not moved forward?
Correct; no longer being. Value is attained through Self-discipline of vibrational change occurring within, going with the matter flow and existing within the plasmatic field.

Q: We were told many species would become extinct. Is this to make way for a new and higher vibrational DNA expression?
True. Nomenclature is coming. Prepare for worst-case-scenario. You can conquer this. Release abjective thought.

Our understanding: Ever-lasting spiritual life exists for those who conform to the purpose of creation and universal law, which dictates ever-expanding conscious evolution. The soul seeks cause: the learning. There are those who are allowed to continue with the knowledge that they must change their course and begin to expand their understanding. There are also those who have continued to exist on Earth, despite their operating at a lower level, to push humanity forward in their understanding. Once understanding is achieved, the beings are no longer necessary. All energy that does not conform to expanding universal consciousness is recycled, where it has no conscious value at the time of recycling.

All matter must evolve to higher states of vibration. The changing vibrational field will also reflect upon the species expression for Earth, resulting in the extinction of some species and the introduction of new species. All life must fit within the new vibrational parameters.

Perilous times ahead

The earth is tuning now.

Kent describes a vision, "They are showing me a tuning fork with a certain sound."

Harmonics are beginning to prevail. Increase in ocean volcanos. Fish pattern changes—mixed up. Tide changes not normal; as if there were two moons pulling. Muscles falling off in the ocean. Rocks quiver to the sound of Earth Mother. Springs change.

Circumference of equator—which will change and will help lead you in this—five degrees center drop.

Future is in consequential movements. Those that want to tell the future add in their own understanding or interpretation. They do not put the consequential coordination of events in perspective to what events are happening then. They add rather than taking things as they are told. Sequential events are ordered. Sequences of events are pervasive on the natural understanding of natural events. Sequence of events will influx to the temperate rhythm of Earth Mother. True concordance is the weight of the soul to the understanding of the universal consequence.

Our understanding: It is difficult for humans to accurately predict the future, which is determined by the order of events, designed to produce consequences of understanding in each sequential step. We tend to add to the narrative, rather than sticking to the dictation from other entities—as it was given. The sequence of events upon us are coordinated with the natural rhythm of Mother Earth. The understanding of the soul must be in agreeance with the universal understanding.

The following paragraph is taken from a communication in October 2007, showing the beginning:

God, the Creator, has spoken the truth. The beginning has begun. The tuning forks are beginning to sound. Almost all in place. They're waiting for the Native Americans to open the door, and then it starts. They still argue about the timing. Irrelevance of time, based on their interpretations.

The Native Americans have been given the task of the ceremonies that will open the door to the fifth world of conceptual learning.

Peace and tranquility of love of God, our Creator, is the key to pervade those of the enlightened hemisphere. The character of the knowledgeable ones to arise, written upon the path of time. Unforseen circumstances prelude the event.

Mankind, human race, is in a renaissance of change and discovery, but difficult to penetrate the veil of antiquity. Absurdity will abound. Correctional behavior will begin to those that do not adjust a mindset in the making: You will have to be forced to be guided by thoughts.

Q: How is thought controlled?
Through vibrational influence—a consequence of being interpretation—your communication.

We were told in October of 2008, that absurdity would become widespread, obvious by the time of the completion of this book in 2019. The human-created chaos has begun. We are in a period of great change and discovery, but it is still difficult for us to penetrate the ancient veil that hides the higher self. Those resisting the change will have to be influenced by other's thoughts to push them forward.

Sufferous to the nature, serendipitous is your word to survival. Imputousness will prevail one to a box, an insecure cornice of the mind, loss of identity. All this is coming—will not interfere—all in motion. The Creative forces will prevail only at a time of insolence. We have forgone the conclusion: *It is a must to prevail the new humanity.*

The Mountain of Dominion will rise, as required, a key to understanding the ancient lost languages. Water and fire, the outside entity influence, complete discharge of electromagnetic energy, remolding [and] reshaping Earth, as now known:

reconfiguration is due.

Harbinger of peace is a true disconnection to the prevalence of mankind. Peace will not prevail: abstract, irrelevant to cause.

Sense of dispair help[s] create a path to purpose. Beings that have died before, mankind, have come to try to help them. Your fellow counselors are corrupt: litigious behavior, exorbitant pathetic non-sense. Disparity can be of value when looked at the function at which it is perceived—not as you think. Disorientation will begin to prevail. Obnoxious behavior will arise within the mass-density areas: people. Irritation will increase. High energy source will be released. Perplexing behaviors. Medical conditions will develop: new items of antiquities will prevail. Center erosion of atmospheric conditions. Transcontinental shift. Warnings will be missed.

Awareness will increase, but not to needed amount. Confidence and attitude must be held. Maintain strength. Perceptive activities to be analyzed. Congruent behaviors, perplexed by most. The oculance: purveyors of unseen.

Much confusion to what's going to happen; no direction given. Anticipation causing obstruction—too high. Variances will occur within the quantum field; missed on most, on others. Alpha field generation of mind thought: a cornerstone which [is] to come.

Give credence to your understanding of All That Is. Preparation is always correct, good. Changes shift as events occur. Always be prepared for change. Aptitudinal effect has changed the curve.

Causation will cease.

Q: Is that due to all the changes?
Yes, clarity difficult at this point.

Correctional value ahead by reflection of self.
Humanity, a change in direction of humanity.

Intellectual ability has changed the learning curve. The cause, the teaching, will cease due to all the turmoil, making clarity difficult. Humanity's correction and change in direction lies in our self-reflection.

Kent describes a vision of August 2017, "I'm seeing lower level entities pushing forward and higher-level entities stepping back in this time period."

We are letting them come forward to create the chaos
of misperception so it can be completed.

Our understanding is limited in that we have certain expectations for how people are supposed to behave. God will use all those who can fulfill the task to accomplish the desired outcome. We live in unusual times, requiring unique processes to redirect humans to the true learning path. The goal here is to eventually destroy our misperceptions through the chaos, reuniting humanity on the other side through a new understanding. The following lesson reflects the concern of the entities directing the change, "What to do with the humanoids?" In other words, how do we push them forward? The next session starts with a single word:

Pluckarian.

Q: What is the significance?
An age of consent has passed.

Q: Can you elaborate?
Single definition: conscripted.

Q: Does this mean consent by the humans is no longer needed?
No consent available. Predicious conglomeration of emotion has taken place. Conceptual agreement is in place. Aquarian charge is in place—war repercussion—displacement required. Perceptual being resistance is gaining; non-functional in universal law. *What to do with humanoids?* Conscript given for purveyance of emotion.

Conditional atmospheric change. Rush, rush to urgency, not knowing why: perceptive change. Changes in atmospheric conditions bring hostile environment. Maintain Selves, [the] conditional representation of who you are.

Q: What is causing this?
Vibrational: both polarities will be magnified and prevailed. The chaos will continue until mathematically settled on the other side; an agreement given by those that cause the chaos. A surrenderous atmosphere will begin.

Closing of the ages, a new parameter will develop. Justification for all things are happening now. Fluctuations are beginning, a spherical degeneration to cause effectual understanding of All That Is. Clairvoyance will become widespread.

Our understanding: The polarities within the human race are being magnified, the effect of a changing vibrational atmospheric field. The chaos will continue until the mathematical balance of true understanding is achieved and man finally acquiesces, an agreement by those who came to create the chaos. There are entities normally from other areas of the universe, now incarnating as humans, who agreed to come here to help facilitate the change. Things are not as we see it.

Rules of consequence

This section is a compilation of multiple communications of common themes received over the course of about four years. We are assuming that they are separate human-created events that will work in synchronistic fashion to correct the direction of mankind. We are not completely sure if these are world events, or specific to the U.S. Time and the sequence of events will reveal the truth.

The following, from a reading in May 2014, started with Kent announcing, "Twice now, I heard we are in the Galactic Center."

> Variations will begin: hotter will be. Consternation has begun to repudiate—the correction at hand. Elevoracious in nature, recipetory upon previous cause and effect. A learned behavior cannot continue to exist without repudiation effect. Lackatory to Self-meaning; will now reflect on Self-worth of value. Weeping and anger among the inhabitants will increase hermetically. Imposed declaration of Self-rule to begin literation among those of consequential behavior. Three months of your time, literation procedure to begin. Self-accumulation to understanding consequence will arise within human nature—many not understanding why—to completion of all within Self-derived instincts driven precariously by unknown Sources within Self.

> Must adhere to the rules of consequence; consequence of events must take place. This is as before, millennia ago. A cycle will reappear, giving birth to causation and effect.

In April 2017, Kent begins the reading, "I keep getting 'a surplex surface.'"

Q: Can you elaborate?
Arogon: a surface of inconsequential behavior to be studied by those of arrogant behavior. A surplex of events to occur, will give way to consequential behavior of those that want to be part of this. All are irrelevant to the cause of events about to happen. The word irrelevance: give cause to understanding. Contemplate this. Human understanding of this event gives cause to disunderstanding; a fallorious puzzle to occur.

Given the outcome of the experiment, vulnerability will weave through your society. Do not attempt to divert it. This is the true meaning of cause and effect. Repetitious behavior exists.

Q: What is the desirable effect of the vulnerability?
Teach the last stanza here. Octacious is the cornerstone of this learning. We cannot predict the outcome of this human race. Theoretical attributes are at play; consequence of past behavior.

The following paragraph was from a message of April 2018:

Autocratic incident will take place, work to confusion of language. Transformation a must for the human species to exist. A non-molecular structure of consequence to begin the refraction of the species.

Later in the same month, Kent announced, "Third time I heard, 'preliminary.'" We sat down to meditate for answers:

Prerequisite to what's coming: preliminary procedure. A correction is due.

Q: Can you tell us what the preliminary procedure will be?
Ligatory in the consequence, aspiratious influx of procedural assets. A quintessential analysis, procurement by quizitory process. Analytical exchange due. Reflectatory upon Self-analysis within the event coming.

Our understanding: Tied to an event consequence, the longing will continue forward, flowing with the process. The perfect embodiment of analysis, the truth is secured by a process of questioning, a result of our own reflection on the coming event. The last of the messages comes from a reading in September 2018:

Projectile of prognostic fortune is coming. Everline is taking place. Quassational effects are in place: redundant behavior at rest. Aptutional requests have gone unheeded.

Q: Can you further explain "everline is taking place"?
A link to the other side. Capture the essence of humanoid relection. Advanced technology to be opened.

Quassational is the event about to take place. Merringer is the word to be used bearing this event.

Q: Does merringer describe a partial event?
A reliance to truth. Perceptive outcome will be deception.

Our understanding: Humanity is being brought forward to a new truth from a previous lower level of understanding. An event will cause shock and confusion that will result in the rejection of past choices. It is designed to lead humanity to a correction in our thinking process. We cannot move to a higher understanding without the rejection of old behaviors that lack meaning to the higher self. This event will cause people to become angry and tearful but deliver a more expansive understanding of the value of our Self-worth: the knowledge. Those who have learned from it will declare Self-rule, instinctively driven by the cumulative understanding at the soul level and the guiding Source within, not really understanding why, at the physical level.

By May of 2017, a sequence of events was being set up to give cause to our understanding. This evidently is an experiment designed to awaken the human race and change our redundant behavior. Theoretical assumptions are made based on past human behavior, but, in reality, they cannot predict the outcome. In the end, many still may not understand what will have taken place, creating a false narrative. We were being instructed to not interfere, that it would continue until vulnerability weaves throughout society, creating the cause and effect in the last verse of the poem to bring the final understanding. It is through angular learning that we come to see all sides of an event that gives the most complete understanding. Cause and effect will return again with a new understanding of why rules of consequence are so important to our learning process.

An event created by an authoritarian ruler will work to the confusion of the people, transforming our thought process and redirecting the course of humanity.

We were being forewarned, in September of 2018, that a driving force creating an event was coming, creating a link to the other side, unifying humanity. The trembling effects will put redundant human behavior to rest. Appropriate requests have not been given any attention. We will have to trust the truth; yet many will perceive the event to be deceptive.

The austrafier

Again, we live in unusual times, requiring unusual measures to redirect humanity's path. These messages come from multiple readings between March of 2012, and February 2018, and are in chronological order:

> Austrafier is at hand for many that do not want to partake in the coming events.

Q: Who is the austrafier?
One that has not been but will be—comes from the other side. A prelude to events of happening, he quietly exchanges to himself to the proper mode given to a task on humans. Has always been there, unseen.

Q: Is this a non-physical being?
As needed.

Q: Where will the austrafier arise out of?
Chaos, to come soon. The planted One. Step[s] on world stage of triumphant beings. Only a night light will show his cause from the darkness. Austrafier is a must to procreate the understanding and protection. November fourth, the austrafier to begin. Coagulate your thoughts into a diametrical understanding of the human events to occur. Contrast the behavior.

Secularism is amended on the horizon. Unity will be separated by the masses due to secular information given by the austrafier; a deception of cause and effect.

Q: What is the austrafier's purpose?
Separation of internal being, bringing together the whole. Separating the individual, reuniting the

magnitude of the whole. Separation *and* unification in the same sentence.

Quiet your thoughts to what you know or think you know. Quillerian diagram of conceptual events can fill in the blanks to your being; a contemplate to understanding.

You cannot stop the continuing circumstance for a trail of deception: must take place to begin the lockdown. Truth shall raise its head during chaos, the austrafier at work. Darnacious: know latitude for understanding structural collapse.

Polarization is beginning to cause effect. Euthyritic is a desire to reach a higher self for reflection, [a] reflective cause of why you exist on this plane.

February 2018, the austrafier was at work revealing the truth of our perceptions:

The austrafier is in play.

Q: Is this still the separation phase?
No. Realization of truth beginning: truth of perception. Ocularian phraseology at hand.

The austrafier is at hand, precursor to numbness. Pluckarian attitude, adapted from the realm cause. Minosis will take place to proceed the event.

Our understanding: Time to widen our parameters of thinking and what we see. This is a being who comes from the "other side," entering the world stage, quietly exchanging to himself the task to be taken upon humanity, to produce an effect of first polarizing, then unifying the masses. By shining light on our perceptions, the events created will instill a desire within humanity to reach for a higher truth. A more widespread understanding of the truth becomes the unifier for the masses. Through this lesson, we learn that certain behaviors and tactics may be utilized to advance the understanding of humans. Yet, we often confine our thinking to a box, having certain expectations of how a person *should* behave, unaware that certain tactics are being used to reshape our thinking process.

Accepting the outcome of the whole

Resonanic vibrations beginning to accelerate. Those that need to know coming from the past. Must be austrafied in order to accept the outcome of the whole. Individualism is not of value at this time here on this sphere, in order to complete the cycle of communicative value within the Universal Concepts and Laws, attained through a whole of eternal documentation from the beginning to the end of this cyclic value.

Severity of ignorance to value is now taking place. Scopulation, scopulation of this event: a forerunner to the coming changes in cycle, preclude event of nefaracious title. Aspirations of singularity opening way for understanding to be as One.

I tremble for those that are eclectic in nature. Preparation is at hand for causation in fact: preparing the people as One.

Astute, exacerbating reflection: a significant value of the coming event. Humans wrapoflate their existence to human control. Renunciation of Self is among most humans. Lavornatious is the cosmic opening to be used in Earth's change. Neutron particles entering next four days. Aggressive enosis will prevail in the winds, created by the event. Volcanic thrust is due. World enunciation upon itself: gargantuan synosis will prevail upon the hitlist. Unity is of most value here and now. Green accentuation of the paragonic parameters. Open your heart-felt being. When the moon becomes red, a significant change is upon this plane. Sedatiousness is at hand.

Our understanding: Intense reflection will have great value in the coming event. Humans have a tendency to hand over their protection to others in control. Most humans relinquish their rights of the higher self and their higher learning. An opening on a cosmic scale, an enhanced cleansing process, will be used in Earth's change, setting the stage for a movement toward a pervasive unity. Perhaps green is the energy associated with this energy pattern of excellence. A red moon signals a time of significant change.

Unity and common direction

The following lesson began with personal guidance. Kent starts, "We may cause disruption in unity."

Be careful of your words. Teach direction. Think about this: You cannot have unity unless you are in the same direction.

Kent describes his vision, "I saw a preacher talking about unity and the people leave and go in their own direction, displacing unity."

Direction and cause; not want and unity. An exploratory configuration, anewitous to the presentation.

Our understanding: To have unity, we must have a common cause and direction. Without having a common process to achieve a goal, unity disintegrates. The goal must include a plan of action so that all work in unison to accomplish the desired end result.

The transformation

Q: Can you tell us more about the cycle?
A shift in consciousness. Every cycle a pertrance of human DNA, insertion of new species attributes and coordination of universal law and acceptance of other dominant entities. A magnitudinal change of entity thought patterns, creating a new nebulae, thought vibration, corrective to align with universality: a vibrational alignment of all living matter. There will be an ocean shift.

Awareness to Self be taught, a must. Oscillate towards Self-awareness. Universal center vibration to occur. Spiritual release of universal souls will happen—center of connectiveness, the alignment of universal vibrations—creating a new Self-consciousness of inner transformation. Many earthly events will occur soon. You will know when the transformation is beginning. Create evidence to event: not natural, not universally connected. Time to release: let go of other's thinkings. Open to antiquity, knowledge: basis for all conceptual understanding.

Q: Can you clarify for us what the "universal release of souls" is?
Movement to new levels of attainment: A periodic shift in the universal magnetosphere hold[ing] all together. Periodic movement of plasmatic force field in the universal plane—not a time field. A life force magnification determination within this field, then shift occurs beyond your home of human existence. Dissolvement of the now-human race. Make room for new species.

Many will vibrate to cause ascension among the lower vibrational entities. Unaccustomed to unfamiliar feelings, cause[s] imbalance and character assassination—some cannot handle.

Five years of massive learning. A Creative influence shall arrive. Not *the* Creator, a Creative influence upon humanity to learn from misperceptions.

Our understanding: Our transformation starts within the universe and the magnetic field holding all together, having an influence on our life force that extends beyond our physical existence here on Earth. Periodic movement of the energy within the atoms of the universe create a magnification of the life force energy coming from Creator that gives a boost to all life forms, making way for new species.

I am the cursor of another. The beginning of a new revelation…this dark time of enlightenment.

Learn the gestation of the being—redundancy abounds—prolific education of Self-analysis.

Pheromones of equal strength will prevail in the near future: love one another to justify your being. Time is short for the duration of humans, as you know them.

Perhaps this guide was acting on behalf of one of our regular guides, disclosing that we are entering a dark time of learning. Humans are redundant creatures and we must move in a direction of beginning to process ideas in a highly productive education of the higher self. Each of the sexes will release pheromones of equal strength to influence one another and we are reminded to love each other to justify our existence, as time may be short for others in our lives.

A vibrational shift

There will be an oscillation change of the earth: slow down your aperture.

In December 2014, we were given the following message, forewarning us of the coming vibrational changes:

The deflectors have come, they are here.

Q: What do they deflect?
Incoming vibrational fields—a temporary deflection until all is ready.

Q: Do they assist with the coordination of events?
Capitulation of events.

Communication with the Ancients had been sparse. They were obviously busy with more important matters. Lower level entities had taken advantage of the situation, leading us astray on many occasions. By October of 2017, utterly confused, we finally called on the Ancients in desperation to set us straight. They explained the work they had been involved in, confirming our thoughts:

Q: Are the Ancients involved in changing the vibrational parameters here on Earth?
Yes. Temporal system is being reset.

Kent recounts his vision, "I see a pulsation in the universe."

The temporal pattern is changing. Universal concepts are adhering—[a] confluence—the magnetic field operates under the conditions of the new panoramic sequence.

Q: Is this a mathematical sequence?
Consortium sequence of reverberating patterns. A
consequence of irrational behavior will take place in
some areas of the universal conscript. This would
be, as you call it, 'a cleaning out.'

Kent, "The whole universe is changing. We are not the only ones."
The earth pattern is changing; the magnetic field is conforming to
the new universal vibrational sequence and universal concepts are
starting to take hold here on Earth. There will be some areas within
the universe of new vibration that will not conform, necessitating a
cleansing of those places to bring uniformity.

Attune to universal understanding

Lean toward the lament of purpose. I show you
nothing and nothing is full of All That Is.

The hand of God is with perpetuating conciseness;
hand moves of relevance: resonance of life's
perpetuating existence.

Kent describes a vision, a metaphor, "I see a human baby inside a
cocoon."

Projected correction of mankind.

Try to tune your vibrations. Look at the mountains.
Try to focus on their vibrations. Do not turn aside
what is felt. Listen when we speak to you, it comes
from inside—all of you.

Conscious behavior, serenity of mind: the edifice of
perception due to the quantessential understanding.
Human behavior: human understanding to the
consequence of the magnitudinal change of direct,
the essence of the universal vibrational tones.

Correctional variance of the universal vibrational sounds will effect the behavior of men, upon themselves, in the coming months. Variance of aptitudes toward man's ability will digress to a perception of incongruent and incorrect realities. Ostentatious behavior is forthcoming.

Do not premap condition before connection. Universal cognizance can be captured here by all. A lull is now; purveyance will prevail at fall. True cognizance of understanding will manifest itself through truth *to* oneself. Be prepared; close to fulfilling for the change. All is on the path: all is as is, all is as was and will be.

Protect yourself with vibrational tones, vibrations of inclusive resonance: attain. Knowledge will increase—the key.

Our understanding: The vast amount of information to come will create a calm and composed behavioral change *for those who understand*. Various degrees of comprehension among the people will produce a variety of behavioral results. Human behavior directly relates to understanding the consequences of the enormous changes, the result of the vibrational tones being introduced. These vibrational tones will have an effect on humanity and their behavior. Ostentatious behavior will be seen in those *unable* to capture the true understanding due to their inconsistent and incorrect perceptions.

We are reminded to not assume an outcome. Eventually, universal understanding will be had by all here on Earth. We were being told there was a lull in our communication at the time, but that it would increase in the fall. As knowledge increases, so does vibration, which gives a degree of protection.

Regaining trust

Kent describes a vision, "There was a snake held in a basket; not of its own free-will. I was able to talk with it. I helped him escape by plugging his ears with cotton so the musical flute that was blown by the snake charmer did not affect his being. When the flute is blown, it holds them. I was able to block the vibrations of the flute and the snake was able to escape. He was hiding in the hole next to a building until I was able to come along and tell the snake it was clear to leave. The snake said to me, 'Let me bite you and not inject venom, so I can recognize you later in life and not harm you.' I held out my arm and the snake bit it and then said to me, 'I injected three times the normal venom because I do not trust mankind.' When the snake understood that I was not deceiving it, it called upon another snake to bite my arm and counteract the poison injected in me."

Kent then settled into a trance and the mentor finished the lesson:

> The deception story is what those tell you, not what they do, of the heart. Deception is achieved through thought, not deeds. The snake is a trust-worthy adversary.
>
> **Q: What can this lesson be applied to?**
> To all, all things of organic nature. The vibrational thought pattern is read by all living. This is a lesson you must learn.
>
> Humans must learn the value of these disciplines. Trust in all that surrounds you, even those of the smallest units must relearn thought [and] vibrational trust.
>
> **Q: We must relearn how to interact with all that surrounds us in this world?**
> With caution. All have come to distrust each other. Relearning a must.

286

Releasing Innocence

Kent describes a vision, "A large building: in the center of the building, on a chair, sat a young woman. The building was full of poisonous spiders. The spiders were not harming her, but were keeping her from leaving and keeping all others out. I asked the question, 'who is in the chair and what are the spiders'?"

> The woman in the chair is Innocence. The spiders are those of the world keeping Innocence from the world.

"When we knocked down the webbing around the door opening, the spiders would immediately reweb over the opening. We managed to clear the door opening. But, as we looked inside, there were millions of spiders, which kept us from entering."

"I asked, 'how are we to get to Innocence, the girl'?"

> Strip away the building one panel at a time. Destroy the spiders on the walls. They will be destroyed by fire and their own poison.

"As we stripped the panels from the building frame, the spiders began to die, the flames erupting around them on the panels."

"I asked, 'how do we protect the girl from those on the ceiling and floor'?"

> Slide clear panels into the building around her, boxing her in. There will be a limited supply of air for a short period while the spiders are being destroyed.

"We slid the panels into position, each having a groove for the panels to slide. This created a protective clear box around Innocence. The spiders on the ceiling and floor were destroyed by fire. It got warm in the box, but not harmful to the girl. When all the spiders and their poisons were destroyed, there remained only the building framework and Innocence. Innocence was then released."

A new beginning

Transitional change is due, ask the new ones to help project the universal thoughts of the Creational apron.

Q: Who are the new ones?
Ones who will emerge at the beginning transformation of the New World. They have thought of value tied to the animal kingdom. They still speak to their Mother: this sphere. Listen to the sounds of the children of Earth Mother. Silence is deafening to their procurement of what is to come. Stranded is the opulent behavior.

Our understanding: Many of the children being born now have come from other places in the universe, here to project a universal understanding. They are tied to the animal kingdom and our Earth Mother. They will be the beginning of telepathic communication. They will mark the end of materialism and our beginning transformation into a New World of exceptional learning and will have much to teach us.

Closing of the ages; a new parameter will develop

NOTES

"The Light is the contemplation of Self as a higher being, which brings forth the structure of what you are on a soul level."

"You are a part of the universe, a part of the stars, and all that exists on this planet. Strive to be happy, learn and understand All That Is."

—The Ancients

AFTERWORD

It is with great excitement that we bring this new understanding to you. Humanity is on the cusp of a diametrical overhaul. We live in pivotal times. We have much to look forward to. It is a great movement, bringing humanity to a higher genetic expression, a new peace through a greater understanding and a new and exceptional desire for learning. It is one in which we will, once again, live in harmony with Mother Earth, and one where we will finally meet our star brothers and sisters. Our desire of the material world will be replaced with a desire to learn about All That Is. A new thought process will occupy our minds and a new conceptual understanding develops, allowing a full panoramic view of all that we see. We are being awaked from within. It is our transformation with the realization of our true higher self, that which holds the key to who we are in all of time and where we are going.

All events currently unfolding have purpose and are designed to lead us through a new conscious evolution. It is a rocky one, filled with chaos and uncertainty, and that leaves one in doubt that the entirety of creation is moving upward in vibration, growing in consciousness. But out of the chaos, humanity will reach out to our Creator, reconnecting with our soul and our true purpose. We will see a more perfect truth, one more aligned to the universal truth. Our expanding consciousness, and that of the universe, is mandated by universal law and the survival of any race is dependent on its ability to move forward within this directive set forth by our Creator. It is imperative that we make the conscious shift for the continuance of our species. We must now be responsible for our own enlightenment through research and study, and through reflection and contemplation. Surrendering to the flow of communication, the Light, we will find amazement in a new world within to explore.

Our world is changing, Earth is rebalancing, and a wonderous paradigm will arise out of what was left behind. A new genetic expression, the result of a multitude of changes that impact our DNA, will lead humanity into the next cycle, prepared for the conceptual learning to come. Observe the children now being born; their intellect and talents will leave one speechless. They will lead humanity into a new world of inquisitiveness, understanding and psychic abilities beyond what we can now imagine.

Peace be with you on your journey,

Kent and Renee Miller

Glossary

abductive behavior: The act of leading another astray.

abjective thought: Hopeless thoughts.

abound: To be filled with; richly supplied.

abscessed: A collection of pus in body tissue, often caused by a bacterial infection.

absolute: Certain. (Physics) Dependent on laws and particular properties of substances or units. Not dependent on external conditions for the conditions of its nature.

abstain: To voluntarily hold one's self back from something inappropriate.

abstinent space and time: Outside of space and time.

abstract: Complicated. A text summary, scientific article, document or speech. To embody or concentrate in oneself the essential quality of something more general.

absurd; absurdity: Lacking meaning or sense.

accentuate: Give emphasis to.

Achilles: A particularly vulnerable area.

acquiesce; acquiescence: To surrender or agree to, consent.

acquilliate: A bed of nerves about the stars with extreme relevance to the structure of **universal consciousness**. "Astrosphere: **neurolectic** assemblage worn of the stars...is several times past relevance to understanding the prevalence of **ot** (a specific field of matter), a **consequential** configuration."

acquisition of the field: To take possession of the energy field.

acquisition: To acquire or achieve mastery of.

activation: To cause to act, react or excite.

actuate: To start a process; move into action.

acularian: One who hears or listens to. An entity or person who delivers a sting, or acts as a thorn (in ones' side).

aculate: To sharpen. Hear, heard or listen to.

adhere: To make stick; unite.

adjunctive connections: Connections with lower levels (of thought patterns).

adversary: That which attacks; an enemy or foe.

adverse: Unfavorable.

affinity: A natural attraction. Attraction of **atoms** to each other in a chemical compound.

affirmation: To express an agreement with, commitment to; or to maintain as true.

afflation: The communication of knowledge from a divine **Source**; the driving inner force.

affluence: Flowing toward; a plentiful supply of thoughts or words; profusion.

agulation: "Planting of the seed of knowledge and understanding."

alchemist; alchemy: The power or process to transform something from one form to another, such as a base metal into gold.

alignment: To draw into a straight line. The state of agreement among persons, matter and **concepts** with a cause of achieving complete understanding.

All That Is: "The **vibrations** of All That Is. Multiples of energy: Fluxionable increase in value as it obtains its various goals [of understanding]. Coursation of energy dictated by the Creator [with a] causation of understanding. The **Q**, the quantum of all understanding, the **Creator**, God."

All To Be: Yet to be a part of **All That Is.**

alpha field: Relating to the alpha brain wave activity within the nerve cells of the brain, in a frequency range of 8-13 Hz. It predominantly originates from the **occipital** lobe at the back of the brain during a wakeful, relaxed state with the eyes closed, such as during a **meditative** or **trance** state.

amend: To remove, change or correct for the better.

amplification: Expansion. (Elect.) Increase in strength of current, power, voltage.

amplitudinal tonic wave vibrations: (Phys.) The maximum deviation of a **vibrational** sound wave from its zero point during one **oscillation**.

analogous: The comparison of like features between two things.

analytical: To separate out the constituting parts to examine key factors and possible results.

anaphylactic: A severe and often fatal allergic reaction from a foreign substance.

anatomical entities: Referring to the anatomy of other beings (greys).

Ancients: "The original ones," created in the beginning of all time. "Spirits of universe—the knowing ones." "A **Creative** entity of spiritual form," never having had physical incarnations. "They are the knowing, the knowledge **preceptors**: interpret, understand, transfer understanding directly from **Creator**." Hierarchal significance: Creator, **Light Beings**, Ancients.

androidal: A human-appearing automated technology.

anewitous; anew: Completely new in form or manner.

angle: Point, aspect or angle of view.

angulated; angulation; angular learning: An angle of view, a viewpoint. The ability to view an event from various angles. "Mathematical equations of angulation: Each concept has a mathematical equivalency."

angulation of consequence: The angle of view, or quantified understanding, following as an outcome to an event.

angulation of proclamation: A communication reflector: Angulation of various degrees protrude the energy field **protoplasm** delivering communication of universal **cognizance** within each culture in response to a movement in the energy field, which dictates the proclamation to be set forth. "An angulation of **conceptual** experience along the **neuronetical** field of concepts dictated by **universal laws: Cause and effect** stipulated by reasoning through laws of variable experience, a universal **concept**; an experience field to understanding behavior of various cultures within the universal standard of laws."

angulation: The angular position; a measurement of angles. An angle of view.

annihilation: Utter destruction. Wipe out the existence of. To void, nullify.

anomaly: A deviation from the normal course.

anti-matter: (Physics) Matter composed of only anti-particles, esp. those of antineutrons, antiprotons and positrons.

antiquated; antiquitous; antiquities; antiquity: Belonging to ancient times.

anxieties: Intense desire or eagerness.

apartions: Literally, lying side by side. "Sequence movement."

aperture: An opening on an optical instrument that limits the amount of light entering.

apprehendible; apprehend: To understand or grasp the meaning of, esp. by perceiving or by intuitiveness.

apprehensious; apprehension: To be fearful or uneasy.

appropriate; appropriations: Suitable for a specific purpose, event or person. Monies allocated by a legislature to be paid by the Treasury for a specific use.

aptitude; aptitudinal: The natural or acquired ability. The inclination to learn or acquire intelligence.

aptitudinal being: A conscious, mortal person capable of natural or acquired abilities to learn or acquire intelligence.

aptutional; apt: Appropriate.

aquafier: An entity associated with water.

aquarian effect: A water effect.

Aquarian: Referring to Aquarius, a constellation between Pisces and Capricornus, also called the Water Bearer. Reference to water.

arbitrary: Subject to individual will or judgement, unrestricted. An unlimited power, unrestricted by law. (Math) Not assigned a specific value.

arbiture: See **preemptive arbiture**.

archaeological: The study of ancient history.

archaic: The earliest stage of development. Antiquated; belonging to a previous time.

architectural dispersion: The structure going out in various directions.

architectural exposure: The appearance of the structure (of DNA).

Arcturian: The inhabitants of the planet Arcturus, or Alpha Boötis, of the constellation Boötes.

ardent: Extremely devoted.

argarious: The state of being fully shining, bright.

arogon: The outward appearance of **inconsequential behavior**. Literally, to educate by the viewing angle.

arterial infusion: Literally, to pour into an artery. A metaphor referring to an intravenous infusion or IV.

arthropic: A sphere for speech or communication; perhaps referring to the **neuronet**.

articulation: Expressed, formulated or written clearly and precisely.

artifactual: Made for subsequent use.

arvadarian: Reflective of a field.

ascender; ascending; ascension: To move toward the **Source** or beginning. "Correctional relationship: Not up—as peering through—[in] relation to location and directional self-viewing, a directional relationship to **Self**-position."

ascertain: To seek out with certainty.

aspect: Visual or mental appearance. The angular distance seen between two astrological points and/or the influence of the planets located at these points. The angle of view.

aspergar: Rough, crude.

asperian: A rough, disorderly, unpleasant and unrefined or even violent person.

aspirate; aspirations; aspiratious; aspire: To eagerly long for or seek out something of great value.

asset: Something viewed as valuable or useful.

assimilation: To conform to or adopt as a part of one's beliefs or customs.

asterical: Pertaining to the stars, or those of the **celestial sphere**.

asteroid: Any of the numerous small bodies of mass, less than one mile to 480 miles in diameter, that **orbit** around the sun, mostly in the asteroid belt between Jupiter and Mars.

astronomical: Relating to astronomy. Extremely large.

astrosphere: The area of the **cosmos** encompassing the celestial bodies.

astute; astuteness: The distinct ability to discern.

Atlantis: A legendary island in the Atlantic Ocean, first mentioned in Plato's dialogues *Timaeus* and *Critias*, in which the island sank after falling out of favor with the deities.

atmospheric platitudes: Excessive repetition within the atmosphere.

atom; atomic: The smallest unit of an element containing all the characteristics of that element and having a nucleus and combinations of **neutrons** and **protons** with one or more **electrons**, attracted to the nucleus by electricity. The number of protons designates the identity of the element.

Atore': An ancient language of the star beings.

atrocious: Extremely bad.

attribute: A result from a specific cause. A quality or characteristic.

attune; attunement: To bring into harmony with. "**Vibrations** are attuned to the magnificence of the human body; corrections are attunements."

auditory system: (Anat.) The system associated with the organs for hearing.

augment; augmentation; augmenting: Increased, expanded or enlarged.

auguration; augur: To **converse** or discuss.

aura: The subtle emanating field around a person or thing. "Reflects the **essence** of the soul, the **shadow** of your **life force**, what you see."

auspication penned: Divination that has already been written or completed.

auspicious: Favoring success; fortunate.

austeriosis; austere: Uncompromising. A condition of "what you do not own or recognize, or recognize as a worthy project."

austerity: The strict discipline of oneself.

austrafied: To separate; isolate.

austrafier: A being who comes from the other side of the **veil**, arising out of chaos onto the world stage, assigned a task to take upon humans to produce an understanding, by separating, then unifying the whole.

austromolization: To render or make extreme. "The most extreme part."

austromolosis: A most extreme condition (sensation, sense of well-being). "Most extreme part."

authoritic; author: The creator or maker of anything. The person who produces a literary work.

autism: According to current psychiatry, a developmental disorder in which difficulty in communication, excessive rigidity and emotional detachment are characteristics.

autocratic incident: A seemingly minor event created by an authoritarian ruler that leads to strained relations between nations that could lead to more serious consequences.

autoimmune disorder: A disorder of the immune response of a body against any of its own cells or tissue.

awaken: To come into awareness or realization; arouse from a state of sleep. "To awaken is to dissolve self." To dissolve the notion of self as being separate from the whole of creation.

axis: A central line around which a rotating body turns.

ayahuasca: A herbal drink traditional people of the Amazon basin and other native tribes brew that has a psychoactive component used in ceremony and for spiritual purposes.

band width: (Telecomm.) The smallest frequency range that forms a band that contains a signal that can be transmitted without distortion.

beacon: Used as a guiding signal.

behavior: The action/reaction of any entity or material under the influence of any given circumstance.

behemoth: Any thing or creature of enormous size or power.

behest: A strong request, **directive** or command.

belied: False.

benign: Gentleness. In this instance, it was inferred in a sense of being inactive.

bequeath: Bestow, impart.

beset: To surround or place upon; attack on all sides.

besiege: To siege or crowd upon.

bestaves: To ward off. The verse or stanza of a poem or song.

bestowing: To present or give.

biased: To be partial to or have preconceived opinions about.

biobonic messages: Good or beneficial life messages. "Messages of the Self."

biochemical: The chemistry of living matter.

biofield: Life field.

biological entities: A living physical entity.

biomass: Organic, living matter.

biosphere: Life sphere.

blue ray: "Integral part of change. Star entity's **conceptual** agreement to come here. **Unitarian aspects** to cause: bring forward ambition for unifier." The new introduction of star entities, through an incarnation of higher human **genetic** expression producing a higher, concentrated learning and unification of humanity. The blue ray children follow the introduction of the **endigot** and come before the introduction of the **magniferious** children.

blueprint: A detailed plan of action.

bombardment: (Physics) The directing of high-energy radiation or particles to. Attack with artillery.

caldarium: The heated pool of a Roman bathhouse. The bathhouses often had adjacent libraries and reading rooms. It would be natural to assume that it was a place where social discourse also took place. "Place inhabited by a previous race. Sympathetic to peaceful understanding. War-like synopsis misunderstood."

capitulation: To surrender to or release resistance.

capricious: Unpredictable.

carcanian atmosphere: "A **concept.** First used: **perceptual** understanding. Universal waves of intelligent **cognizance** on a level elevated to perceive a higher intelligence pattern attained by relevant entities to regulate individual thought patterns when the whole of one has not yet been achieved."

carnarian attribute: A result of being human, or of the flesh.

carnivorous effect: An effect of eating the flesh (of the earth).

castronation: The deprivation of generative power of the nations.

cause and effect: The relationship between actions and events, such as the action providing a teaching opportunity and the resulting event of the actual understanding gained.

cause; causation; causational: The producer of an effect or reason for an action. In these teachings, cause is the action taken to produce an understanding.

causeway: A higher path or road; a highway.

caustic: Sarcastic or severely critical. Harmful to flesh.

celebratory distress: To celebrate the misfortune or infliction of suffering upon another.

centrifugal oddity: An unusual movement from the center outward.

cerebral cortex: The outermost furrowed gray matter of the brain that is responsible for higher functions, such as intellect, learning and memory, as well as voluntary movement and the coordination of sensory information gathering, resulting in the ability to "connect the dots."

ceremonial ordinances: Ceremonial laws ordained by a deity.

chakra: "Step ladder to communication, chakras are understanding. Only five chakras, five energy centers. The crown chakra attaches to the universal cords. Chakras are only valued for communication with the **Creator** and the **Ancients** to better understand life's energy flow, based on universal patterns of energy flow."

channel: Entering a meditative state to receive messages communicated from a spiritual guide.

character: The various traits that form the nature of a person or thing. Qualities of morality, honesty, ethics, courage and integrity. A reference to the behavior or personality of a person.

charge: Rushing violently against, as in an attack. To lay a command upon another. To put a load or burden on.

charlatan: One who poses to have more knowledge or skill than what is actually possessed.

chi: "A universal life force to all cultures. The chi controls the lower **vibrational** force, the instinct of life. It is not a **chakra**; the chi is the representation of life itself. A collusion of mass reflectors: your interpretation of nerves. The chi is a **portal** into the human body and allows various things to come in. It allows a **life force**

302

to come in...but it is not *the* life force. It allows an intricate value of emotion [to come in]."

chivalry: Having the qualities of courage, loyalty, generosity, graciousness.

cipher: The use of symbols or numerals in arithmetic.

cipherious: Possessing mathematical or coded messages.

circuit: To move about or around. Traveling a round, winding or circular journey, beginning and ending at the same focal point.

circumference: The extent of the boundaries.

clairvoyance: Having intuitive knowledge of people and things. Being able to see things beyond natural vision.

CME: Coronal mass ejection.

coagulate; coagulation: To bring together into a single **parameter**.

coagulation resolution: The bringing together of separate parts, conversion or intent.

coalescing: To blend together.

cognizance; cognizant; cognitive: The method by which results in the knowing, knowledge or awareness of an individual. The mental perceptiveness or knowingness of a person.

coincidal; coincide: Happening at the same exact time or occupying the same space and time.

co-lingering: To dwell in a place with others longer than expected with a reluctance to leave.

comet: An envelope of gas and dust surrounding a central mass, rotating in an unusual **orbit** around the sun, often having a tail that moves away from the sun.

communal release; communal understanding: The shared understanding between two or more entities.

community: A group of people sharing common interests apart from a larger society in which it exists.

complex: An intricate association of many parts.

compound: Made up or composed of.

comprehensive understanding: All-inclusive understanding.

comprehensive: All-inclusive.

concave: Roundly curved inward like the interior of a circle.

conceived: To form an opinion, idea.

concept conceptual; conceptualism: The mental combining of separate ideas to form a concept. An intuitive thought.

conception: Idea or concept.

conceptual aptitude: The natural or acquired ability to combine separate ideas to form a broader **concept**.

conceptual being: Beings whose purpose is focused in learning and understanding **Universal Laws and Concepts**; **conceptual** understanding. "Entity of thought...adhere to the **perceptual** truths as written by ancient law."

conceptual intercourse: The sharing of communications of **conceptual** ideas between cultures, individuals, groups, etc.

concerted: Performed together in cooperation.

concerto: A composition of one or more instruments.

conciliatory: To overcome hostility or distrust. To reconcile or make compatible with.

conciseness: Broad in scope, expressed in brief form.

concordance: In harmony or agreeance with.

concourse: A path; an act of coming together, assembly; a **confluence**.

concurrence: Agreement.

condensation: To condense or make denser.

conditional void: The empty space that depends on the prevailing conditions.

conductive material: A substance's ability to conduct an electrical current.

configuration analysis: The analysis of the arrangement of the parts or units of a thing. (Chem) The analysis of the spatial arrangement of **atoms** created by the chemical bonds in a molecule, that cannot be changed without breaking the bonds.

configuration: The arrangement of the parts or units of a thing. (Chem.) The spatial arrangement of atoms created by the chemical bonds in a molecule, that cannot be changed without breaking the bonds.

confluence: The junction where two or more streams flow together.

conglomeration; conglomerate: Composed of many parts or elements.

congruence; congruency; congruent: Agreeing, congruous. (Geom.) Coexisting at all points while superimposed.

congruenial coexistence: An agreeing, congruent, coexistence.

congulated: Literally, with the throat. Possibly a reference to when speech was introduced into the human genome with the FOXP2 gene.

conjugal; conjugate: Representative of marriage. Blending of different elements or parts.

conjunction; conjunctional: Associated with. The combined events or circumstances. (Astrol.) Two or more **celestial** bodies existing in the same celestial longitude at the same time, characterized by the unifying of planetary energies; the angle of view of the coordinating celestial bodies.

conjunctive alignment: An adjustment in a connection; to line up.

conjunctive: Connective.

connected species: The communication between two or more species.

conscience; conscious; consciousness: That by which one is aware of their thoughts, surroundings and/or existence; the collective awareness of a group. The internal knowing or awareness for what is.

conscious behavior: The behavior associated with one who is aware of their thoughts, surroundings and/or existence, or associated with the internal awareness for what is.

conscious collective: The collective awareness of a group or whole.

conscript; conscriptatory; conscriptical: To compel or force into service.

consecrated density of matter: Matter dedicated to the service of a deity; sacred.

consecrational; consecrate: To dedicate one's service to a deity; sacred.

consequence; consequential: Following as an outcome or conclusion to an event, such as an understanding.

consequential behavior: Behavioral change as a result of a **consequence**, outcome or conclusion to an event.

consequential being or entity: "You have to understand all the laws consequential to the event. Of **conceptual** nature; each physical life cycle will have **cause and effect** to nurture the structure of **Self**-being."

consequential movements: The actions, activities or events that create the consequence of an outcome.

consign; consignment: To transfer; hand over to the custody of another.

consoling: To give comfort to; lessen the grief or sorrow of.

consonant: Consistent with.

consortium; consorted: In partnership, agreeance or in harmony.

constance; constant: Reoccurring and continuous.

consternation: The shocking astonishment and/or dread, throwing one into a state of confusion.

constitute: Forms.

contemplex realities: The existence of a network of thought patterns within a given culture.

context: The circumstances or facts surrounding a circumstance or event.

contractual: Obtained by contract.

contrived: To plot or devise a plan for/through ingenuity.

converse: Familiar conversation. Opposite direction.

convex: Roundly curved outward like the exterior of a circle.

convexing diagnostic behavior: The presenting analysis and interpretation of life events.

coordinates: (Math) Any of the **magnitudes** or **dimensions** that define the position of a line, point, etc.by referencing a fixed system of lines or figure, such as longitude and latitude.

coourzonian: Literally, together with the tail of the belt; a reference to the area in which the atmospheric disturbance is occurring. "A **nefarious coagulation** of atmospheric effects. Centralized plane to the **neuromagnetical** field relating to **consequential** behavior of various energy sources, coming soon to affect a single body of this planetary field (Earth). A numerical value to be used as a source of concentrated energy: n-5 (**neutrons** to the fifth power)."

copulation oscillation: The vacillating use of connecting words used in a language.

corazonian aspects: "A single thread thought among many." Where many are viewing an event or field of study from the same angle/s, having the same understanding.

cordessential: **Quintessential beings** that are attached by a cord.

cornerstone: Something that is basic, essential or indispensable.

cornice: A decorative horizontal molding appearing between a wall and ceiling, over a door or window, or below a curtain rod to conceal the hardware.

cornucopia: Representing an abundant supply.

coronarial; coronary: Pertaining to the heart.

correlate; correlation; correlator: A mutual or reciprocal relationship.

correlean effect: "Universal correlation within planetary sphere."

cosmic rays: High-powered radiation energy originating from outer space.

cosmic; cosmos: The organized and harmonious universal system.

cosmology interface: The philosophy of the shared common boundary of two bodies, spaces, systems or peoples within the origin, structure and laws of the universe, especially that of space, time, cause and freedom.

cosmology: The study of the organized and harmonious universal system.

Council; Council of Nine: "**Supersedes** the judgement of any one individual. Sets the **parameters** for correctional behavior. Those that are wise and just guide the Council. Invested interest **manifesting** the correct energy for all universal understanding and guidance. Maintains order within its objective. Oversee **universal laws**. Representing eight sections, one for each of seven universes, plus the eighth for the Seventh Creation and the ninth represents the voice of love, **All That Is**."

counselors: Those who advise.

coursation; course: To advance or progress forward or in a particular direction.

coursational aptitude: The course to learn or acquire intelligence.

coursational aspect: Referring to the angular distance seen between two astrological points in an **orbit** and/or the influence of the planets located at these points.

courts: A body of those qualified for membership on a council or board. Special or concentrated focus in order to gain favor.

covenant: A usually formal agreement between two or more persons for a specified purpose.

created stock: A created race of people.

Creational apron: The apron to the **Creator**.

Creational concepts: Concepts of "universal understanding as proclamated by the **Creator** and under **universal law**. Concepts of "higher **consciousness** of universal law derived from a **Source** given by Creator—pass-down effect."

creatious: To give rise to.

Creative aptitude: The ability to learn or acquire intelligence from a **Creative**, or higher **Source**, entity. See **Creative force**.

Creative cognizance: "Higher **consciousness** of **universal law** derived from a **Source** given by **Creator**—pass-down effect."

Creative/Creational energy, force, guidance, influence, or understanding: The power or energy exerted by a higher consciousness directed by the **Creator** to create an effect on a given population. "Higher **consciousness** of **universal law** derived from a **Source** given by Creator—pass-down effect."

Creator: "The vibrations of **All That Is**." The knowledge and Creator of all things. The many names that encompass the Supreme Being; God.

credence: To give credit to.

crescendo: The gradual and steady increase in intensity or force.

crested: The highest point.

criterion; criteria: A rule or standard of judgement or criticism.

Cro-Magnon: The human prototype of the modern Homo sapiens, named after a cave in France where the first skeletal remains were found.

croptic; crop: A group of people appearing or occurring together.

crossover: The crossing from one point to another.

crudacious: Completely crude. Undeveloped and lacking intellectual acuteness of mind.

crusade: The aggressive or vigorous movement in the defense or advancement of an idea or cause.

crustacean: "The hard-shelled ones." Those who are difficult to teach due to the hard shell they put up around themselves; or, a similar reference.

cryogenic matter: Matter held within very low temperatures.

crypt: A small subterranean recessed area used as either a burial site or a location for secret meetings.

culmination: The highest point or state.

cultural dimensions: The analysis of a particular stage of civilization within the space of a nation or a period of time.

cuneiform clay tablet: Clay tablets on which ancient humans inscribed cuneiform characters while still wet, using a wedge-shaped tool.

curelacious events: (kyoor lā shē us) The many events correcting all that is troublesome or detrimental.

cursality: A condition of being cursed.

cursor: A runner, courier.

curtacious; curt: Completely brief and concise.

cycloneuretic: Repeating cycles within a nervous system.

damperings; damper: To depress. That which keeps **oscillations** from vibrating too excessively.

dark matter: A hypothesis that states that there must exist matter, unseen by **electromagnetic** radiation, that accounts for the universal gravitational forces.

darnacious; darn: Possessing the nature of mending.

deflectors: Beings who bend incoming **vibrational** fields away from the earth until all is ready, then the vibrational field will be allowed its straight course toward Earth.

degrees: (Geom.) A unit of measure of an angle or turn, represented by the symbol °; the circle having 360-degrees.

delusionment; delusion: The deceived, misled or false deduction.

denature: (Biochem.) To treat a protein or the like with a chemical or by other physical means to change its original state.

densified; density: The component parts tightly compacted together.

derision: To mock, ridicule or make fun of.

derivative; derived: To originate or come from another source.

descential being: An ancient being; possibly descending, as in moving down toward Earth.

destination of intercept: The final place in which the energy stream is transmitted to.

detention: To prohibit from moving forward.

detrusious; detrude: To force down.

deviation of variance: A departure from the standard **variance**.

devoid: Lacking.

diagnosis; diagnostic: The analysis and interpretation of the cause of a problem or situation.

diagonal convexes: (Math) Having an outer curved or rounded surface with all the interior (concave) angles (diagonal) less than or equal to 180-degrees.

diagonal transcourse: Across or through a diagonal course.

diagonal variance: The degrees of variation of a diagonal angle.

diameter: A straight line passing through the center of any body or thing, spanning from one side to the other.

diametrical field geometry: The underlying **geometry** of a specific field.

diametrical field poles: Having opposite poles, possibly **electromagnetic**, within a given field.

diametrical life pattern: The **parameters** of, or the area which encompasses, the **sphere** of the **life pattern**.

diametrical pattern: A pattern being of the opposing side or extreme.

diametrical perceptual participation: To actively attempt to grasp the entirety of understanding through mental, cognitive or sensory means.

diametrical understanding: Encompassing full scope of or complete understanding.

diametrical: Being of opposing sides or extremes; completeness.

dianectical divergence: The amount of water flow over a surface that has escaped, separating from the infinite volume of the seas, relative to the **orbital** change.

diatomaceous: The fine silica formed from the cell walls of numerous dead microscopic algae.

diatribes: Sharp and abusive denunciation or criticism.

differential: That which distinguishes as different.

diffraction: The bending of (light or sound) waves around objects in their path.

diffused pattern: Scattered pattern.

digest: To collect data and assimilate mentally.

digress: To wander off the main topic; to turn away from.

dilapidate: To waste, neglect, misuse.

dimension; dimensional: To define a location as a characteristic of space. Space-time is defined by the three dimensions of space including length, width and thickness plus the dimension of time. Dimensions are further defined by the Ancients as specific learning spheres.

dimensional change: A change in spatial placement.

direct: To manage or guide by instruction or through information. Channeling the course to a desired result.

directional being: Giving direction to self.

directional equivalence: Direction is equivalent to.

directive: An authoritative order or direction given.

discern; discernment: The recognition of something separate & distinct.

discipline: The activity in accordance with a set of rules.

disdain: To regard as unworthy of notice.

dispensation; dispension; dispense: The distribution of, or particular order, arrangement, placement, system or management.

disperse; dispersion: To cast or scatter in various directions.

disproportional: Lacking the correct relationship in size, number, etc. Not in proportion.

dissension: To disagree with the opinions, goals, doctrines of a government, church, political party or majority.

dissipation: Scattered or dispersed. (Physics) The energy spent without accomplishing useful work. To dispel or disintegrate.

distallation; distally: Positioned distally or out from the point of origin or point of attachment.

distillance; distill; distillation: To draw out the essential ingredients from. To refine.

distortion; distortional: To move out of shape; twist. To misrepresent or falsify.

distriangular dispersion of truth: A consequence of receiving an understanding of the truth in a direct manner. "An angulation of consequence relating to thought truth. Not a **variable** to understanding—actual consequence. A variable to understanding its value, **recipical** in nature."

distributional circumference: The boundaries of the distribution.

disunderstanding: Separated from understanding.

diverge: To move away from or differ in opinion.

diverse; diverseness: Variety in (understanding the many **Creational concepts**).

divert: To direct from one path to another.

divine: Of, devoted to or pertaining to God, the Creator.

DNA: Deoxyribonucleic acid. Two nucleotide strands running **parallel** to each other, forming a ladder-like appearance, coiling up around each other containing and transferring the genetic characteristics of all life forms.

dominion: The sovereign rule over; especially that of a large territory.

duality: Two separate states. The belief that we are separate from the whole.

dullatarious: Having no depth.

dyareous: Occupying two spaces.

eclectic: A philosophy drawn from the desired elements of different sources as opposed to following one system.

eclipse: (Astron.) The **orbital** movements of **celestial** objects that intersect and align in a straight plane, one of which crosses the center, such as when the earth or moon eclipses the sun, blocking sunlight to the other.

edifice: A large complex system.

edit: To correct or revise.

effervescence: Full of vital energy or life; enthusiasm.

ego: The oneness of self as different from other's thoughts, beliefs; self-image, self-esteem and importance; conceited.

egotistical: Excessive and offensive reference to oneself (as separate and different from others), self-centered.

elate: To make proud or happy.

electrical conductivity: The measurement of the ability of a particular substance (the brain) to channel electricity.

electrical-magnetic field; electromagnetic field: The field where varied time currents and increased charges create a combined electric and magnetic field.

electromagnetic energy: Varied time currents and increased charges that create a combined electric and magnetic field.

electromagnetic field energy: The flow of charged **atoms** within Earths' molten core creates an electric current. The current creates a magnetic field possessing positive and negative poles.

electromagnetic flow: The flow of varied time currents and increased charges of a combined electric and magnetic field.

electron; electronical: A negatively-charged elementary particle that, together with other elementary particles, forms the basis of matter.

electron-base net system: A networking system that forms the base for **electron** activity.

electroplasmatic field: The **ion**ized gases within the atmosphere around Earth that react strongly to **electromagnetic** fields.

elevoracious: The raising of **vibration** through the voracious appetite for learning.

elixir: A sweet and alcoholic syrup containing a medicinal property. A remedy.

ellipse: (Astro.) Pertaining to a **sphere**- or **ellipse**/oval-shaped galaxy, instead of a disk-shaped galaxy. Possibly relating to the curvature of time-space.

elongated field: An extended, longer and thinner field.

emanate; emanates: To flow out from a source or origin.

embodiment: The act of providing a body.

empirical: Guided by experience or observation without the use of the scientific method.

encapsulate: As if placed in a capsule.

encirclement: To surround.

endigot: "A learned culture of variance: [a] higher learn." A higher genetic expression being introduced to the human race since approximately 1960, expressing a higher state of learning. Also called *indigo*.

enhanced disclosure of Self: A higher level of revelation (from the **higher self**).

enhancement: To raise the value of; to a higher degree.

enlightened; enlightenment: The state of possessing intellectual or spiritual knowledge of; spiritual **Light**.

enosis: A movement to solidify political union, to unify.

ensigneous; ensign: Formed by a conspicuous leader.

entity field: A livable **sphere**.

entity: That which has real existence as distinct or independent.

enunciation: To declare with certainty.

equatic center; equator: A circle within the great **celestial sphere** that passes equidistantly and perpendicular between its' two poles.

equation; equational: (Math) A mathematical expression, often algebraic, that expresses an equality of both sides.

equatious; equate: Possessing equality; equal to. (Math) A mathematical expression, often algebraic, that expresses an equality of both sides.

equinox: Pertaining to the **celestial equator** of the great celestial spherical circle, where the equator crosses the **axis** perpendicularly and equidistant to the two poles and which also lies in the same flat plane as the earth's equator.

equivalation; equivocal; equivocate: The state of having equal value.

eradication: To utterly destroy or remove.

essence: The basic and unchanging nature of a thing, esp. that of a spiritual entity. "Your essence is your **life force**. The life force creates the soul and gives it the essence. The essence is the character of the soul."

essential life force: Life force from **Creator** and **Light Beings** that is essential to all organic life.

essential life pattern: The pattern absolutely necessary for life.

estuarian; estuary: Where the mouth of the river meets the ocean. "The distance between (energy) flows designates a **variation**...It is a bridge to the other side—a comprehensive understanding of the solarsphere—an opening within."

ether; ethereal; etheric: Having the characteristics of ether; in reference to the upper regions of space or heaven.

euphoric: A state of feeling well-being, happy, confident, often associated with mania.

euthyritic: Straight, direct, correct, honorable, virtuous. "A desire to reach a **higher self** for reflection; [a] reflective cause of why you exist on this plane."

evasive: To avoid directly answering to.

everline: Literally, a lasting line. "A link to the other side."

evisceration: To remove some of its vital parts.

evoke: Produces feelings.

exacerbating; exacerbate: To increase the severity of.

existive value: The value of life.

exonerate: To free from guilt; to relieve from obligation.

exonerating platitudes: Excessive or cliché remarks to free from guilt; to relieve from obligation.

exorbitant: Excessive.

exotic: Unusual.

exploratory configuration: An investigation of the association of various parts.

exponential: (Math) The power to which a value is raised, multiplied by itself. That which a person explains.

exposition: A large scale show or display. The act of being exposed.

exposure ratios: The proportional relationship of the rates of exposure measured by the number of times the first contains the second and expressed as a ratio, such as "one in three people exposed will..."

faces: The outward appearance; outer surface or presenting parts. Many aspects of; referring to the angles within a **geometric** form.

fallorious; fallacy: A mountain of fallacy.

farcical: A light-hearted play which incorporates a plot to skillfully exploit a situation, rather than to focus on the development of character.

fasting: The abstaining from food for a period of time.

federation: The uniting of separate entities or representatives within a league with a central governing body but where each entity or representative retains control of its own internal matters.

fiber optics: A branch of optics where pulses of light are transmitted through transparent fibers in the transmission of images, data and communications.

field complex: All the interrelated parts encompassed within a vast area.

field resistance: The opposing forces within the (energy) field.

fleeting: (Naut.) To shift in direction; change position.

flourish: Prosper, to make successful; thrive.

fluctuate; fluctuation; flux; fluxionable: The continuous variability in a flow. (Physics) The quantified strength of a force field of a fluid, particle or energy; **fusion**.

fluctuation of time variance: The continuous variability within a set of time variabilities. (Math) Having a quantity or function that may be assigned any of a set of time values.

forbearance: Patience; to pull back from the enforcement of a right.

forerunner: Precursor.

forgone: That which has been determined in advance.

formic field: A creational field.

formulation: To systematically develop.

forthcoming: Approaching in time.

fortitude: Courageous mental and emotional strength.

fortuitous: Accidental; happening by luck or chance.

fortunate: Favorable.

forward lapse: A decline in forward movement.

fourth dimension: "The **dimension** of time."

fracturial events: Breaking or cracking events, possibly earthquakes.

fracturing: Breaking.

fray: Quarrel or competition.

freedocks: "A **conceptual** understanding of the particulate matter contained within the **DNA** helix of those **subatomic nanomatter** within the constraints of all DNA on this sphere flowing within the **ionic** pattern of all living matter **organic**."

fruitility: Fruitful, good or abundant results.

function; functional; functionality: An action or activity relative to a person or thing. A factor dependent upon other factors. (Math) The relationship of two sets, where one element of the second set is also found in each element of the first set, such as $y = x^2$.

fundamental: Serving as the most essential part or basic foundation of any given thing.

furoration: "Concept of being **astute** to understanding right from wrong. **Conceptual** misperception of word [furor]."

fusion: To unite or blend into a whole. (Physics) The sun generates its energy through nuclear fusion, a thermonuclear reaction in which the nuclei of lighter **atoms** join the nuclei of heavier atoms.

Gaia: Earth.

galactic meridian: (Astron.) The great circle within the galaxy that passes through its poles and the point directly above the observer.

galactic; galactical: Pertaining to the galaxy.

gamma particles; gamma rays: An **atomic** nucleus radiating a photon of penetrating **electromagnetic** radiation; the internal conversion of an **electron** resulting in the emission of a photon.

gargantuan: Gigantic.

genetic: Referring to the basic units of **DNA** that determine hereditary characteristics.

genetical beings: Physical beings that contain a **genetic** expression. Perhaps referring to reproduction.

geometric; geometry: A division of mathematics that deduces from defining **parameters** of assumptive properties of space measurements and association of points, angles lines and objects in space.

geometrical life patterns: A division of mathematics that deduces from defining **parameters** of assumptive properties of space measurements and association of points, angles, lines and objects within **subatomic** life patterns.

gestation: The process of thinking and developing ideas.

gradient radiation: The ascending or descending in degree of **inclination** in respect to a radial arrangement of outer **celestial spheres**. The curvature (of the **orbit**) representing the change in distance relative to the radial arrangement of outer celestial spheres.

gravitational field: The area surrounding an astronomical body which is under the effect of a gravitational force.

grid: (energy) "Forms the **parameters**, like banks of a river, to keep the energy flow along the **neuronet** intact and concentrated so as to not dissipate or dilute. It is related to the atmospheric gases along the neuronet stream throughout the universe and ionization of fuel content within the atmospheric gases to obtain the fixture of **subatomic** particles that contains the communication within that sector."

harbinger: A person who makes known the coming of.

hard-line: An uncompromising stand, esp. in politics; adhering to a rigid dogma or plan.

harmonics: The reduction of the fundamental tone combined with the elevation of an overtone.

heliosis: A condition of the sun.

helix: A reference to the **DNA** spiral.

hemisphere: The area in which something happens. Either of the two halves of the brain.

herald: To publicly declare or announce.

hereditate; heredity: To pass certain genetic characteristics from the parent to the next generation.

hermetically: Not influenced by outside factors.

hexagonal distribution: To disperse in six directions.

higher self: "The Self, the receiver, the messenger of **conscious purveyance**. The **Source** of **All That Is** within Self, the eternal being. The **essence** of understanding the true Self. The **veil** within separates the movements between the higher self and the physical self. Continuation into the world of order, order generated by your highest being. It **supersedes** the mind track to completion of Self, directs your learning process. The highest direction of one's own Self, it predetermines **cause and effect**. Determination of Self affects events to one's path, recognizes course; a predetermination of will, that which is not embedded in your soul, the cord to **Creator**. A higher state of being." The capitalized Self refers to the higher self, as differentiated from the lower-case self, in reference to the physical self.

holdings: The act of being held.

hologram: A negative projected onto a coherent light beam producing a three-**dimensional** image of the subject.

Hopi: A Native American tribe situated in northeastern Arizona.

horizon; horizontal: The line that forms the demarcation between the earth and the sky. Of or pertaining to the horizon. The range of perception, knowledge or the like, as seen off on the horizon, or at a distance.

horizontal dispersion: To scatter along the demarcation between Earth and sky.

horizontal latitudinal adjustments: Adjustments relating to the horizon and latitude of Earth.

hostility: Antagonistic.

hyper-bolster system: A tunnel-like system of the **time-space continuum** that provides the stability of a **dimensional** field.

hyper-space tunnel: A tunnel containing greater than three dimensions.

ideology: The belief or doctrine that drives an individual, social movement, group, etc., and may include a political and social plan to put it into motion, such as fascism.

illusion; illusionary: Deceptive or misleading.

Immanuel: A prophesized great leader to deliver the people.

immaterial: Irrelevant to.

impervious: The inability to be penetrated. The inability to be influenced.

implications: Related intimately. Incriminating involvement.

imputousness; impute: To attribute from one person to another person vicariously. To cast blame to another.

incandescent: Extraordinary understanding. Aglow with purpose.

incarnation: A physical presentation of life.

inceptions forbearance: The beginnings of patience, **Self**-control.

incessant: Without end.

inclination: (Astron.) The angle between the **orbit**ing plane of one planet and the plane of another given plane or **ecliptic**. To have a tendency toward a particular preference.

incomprehensible beings: Those who are incapable of comprehending.

incongruent behavior: Behavior inconsistent to the true nature or emotion of a being.

incongruent; incongruity: Not in agreeance; not **congruent**.

inconsequential behavior: Unlearned behavior.

inconsequential beings: Those who do not realize a consequence of logical understanding relative to the proper sequence of thought.

inconsequential life attributes: Not a result or consequence of life's events and circumstances.

inconsequential: Does not follow the proper sequence of thought; lacking logical sequence; lacking the consequence of understanding.

indemnity: Compensation for damage.

indenturedness: Contracted to; bounded service to.

indulgence: To yield to or gratify one's desires.

ineptitudes; inept: Lacking the natural or acquired ability, or the inclination, to learn or acquire intelligence. Not possessing the **aptitude** for a particular task; unsuitable.

inference level: The level of being able to reason or draw by conclusion.

infinity: (Math) The assumed limit of a series or sequence that continually increases without **parameters** or boundaries.

influx: The act of flowing in.

infractive; infraction: To break the laws or rules.

infusion: To penetrate or introduce into.

inherent: The state of being an inseparable attribute or element of.

innocence: Lacking knowledge or understanding. Simplicity. Free from guilt; pure.

inoculate; inoculation; inoculus: To infuse or inspire a person with feelings or ideas. "The understanding of the Great One: **Serendipitous** behavior of all that surround the energy of the Great One (Creator).

insolence: Boldly rude, insulting and disrespectful.

insonation: Occurring upon a particular sound made by an energy release.

intact: Not swayed or influenced.

integral: A necessary part for the completeness of the whole.

integrity: Being a part of the whole. Expressing a moral code of conduct and the principles thereof.

intellectual absolute: Perfect in its higher mental capacity. Intellectually independent of outside influence.

intellectual being: A being possessing a capacity for thinking and understanding.

intercede: To act on behalf of, intervene or influence.

intercept; interception; interceptual: To see or overhear. To stop or interrupt the course.

interceptors: The area between two points, such as the small area between nerve cells, called a **synapse**. To seize a transmission.

interconsequential being: Among other beings of **consequence**.

interdiameter: Between each side of.

interdimensional being: Between the physical self and the **higher self**.

interface: The shared common boundary of two bodies, spaces, systems, concepts or humans. The direct shared communication or interaction.

interferal: Having the characteristic of interfering.

interloculence; interlock: To bring the synchronized parts together. The use of a device that prevents one mechanism from activating while another mechanism is in use.

interpretive thought: Thoughts that give meaning to, explain or understand in a given way.

interspherical field poles: A field between celestial spheres that contains magnetic poles, creating a pulsating, repelling field.

intunable sequence: Inability to **attune** to a higher understanding as a result of an action.

invasive procedures: The action taken to recover damages from the injury.

ion; ionic; ionized: Electrically-charged **atoms** created by the loss or gain of **electrons**.

ionic dispersion: The evenly distributed or scattered charged **atoms**, or **ions**, within the field.

ionic particle beam: A beam of electrically-charged **atoms**, having either a positive or negative charge.

ionosphere; ionospheric: the **ionized** (charged atoms) layers of Earth's atmosphere between the stratosphere and the exosphere.

ionospheric damperings: To somewhat suppress the **vibration** of the charged **atoms** in the **ionosphere**.

iridational metal: Referring to **iridium**.

iridium: A precious metal element used in platinum alloys; similar to platinum.

irrationality; irrational: Without reason. (Math) (ratios) No relationship between the characteristics of two similar magnitudes with respect to one being a partial subset of another. Incapable of being expressed as a ratio of two integers. In other words, the two comparables have nothing in common.

irrefutable: Cannot be disproved.

isometer: An instrument used in measuring the equality of two heights relative to sea level.

isometric configuration: To design a specific arrangement of relative heights for a specific purpose; a metaphor for an elevation of genetic expression to a higher level.

isospheric particles: Particles of equal spherical shape and/or size.

isotonic: Equal tones.

isotopes: A chemical element having two or more forms that have the same number of **protons**, but a different number of **neutrons** in the nucleus; many of which are radioactive.

junction: A union; that which joins other things together.

justification: The reason for.

karma: "Karma is a stream of uninterrupted **essence** of thought to be corrected, as needed, of the beginning to the end: the thought of one Self-entity. The thought is the beginning of **Self** and ends in the **enlightened** state of completeness. Karma is learned to obtain a higher vibrational Self; process varies, legitimacy of **aptitudes** a must. It is not directional. It is learning and behavior modification...as needed, from surrounding **vibrational** events involving the flow of this energy, crisscrossing other energies to attain a correct dimensional flow of energy."

kiva: A subterranean room used by many Puebloan Native Americans for ceremonial planning and rituals.

laborious: Labor intensive. Requiring much work.

lackadaisiness; lackadaisical: Lethargic, without determination, interest or vigor.

lackatory; lack: A condition of something missing.

lackluster: Lacking liveliness or enthusiasm.

lactavius: A plant substance, high in potassium that lets off a **pheromone** that blocks weeds.

lament: The burden of; to lean toward the burden of purpose.

laphyrasarian extension: The extent of one who robs or takes wrongfully.

lateral: To the side.

latitude: Unrestricted action or opinion.

lavornatious: Possessing an enhanced bathing quality.

Lemuria: Proposed initially in 1864 by lawyer and zoologist Philip Lutley Sclater, who wrote a hypothesis in The Quarterly Journal of Science about a lost continent that must have existed in the Indian Ocean, in an effort to explain how some species of lemurs, having greater numbers of species in Madagascar, may have crossed this landmass to Africa, while other species crossed to India. This land mass was given the name Lemuria. It has since become a part of pop-culture, particularly after *The Secret Doctrine* was published in 1888 by a Russian occultist and medium, Elena Blavatskaja.

lethargic: Inactive; drowsy.

levator: A lifter.

levying: To enlist, conscript.

life field; life force field: The **life force** existing in and defined by the influence and force it exerts at all points in the space it occupies.

life force parameter field: The limits or boundaries of a **life force field,**

which include a corresponding mathematical formula in which the values of the variables represent different distributions.

life force: "Life force, created by **Creator** and **Light Beings**, is universal. Your life force within you is the life force of God. Your **essence** is your life force."

life geometry: A division of mathematics that deduces from defining **parameters** of assumptive properties of space measurements and association of points, angles, lines and objects that make the pattern for life form expression.

life pattern: The pattern for life within the **plasmic field**.

life signature: The distinctive set of characteristics for life forms.

ligatory: Tied to.

Light Beings: "Between the **Ancients** and **Creator**. Highest level of pure truth and understanding; level beyond what you can attain here. Level devoid of emotion, pure truth, abstinence of sickness, devoid of misunderstandings. Set the **parameters** of the universe, creation with the Creator, continuous creation of universal thought that **pervades All That Is**, manifestation of the Creator. The cordessential beings: Communication travels on a Light cord, crossing the paths of higher entities for learning that are eventually connected to the Light Beings."

light crystals: Particles of light having a structure of symmetrically arranged plane surfaces that intersect at characteristic angles.

Light: "Light is a communication tool that is a strand across all universal boundaries. Light is not obstructed or deflected, it carries all communicative processes, even between universal connections beyond your comprehension."

lindacious: Lineal field; being in direct line.

linear extension: (Math) An addition or magnification having the same effect on the sum as each individual part of the sum.

liquefication: The process of turning into a liquid.

listless: Showing little or no interest in anything.

literation: To script or write.

litigious: Inclination toward a lawsuit.

lockdown: The confining of prisoners to their cells, usually the result of a riot or other disturbance.

logarious: The release of the vibrational underpinnings of the mathematical codes.

logarithms: The exponential power a base number must be raised in order to equal an assigned number.

longerian plasmic movement: The much-elongated movement of **plasma** within a field.

longerians: Ancient intruders from outside Earth, whose sole purpose is to interfere with our learning process. May also be used as a **parallel**.

longitudinal navigation movement: To observe the same planetary object over a period of time as it moves through its **orbital** course.

lubrication: To drink or become drunk (with one's own thoughts).

lucerian: A person who supports or advocates the **Light**.

luciferious: Identified with Satan.

luephorbious: (lū for bē us) Literally, to bear trouble.

lugubrious: (loo goo brē us) Gloomy or sad.

lull: A period of temporary calm. To give a false sense of safety.

magnetic field; magnetudinal field: The area around a magnet, electric current or moving **ion** where the magnetic force acts on another magnet, electric current or moving ion.

magnetic flux: The continuous variability in a flow within the **magnetic field**. (Physics) The quantified strength of a force field of a fluid, particle or energy; fusion.

magnetosphere: The outer portion of the **ionosphere** around a planet or **sphere** where the movement of charged particles are controlled by the **magnetic field**.

magnetudinal lines: The **coordinates** created by the **magnetic field**.

magnetudinal: Pertaining to the **magnetic field**.

magniferious: The third phase of children to be born that will bear a magnified genetic expression.

magnification; magnify: To make greater or enlarge in size (or expand in expression).

magniflux: A large variable flow.

magnitude; magnitudinal: Vast size or extent. (Math) A comparison of quantities, such as length. Referring to the **dimension**, or properties in space, and the determination of an angle within that space.

malcommunication: Imperfect or wrong communication.

malfeasance: The act of an official that is contrary to law, unjustified or harmful.

manifest; manifesting; manifestation: Visually or mentally apparent; to materialize.

Marduk: A chief Babylonian deity. Also discussed in the book, *The 12th Planet*, as a planet.

mechanical: The design, use and understanding (of a **concept**).

meditate; meditation; meditative: To think, contemplate, reflect; engaging in transcendental meditation, devoted spiritual contemplation or the quiet spiritual going within or introspection.

meditational diameters: Encompassing the ability to think, contemplate, reflect within the **parameters** including the entire event or **concept**; engaging in transcendental meditation, devoted spiritual contemplation or the quiet spiritual going within or introspection.

meditative communication: Communication occurring during a state of **meditation** or introspection.

memory stick: Reference to a computer device for storing information external to the computer; a flash drive.

meridian: (Astron.) A great circular flat plane superimposed in the middle of the **celestial** sphere, passing through the celestial poles and crossing perpendicularly to the great celestial **equator**, dividing the celestial sphere in half.

merkaba: In ancient Hebrew means vehicle. Egyptians believed the merkaba carried the spirit and body from one plane to another. In recent times, like the **chakras**, more definitions have been added. The merkaba, according to the **Ancients**, is antiquated and no longer used.

merringer: "Reliance to truth."

metaphor; metaphoric: A phrase, term, or visual that serves as a symbol or parallel that is applied to something else.

meteorlogical event: An atmospheric or weather-related event.

microcosm: Societies as viewed as a miniature of the universes.

migrate magnitude: (Chem.) The movement to a large degree of positively- and negatively-charged **ions** (sodium, calcium and potassium) to the positive or negative conducting ends of a cell. It is assumed that this would change the electrical current within the cell.

migrational delineation: To outline the mathematical movement of genetic expression from where it exists now to a higher expression.

minosis: A threatening condition.

minute: Extremely small; concerned with the smallest of details.

misconceptive; misconception: Erroneous ideas or concepts.

misnomer: Erroneous description.

misperceptive; misperception: Wrong **perception**.

misvalues: Wrong or incorrect values.

molecular dispersion: The scattering of **molecules** in various directions.

molecular dissention: The **molecules** not being in agreeance with each other.

molecular singularity: A unique quality of the **molecular** structure.

molecular structure: The organization or arrangement of **atoms** and their constituent parts.

molecular: The smallest unit of an element, such as one or more of the same **atoms** in an element or two or more atoms in a compound.

monteculiar domain: "**Parallel** flows within each stream...flow participates within each molecule...**Molecular singularity** of one within one."

multi-lingual denomination of numbers: The many articulated **degrees** or grades in a series of designated numbers.

multiplex: Many networks.

myopic: Near-sighted. Without understanding; narrow-minded.

myopscopic: Observance of short-sightedness or narrow-mindedness.

mysipical: Pertaining to the closing of the eyes, turning inward in **meditation**.

nanomatter: Dwarf or very small matter.

nanoparticles: Dwarf or very small particles.

nappeletts; nappe: (Geol.) The thrusting of a large rock along a nearly **horizontal** plane, as in moving planetary bodies. The suffix "lett" indicates a smaller distance than the word nappe implies.

narcissistic: Extreme self-absorption.

Narcolysis: A being whose objective is to loosen or break down the stupor of humans.

nautilus: Referring to the paper nautilus, resembling sails of a ship.

nebulae: A cloud of interstellar gas and dust. May be in reference to thought.

nebular region: The area occupied by a **nebula**, a cloud of interstellar dust and gas.

nefaracious title: Wicked description. Described as against divine law.

nefarious: Bad, wicked, unpleasant.

neonatal positioning: Relating to an attitude or stand of a newborn child.

Nepherum: "Eighth planet of the second solar system outside yours. Your seed of Earth: partial, [a] mixture."

Nephilim: The offspring produced by the "sons of God" and the "daughters of men" before the Great Flood, as described in Genesis.

Neptune: The eighth planet from the sun in our solar system.

neuro: Pertaining to a nerve cell.

neuroelectrical: The combined electrical and nerve-like function.

neuro-electronical electron base net system: A system in which **electrons** are used to conduct a communication over a network that contains components that are electrical and nerve-like. The **neuronet**.

neuroesolence: Within the nervous network.

neuroflex: The flexibility of the nervous network.

neurolectic: A bed of nerves.

neurologic; neurological: Pertaining to the science of the nervous system.

neurological indulgence: To yield to the **neurological** field, or **neuronet**.

neurological inscription: Written upon the nervous system (of Earth).

neurology: The science of the nervous system.

neuromagnetical field: A field that contains components that are both magnetic and nerve-like.

neurometrical: A measurable nerve impulse.

neuron release: The electrical-like release of a message from nerves.

neuron: A nerve cell.

neuronautical: A nerve-like navigation.

neuronectular understanding: Joined with the **neuronet** for understanding.

neuronet; neuronetical; neuronetular: "A network of nerve-like interceptors that produce a signal of corresponding value, similar to a nerve **synapse**, that contains the energy of the communicative **Light** force within the **plasma** cord. Thought pattern communication travels on a Light cord/plasma cord crossing paths of higher entities for learning that are eventually connected to the **Light Beings**. It is the main regulated **Source** of communication for all beings that are essential to the **universal consciousness**. The thought is carried through Light that carries all communicative processes within the nervous network of the neuronet across all universal boundaries." The brain.

neuronetic or neuronetical field or energy field: The field that contains the **neuronet**.

neuronetical field pole: Either of two opposing ends of **electromagnetic** polarity of the **neuronetical field**.

neuronical electrical impulses: Nerve-like electrical impulses.

neuro-stream: A projected stream of intelligent sequential thought patterns.

neurosynaptic energy: The energy carrying a message that passes across the small gaps between nerves.

neurtactic purpose: A procedural system within a nervous network that has an intended, desired outcome.

neutron; neutronal: An elemental particle lacking a charge, with a mass slightly more than a **proton**, and a component of all **atomic** nuclei, except hydrogen.

neutronal field: Referring to a field of neutrons.

New Age: A new cycle. A movement embracing a broad range of philosophies and practices traditionally belonging to the metaphysical, paranormal or occult.

newitarian: One who represents new life.

nexus reformation: The link or means to correct what is wrong.

Nibiru: A word inscribed in ancient Sumerian cuneiform clay tablets and translated as an extra twelfth planet beyond Pluto that has a 3,600-year orbit. Also mentioned in other ancient texts with various references to a sun, a god, a crossing point or a celestial median. Past astronomers witnessed that Uranus' orbit had veered unpredictably and surmised that it might well be due to the influence of a gravitational field of another unknown planet. More recently known as "Planet X," so called because it is a hypothetical *unknown* planet assumed to exist based on the mathematical calculations and computer simulations of two Caltech astronomers who attempt to explain the unique orbits of other planetary bodies in the Kuiper Belt. Our guidance states that Nibiru has a 5,662 Earth-year cycle and that the 3,600-year orbit mentioned on the clay tablets is in reference to a moon that precedes, and has half the cycle of, Nibiru.

nirvana: A progression of freedom from pain and suffering.

node: A center point of component parts. (Geom.) Coexisting at all points while superimposed.

nomenclature: A collection or system of names or terminology specific to those used in a particular science, group, trade, etc.

nomeric: Pertaining to the customs or laws.

non-consequential being: A being that does not understand all the laws **consequential** to the event and who is not **conceptual** in nature. A consequential being: one who uses each life cycle of **cause and effect** to nurture the **Self-being**.

non-consequential: Not understanding all the laws **consequential** to the event. An event not possessing the consequence of a higher understanding.

non-credence: Giving no truth to.

non-linear structure: The relationship of events as an understanding of the whole not seen as sequences on a time line.

non-numerical understandings: Incomplete understanding: that which does not contain the mathematical equivalent of the understanding of an event taking place.

non-perplexible: Clearly understood.

non-secular: The spiritual or religious learning.

nonsensical; nonsense: Having the characteristics of making little sense.

non-sparing: Unlimited.

noostortic: Literally, a twisted mind.

notation drive: A driving mechanism guided by graphic signs and/or symbols, perhaps mathematically.

noticiousness: The quality or state of noticing or observing.

notorious event: An event widely and unfavorably known about.

numerical event: An event represented as a mathematical expression.

numerical value: (Math) The assigned symbol representing a quantity or number. In this sense, the guides are given the mathematical equivalent of the understanding of an event taking place.

numerious: Many; existing in great numbers or quantity.

nupharous: A unification of multiple networks under existing natural law, creating a new system that has the ability to hold the field together.

obscenity: Repulsive and offensive to morality.

obtruse: Projecting out.

occipital patterns: Referring to **neurological** patterns originating from the occiput or back of the brain.

occipital; occipital lobe: Referring to the occiput, back of the head or skull.

occultarian: Beyond the range of what one is able to see.

occupational forces: A body of beings working together in an activity (to correct the **DNA** sequence).

octacious: The quality of viewing from all eight angles.

octagon: A form containing eight sides and eight angles. Dispersed in all (eight) directions.

octagonal movement: The movement toward the understanding of the mathematical equivalency assigned to each of eight viewing angles of the subject being studied.

octanian procedure: A course taken to look at all [eight] sides (of the cycle).

octarian effect: Having an effect of imparting an understanding of the eight angles in which to view an event from, each angle having a mathematical equivalent.

octarian: One who endorses or practices the viewing of an event or subject of study from all eight sides, which is referred to as angular learning. "Eighth planet of the second solar system outside yours: **Nepherum** culture. Your seed of Earth: partial, [a] mixture." The **Anu** of **Nibiru** are also referred to as octarian.

octavian: "See all [eight] sides."

octillate: To pull out in reverse. "Significant change in the directional pattern of the **synaptic** field, the universal **neuronet**."

octuarian: A being who puts into action the sequence of events (leading to a time frame reformation).

oculance; oculation; oculator: Within the eye; the viewing of or perspective. "Pervasive understanding of Self-intellectual thought; consequence of direct behavior to understanding of **Self**, the **parameters** from within."

oculant understanding: The understanding of what is seen.

ocularian phraseology: The style of verbal expression used by the observer.

ocularian: One who sees.

Omniscient One: Creator, God.

oppression: The cruel, burdensome restrictions imposed, usually by an authority figure.

opt-organic field: The visible natural field.

opulence: Abundant, plentiful.

opulent behavior: Exhibiting wealth or an abundance of resources; materialism.

orbital; orbit: The curved path of a **sphere**, usually **elliptical**, traveling around another sphere, such as the earth's path around the sun.

ordinance: Ordered or commanded by God, the **Creator**.

organic: Pertaining to living organisms. Natural. The arrangement of parts within a system.

orgortaneous: Lofty, conspicuous (projects).

orientation mode: The determination of position among the many temporary patterns of **oscillation** that a varying system can express.

Orion: A constellation, represented as the Hunter, that rests on the celestial equator between Taurus and Canis Major.

oscillate; oscillation: The **vibratory** wave for moving to and fro; the one-directional swing or movement of an **oscillating** body.

osculation: The area where two curvatures come into close contact.

ostentatious: The conspicuous behavior designed to impress or attract notice.

ostracization; ostracize: To exclude from social privileges, friendship, etc.

ostuarian bridge: See estuarian.

ostulation: "A covenant between the sectors of a universal dispersion."

palakian concepts: Concepts associated with the palakian field: "Field of containment associated with the dispersion of **magnetospheres** that interwrap itself around specific **spheres** within the **galactic** field, quite specific in cause. Helps move the cause of change for specific spheres."

panoramic field: The wide and extensive field of view.

panoramic sequence: An unobstructed and wide view of a very large area encompassing the sequence of new **vibrational** patterns.

paradigm: Serving in the capacity of a model or pattern.

paradox; paradoxal; pardoxical: A proposition that seems contradictory, but, in reality, is true. Any contradictory nature.

paradoxal field: The field that events take place within that seem contradictory, but, in reality, may not be.

paragonic; paragon: A standard or a pattern of excellence. To compare or draw a **parallel**.

parallel: To proceed in the same direction or course without crossing.

paraloxical: Near-oblique, slightly sloping angle.

parametal sphere: The limits or boundaries of a particular area.

parameter: Extent of boundaries. A mathematical distribution variable that corresponds to differing distributions.

paratication: To ready or prepare.

partake: To take a part in.

particle being: Either physical or non-physical beings, the parameters for which are set by the **life force field**.

particle infusion: An introduction or penetration of particles.

particulate: Pertaining to a specific type of particle.

patternize: To create patterns.

per: By means of or through.

perceive; perception; perceptive; perceptual; perceptorial: To grasp by mental, cognitive or sensory means. Sharp mental perception, understanding, insight or intuitiveness.

perceptive understanding: The understanding gained by mental, cognitive or sensory means.

perceptual anomaly: A different way of **perceiving** something.

perceptual assets: The desirable or useful possession of knowledge.

perceptual being: A being who the focus of learning is within the **perceptual** realm, as in humans within the past learning cycle.

perceptual confrontation: A **perceived** confrontation.

perceptual habitat: A special cognitive environment.

perceptual understanding: To understand how perception forms through the mental and sensory experiences.

percolation: To permeate or filter through.

perilogical: By means of logic.

perpetual; perpetuate; perpetuating; perpetuousness; perpetrude: The force to keep something ongoing, enduring, continuous.

perplexed; perplexing: Complex, confusing, uncertain.

persuasive accents: Stressing a persuasive point or an appeal to action.

pertrance: Transference; a change from one location to another.

pertuitous: Through consideration. "Purposeful."

pervade; pervasive: To disseminate throughout all parts of.

pharoguyance: (par-a-goy-ans) "Exceptional value: extreme **Light** conditions. **Parameter** set forth by **incandescent** stabilization of protracting power. Light given to universal being of higher nature. External beings of extreme value to universal **life force**...dictates consequence of **particle beings'** [physical or non-physical] organizational structure. On-going informational energy derived from, manifesting an energy field, called manipulation of an energy field."

phenomena; phenomenon: The observable facts.

pheromone: A chemical substance normally secreted by an animal that influences the physiology or behavior of the same species.

phraseology: The characteristic manner or style of language.

pineal gland: (Anat.) A small endocrine gland behind the frontal brain which secretes melatonin and regulates the body's biorhythms and development of the gonads.

pinnacle: The highest point.

pious: A hypocritical showing of virtue and/or religious devotion.

placate; placating: To calm or appease by yielding to or by gestures made to overcome the distrust of.

placonic shift: Shift of plate.

plagaceous space; plagaration: A region, zone or space. See **plage**.

plage: An area reflecting light in the sun's chromosphere, appearing near sunspots.   The chromosphere is a red gaseous structure surrounding the sun in which huge amounts of hydrogen and other gases erupt.

plagiarize: The unauthorized use and promotion of another's work, representing it as one's own.

planetarial; planetary: Pertaining to planets.

planetarian: An entity associated with a particular planet.

planetary nomenclature: The mathematical set of terms for a planetary system.

plasma; plasmatic; plasmanic field; plasmic field: An **ionized** gas with nearly equal amount of positive and negative ions, or charged **atoms**. "The **Light** force, the energy field within the **neuronet** system, a bright, connective energy."

plasmanic molecular field: The **molecular** field of charged **atoms**.

plasmic electrical life pattern: A life pattern within the **plasmic field** of charged **atoms** and its' electrical current.

plasmic force or energy: The energy within the plasmic field of charged atoms.

plasmic limitations: "Special **neuron** connectors control then surround the **[Seventh] Apron**...It is the **neuronetical** foundation of all universal connection to everything that has ever been, to everything that now exists, and that everything is brought forth in the future." Nervous limitations allow a timed release of knowledge to descend from beings of higher understanding to those of lower understanding.   It also allows for the contemplation and assimilation of understanding at the human level.

plasmic lines: Charged atoms that form strings that carry the **Light**, or informational energy.

plateau: The state of stability.

platitude: A dull remark, spoken as if it were profound; cliché. Excessive repetition.

Pleiades: A star cluster in the constellation Taurus.

pluckarian. One who moves by force. In this case, this is not an entity, but a forced sound produced by a thought wave.

plunderance; plunder: To loot or rob.

pluracious: Holding many (events).

polarian aspect: Referring to the nature of the poles, or the given direction of the poles.

Polaris: (Astron.) The North Star sitting close to the celestial north pole in the constellation Ursa Minor.

polarities: The positive and negative poles of the **electromagnetic field**.

polarization: To cause to be polarized, having opposing poles. A sharp division of a population into opposing factions.

polutionarian: "The poles release a conceptual agreement for cause…" One who experiences both sides for a conceptual understanding of All That Is.

pompousness: The conspicuous behavioral display of loftiness or importance.

port: (Computers) An area on a computer to which a data connection from a device or transmission line from a remote terminal can be made.

portal: A door or opening, an opening to a tunnel.

potentiate: To make more potent.

power of pnokox: (nox) To "possess the power of hearing the mind without speech. The power to discern the power of others without verbal conversation; all entities. Discernment of corrective thought." Also known as Knox.

precarious: Uncertain. Dependent upon circumstances or the will of another, outside one's control.

precede: To come first in order.

precept; preceptor; precepts; preceptual: Guidance or instruction; procedural ordinance. A **directive** of a code of conduct or action.

precipice: A steep face of a cliff. An event of great peril.

precipitate: To separate out from; in this case, the atmospheric mixture of particles.

precipitous: A steep rock wall; impassably steep.

preclude: To prevent.

precognizance: A knowing, usually from an extrasensory source, of an event in the future.

precondition: To subject a person to a particular treatment or approach in preparation for another subsequent experience or process.

predicious; predicate: To proclaim as true.

preemptive arbiture: (Math) Not assigned a specific mathematical value in advance to allow for a **Creative understanding**.

prelaperious: To understand the significance of cyclic atmospheric changes. To understand the nature of precipitating factors of recurring events. "Attaining the value of looping atmospheric changes into a vibrational complex to understanding its nature."

prelapse: The time leading up to a period where the slipping or declining from an accepted or expected standard occurs. An innocent (lacking knowledge of) or carefree period.

prelation; prelatious; prelate: "Executive event: high order of undertaking."

prelucence: Literally, before translucence, or clarity. "Transparency of love. The key to eternal love. The level of understanding beyond the **self**. A concordance of universal love."

prelude: The preliminary action to another event.

premap: To draw out a course before it is taken.

prepietous: Before giving respect to.

prerequisite: A prior requirement.

prescription: Lay down the rules or course of action to remedy.

presentage: To be present.

presumptuous: To assume as true in absence of proof or fact.

pre-tense: Before the time of.

pretentious: A false claim or showing, esp. that of importance or dignity. An exaggerated outward projection.

prevail; prevalence: Predominate. To be widespread.

preverbious: Before an action.

primordial: Existing from the beginning.

proaxiomer: One who is in favor of the opinion that the statement is generally accepted as truth, but may not be substantiated by fact.

procedural assets: A useful or desirable course of action or process.

procedural: To continue forward in a course of action or process.

proceed; proceedings: To move forward. A course of action or series of events.

processive: Progressing forward.

proclamation: A declaration or announcement given formally or officially.

proclivity: Natural or habitual inclination or tendency.

procreate: Produce.

procure; procurement: To acquire by a particular method or with great care.

profusion: An abundant amount.

prognosis: To predict a likely course and outcome.

prognostic fortune: A prediction of what is to happen in one's life.

prognostic purification: A prediction of a future purification. It is assumed that this is in reference to the purification of one's thoughts to a correct and pure understanding.

prognosticators: Those who predict future events.

progressive process: A series of changes that take place that move one forward in a more successively enlightened state.

prohibition: To prevent, forbid or hinder.

project: To be thrust out, protrude.

projectile: A driving force.

projection: The distinct and forceful communication to an audience. The ability to visualize and contemplate an idea as an objective reality.

proletarian: The poor, non-land-owning, class of (usually) manual laborers; the working class.

prolific: An abundant production of.

Prometheus: (Class. Myth) A Titan who taught humanity many things and gave man fire.

promissory note: A written promise to do something or pay for something.

pronastation: Advancing density (of learning).

propagate: Traveling through space or a physical medium.

propensity: A natural proclivity or tendency toward.

prophetic interpretation: The one who interprets and speaks for a deity or by divine inspiration.

proportion; proportional: A relative comparison between size, quantity, etc., of one unit to another as a ratio.

proportional consequence: The relative comparisons that follow as a consequence (of widening meditation parameters).

proposal: An offering suggesting a performance or acceptance of.

protein marker: Small molecules of protein attached to various places on the **DNA** helix that enable the expression of certain genetic expressions.

proton: An elemental particle having a positive charge and being the basic component of all **atom**ic nuclei.

protoplasmic: First or original **plasma** or **ionized** gas.

protracted; protracting: To extend out. To draw out in time, or lengthen.

protrudence; protrude; protrusion: The act of projecting or thrusting forward.

proverbial: Relating to a wise saying or **precept**. Having become the common mention of.

provincial: The customs, manners and viewpoints characteristic to the inhabitants of a particular area or province. A person of a religious order that presides over an order in a given district.

provocation: To give rise to, call to action, stimulate or incite.

proxarmial: Many arms or branches coming off the original point of attachment.

proximatal; proximate: Following in an order, occurring immediately before or after in occurrence.

prudent: Exercising good judgement. Care taken to provide for the future.

pseudo-essence: False **essence**.

psychic communication: Mental or telepathic communication.

psychic: Mental phenomena obtained outside of scientific or natural knowledge.

Puebloans: Ancient Native American tribes that resided in what is now called the four corners region of the United States of Utah, Colorado, New Mexico and Arizona.

puerdurial understanding: To mentally assimilate understanding through curiosity and practice. "Athenian dialog: To partake in the digest of understanding relevant to **asceration** (wrought with curiosity, to practice) of being." May also be spelled fuerdurial.

pulsar: (Astron.) A celestial object thought to be a rapidly rotating neutron star that emits regular pulses of radiation, such as radio waves.

pulsators: Something that produces a pulse or beat.

purveyance: To provide or supply something (understanding).

purveyor: A person who provides or furnishes something.

Q: The **quantum** of all understanding; **Creator**, God.

quadrant: One of four parts of a circle. In this case, one of four parts of the brain.

quadraplex: "The end result of the quantum paths offered in relation to the **[vibrational] signatures** given off from each human entity. Compartmental decisions: separate." Within **Self-guidance** to higher intelligence. A structural network that directs the flow of energy according to **Creator**'s plan.

quadrical; quadric: (Math) The measurement of the surface of a spherical or ellipsoid/oval-shaped galaxy, as opposed to a disc shape, defined mathematically by a second-degree equation in three real variables.

qualiceptive: A quality of awareness.

qualitative: Relating to the quality or qualities.

quantarian understanding: One who holds a certain amount of understanding.

quantarium: A place where many things (relating to time) are kept.

quantcipital behavior: Containing many critical culminating behavioral events.

quantcipitous: Containing many critical culminating points or events.

quantciprocal orbit: A relationship where gratitude and respect for the understanding that may be given by a Source entity determines characteristics of the mentor received. "To give to **Source** to receive reflective characteristics of mentors."

quantessential: An absolutely necessary quantity.

quanticept; quanticeptical; quanticeptive; quanticeptual: A quantitative awareness; an awareness of many things.

quanticeptive precepts: Guidance or instruction from those with an expansive awareness. A **directive** or code of conduct or action involving those with an expansive awareness.

quanticeptual beings: Beings that have a quantitative, or expansive, awareness of many things.

quantification: To assign a quantity to something thought of as having only quality.

quantify; quantifier: To assign a quantity to something thought of as having only quality.

quantipitous: The many secret or private pieces of information, often used in writing a news story, or in betting.

quantitative values: Estimated or measured quantity or amount, through mathematical sequences.

quantitative: Estimated or measured by a quantity or amount.

quantrasuitrical: The many selves.

quantum field: The field holding the many possibilities.

quantum values: Many values. (Math) The possibilities assigned to symbols representing quantities, **magnitudes** or numbers.

quantum: A large amount. "Many possibilities."

quasar event: (Astron.) An event produced by one of the known extragalactic objects with a star-like appearance believed to be the most distant and luminous universal objects with detectable radio emissions.

quasar: One of the known extragalactic objects with a star-like appearance believed to be the most distant and luminous universal objects with detectable radio emissions.

quasi: Nearly; almost; as though.

quasi-atmospheric changes: Having some atmospheric changes.

quasi-essentialness: Being somewhat necessary.

quasi-fractional: Possessing some part of the whole.

quasi-functional net: Having some, but not all, performance and activities of the **neuronet** (of brain) of other **biological entities**.

quasi-learning field: Possessing some of the characteristics of a learning field.

quasi-magnitudinal shift: Somewhat of a **shift** in the **dimension**, or properties in space, and the determination of an angle within that space.

quasi-truths: Near-truths.

quassational: (kwaz ā shun al) Producing an effect of trembling or shaking.

quatrain: Alternately rhyming poem of four or more lines.

quell: To extinguish or suppress.

quenine: (q' nēn) The **essence** of eternal existence. Of, or pertaining to **Q**, the **quantum** of all understanding; **Creator**, God. The **essence** of eternal existence through continuous growth in understanding.

quiaxle: (qwī ax l) "Similar to a wagon wheel, but has many close lines coming off the center distribution of energy of **All That Is**, representing a center release of energy with many paths, learning paths."

quiescence: Inactive, motionless.

quillerian diagram: (kwil ere' ē en) One who pens in a drawing of all the connecting parts and operations of (conceptual events).

quillerium flap or opening: (kwil ere' ē um) An opening in the **aura** in front of the abdomen through which communication energy enters during a sedate or **trance**-like state when one's **vibrational** level is higher.

quintao: "The course to gain access to the inaccessible."

quinterrium: "Replication of **dimension**, giving cause for understanding the **precepts** of aguarian structure (ancient beings that were once here)."

quintessence; quintessential: The concentrated pure **essence** of a thing. The perfect exemplification of a physical-spiritual entity.

quintessential beings: Beings representing the most perfect embodiment of something; the pure, concentrated **essence** of that being.

quiver: To tremble.

quizitory process: By process of questioning.

radius: The straight-line measurement from the center of a circle or sphere to its outer **circumference**.

raglatarian: A humble person.

ramification: A consequence of. A related subject.

rapidivious: Rapidly spreading.

rapture: Joyful, ecstatic delight.

ratify: To confirm or accept something done or arranged by a representative.

realization: To clearly grasp or understand. To make real that which was imagined or planned.

realm: The region or **sphere** in which something occurs.

recede: To retreat or withdraw.

recipetory: "Receiving value of a lesser degree causing **reciperation** (the act of receiving)."

recipical; reciperation: Pertaining to receiving.

reciprocal addresses: A mutual communication, or, conversely, a communication between one of higher understanding and one of lower understanding.

reciprocal: Mutually given by one toward the other. Opposite, proportional and inversely related.

reconstituting; reconstitute: Reconstruct.

redaction: Revision.

redialing: The reconstruction of the plate that contains the numerical codes (for **DNA**).

reduce: To diminish.

reductiation; reduction: The allowances made to adjust or correct due to an astronomical observance. (Chem.) To add **electrons** to.

redundance; redundancy; redundant; redundiate: Repetitive. To characterize by the use of many words. To make superfluous.

redundancy exchange: A reoccurring exchange.

reflectatory; reflect: Appropriate for reflection.

reflection area: An area to reflect upon events of one's immediate past life.

reflective: Mirroring; one represents the other.

refraction: Changing the direction (of the human species).

rehabilitation, exceptional: To restore to superior function and operation (of the energy field).

reincarnate: To have physical incarnations again in a new body at a future time.

reiterate: To occur or to say again, repeatedly, often excessively.

relapse: To fall back into a previous practice or state.

relative: A comparative in relation to something else.

relection: To reunite.

reliance: Trusting dependence.

relief: The freeing of a closed space from a more-than-desired pressure, such as in a tank.

relinquish: To release or give up.

renaissance: A time of awakening. A time of revival of art, literature and learning.

renumeration of Self: To reassign a numerical value according to understanding of the **higher self**.

renunciation: Relinquishing a right.

repercussion: The indirect result of an action.

replenish: To make complete again.

replicate: To reproduce or repeat, especially as an experiment or a procedure.

replicator: Entities used for experimental or procedural replication.

repose: Peace. To be at rest. (Archaic) To rely upon.

repository: A place within where thoughts and ideas are deposited and stored.

reprehensible: Deserving reprimand or censuring.

repudiate: Disapproving rejection.

resonance; resonanic: The prolonged resounding **vibration** or **reverberation**. The **amplification** of audible sounds or speech. A systemic state where an extremely large vibration is produced from an external stimulus and occurs when the frequency of the stimulus is near-same or the same as the natural background frequency of the system.

resuscitation: To revive from unconsciousness.

retract: To withdraw an inaccurate statement, opinion or promise.

reverberate: Resounding **vibration** or echo.

rite: A formal or ceremonial procedure.

rudimentary thought: Undeveloped, elementary or immature thoughts.

sagarian: (sag ayr e' n) Possessing an acute and practical sense of mental discernment. "Intelligence beyond your understanding at this point. An understanding of the true meaning of 'beyond the **Light**.'"

Sagittarius: (Astron.) A constellation between Scorpius and Capricorn, known as the Archer.

sanguistical: Relating to blood.

sarcaustic: Literally, the burning of flesh. "Non-essential. A **caustic** influence on surrounding others, altering character, their being. Considered negatory aspect, as in negative. Caustic in nature—same relation [as sarcastic]."

sceupharocal; sceupharic: (sū' fayr e kal) Literally, a vessel of **Light**. Entities of various degrees of higher conscious understanding. "The completeness, unending. Various degrees, levels...Higher outside understanding."

scherlong: Occurring one after another in a linear extension.

schizophrenia: A severe mental illness characterized by **delusion**s, disorganized thought and behavior, and/or hallucinations, among other possible symptoms.

scientarian: One who supports and advocates knowledge.

scopulation; scope: (skōp ū' lā shen) Space of movement; range of view.

sectional devariances: Less variances within a particular region during a given lifetime.

secular; secularism: A non-spiritual, non-religious person; a worldly person.

sedatiousness; sedate: A state of being calm, quiet and composed. Often referred to as a meditative or trance state.

segmented: A natural division or portion.

seignoirsis: The act of a lord or ruler.

seize: Forcibly taking hold of.

Self; Self-being: The **higher self**. That part of the soul that directs one's conscious path through cause and effect. The messenger and receiver of **conscious purveyance**.

Self-accumulation: The accumulation (of understanding) within one's **higher self**.

Self-analysis: The analysis performed by the **higher self**.

self-annihilation: To reduce the physical self to a state of non-existence.

self-annunciation: To announce or proclaim to one's self.

self-assertation: To affirm or state to one's self with assuredness.

Self-atmosphere: Within the influence of the **higher self**.

Self-attainment: To reach the course of development or growth of the **higher self**.

Self-attunement: Coming into harmony with the **higher self**.

Self-awareness: The knowledge and consciousness of the **higher self**. The knowledge and understanding of the existence of the **higher self**.

Self-being: The existence of the **higher self**.

Self-clarification: To free the mind from confusion regarding the **higher self**. To clearly understand the higher self.

Self-cohesion: The unification with the **higher self**.

Self-complex: The many component parts of the **higher self**.

Self-concurrence: To work together with the **higher self**.

Self-confidence: Having confidence in the **higher self**.

Self-conflict: The physical self is acting in opposition to the **higher self**.

Self-consciousness: The awareness of the **higher self**.

self-contentions: The debate within one's self.

Self-diagnosis; Self-diagnostic: The examination performed by the **higher self** of the **cause and effect** of events.

Self-direction: Allowing the direction of one's decisions, aspirations and learning path to be dictated by the **higher self**.

Self-events: Events created for movement in understanding by the **higher self**.

Self-existence: The existence of the **higher self**.

Self-guidance: Guidance from the **higher self**.

self-identity: The often-false perception of one's identity, usually associated with the physical being, instead of the identity of the soul.

Self-identity: The unchanging **character** of one's **higher self** under varying conditions or aspects.

Self-ideology: The beliefs or doctrine driven by the **higher self**.

self-illusion: The deceptive or misleading understanding of the physical self.

Self-indulgence: To gratify the needs of one's **higher self**.

self-indulgence; self-indulgent: To gratify one's self; to yield to the pleasures of one's physical self.

self-infliction: Inflicted upon oneself by oneself.

Self-influence: The influence of the **higher self**.

Self-infusion: To introduce to the **higher self**.

Self-interpretation: Interpretation of the **higher self**.

self-mutilation: To injure one's self.

Self-nurturing: To foster the development of the **higher self** through progressive levels of understanding.

self-proclamation: An ostentatious public announcement drawing attention to one's self.

self-prostration: To humbly submit one's self to. Humility.

Self-realization: To fully grasp or understand the **higher self**.

Self-rule: To be guided by the **higher self**.

self-thought: The limited understanding of the physical self (lower case self).

Self-thought: The understandings and thoughts of the **higher self**.

Self-truth: The truth of the **higher self**, the part of the soul that directs the learning process.

Self-understanding: The understanding of the **higher self**.

Self-value; Self-worth: The value of the **higher self**.

self-worth: The usually incorrect perception of self-worth associated with **ego**. (Note: self is not capitalized and signifies the physical self.)

sequential thought: A part of a continuous and connected series of thoughts.

sequential: A part of a continuous and connected series.

serendipitous: Fortuitous discovery by chance or luck.

serengnosis: Clarity of understanding.

serenity: A state of calmness or tranquility; composed.

serrated; serration; serratious: A notched edge. "Serrated edge of events taking place. In other words, the ups and downs."

servacious: Being of great service to.

servitude: Obligatory service.

Seventh Apron; Seventh Creation: "Creation of God's approach, the apron to the **Creator**. The creation derived prior to **Light Being** where order is complete and exact, where order dictates the exactness of the outer universes and worlds. Near the final step of total creation, where order begins to be divine. Our understanding is beyond your comprehension. Center of all the universes, Seventh Creation is the value of **All That Is**—complete. The Seventh Creation, the Seventh Apron, and the Creational Apron are one, not the same. Creation influence: adjust the **diameters** for **cause and effect**."

shadow: A faint representation of.

shaman: One who works between the natural and supernatural world, especially within tribal cultures, to heal others, alter spiritual forces and foretell the future.

Sharausedhien: (sur a sē' din) A culture from **Sirius**.

shift: To move from one place or position to another.

shock treatment: The application of an electrical shock to the chest wall to restart a non-beating heart or correct a life-threatening irregular heartbeat. This term is being used as a **metaphor**.

shudder: To tremble or shake in a convulsive movement, often in response to fear.

signature: The unique identifying features of a thing.

silique: Representing a pod or husk.

singularity: The state of being One.

sipaporious; sipapu: **Hopi** representation of the hole in the earth that their ancestors arose from after the great flood. It is depicted as a hole in the center of the dirt floor inside their present-day subterranean ceremonial kiva, reminding them of the Great Flood and their reemergence.

Sirius: (Astron.) The brightest star in the sky in the constellation Canis Major, the Dog Star.

slavorious; slave: One under the total dominance of another person or outside influence.

solace: To comfort or cheer.

solar flares: A release or loss of charged **atoms** and gases from the sun into the atmosphere.

solarization: The use of solar energy.

solarsphere: The area around a sun.

solstice: (Astron.) The two times a year when the sun is its furthest point from the celestial equator, either June 21, when the sun is at its most northern position, or December 22, its most southern position.

soothsayer: Someone who claims to be able to foretell events.

sorghum: A cereal grass.

soul: "Soul contains particles, **nanoparticles**, of a **life force**. Twinklings, a memory stick. Nano technology built within the **DNA** to represent particles of the life force. The life force creates the soul and gives it the **essence**. The essence is the character of the soul. The soul has a **quantum** informational understanding."

soul's box: The **higher self**.

soul's resonance: The prolonged resounding **vibration** or **reverberation** of the soul.

sound bite: A short, striking, statement taken from a video or audio recording to insert into a broadcast or news story.

Source: "Part of the **Creator** for communicative processes. Directly tied to the Creator for communicative transmission to those that want to learn, understand and have a ponderance of truth from the communication level, but not *the* Creator. It is the beginning of the **neuronet** that creates the pulse to move the communicative energy." Source originates from "The **Creative forces'** natural comprehension."

spatial plateau: A period in time of little growth.

sphere of thought pattern: The particular manner of thought that takes place in the realm of the mind.

sphere: A specified area, environment or field of activity in which something exists; a **realm**. Having a round structure where each point on its surface is equidistant to its center. A globe. In reference to a sphere or heavenly body.

spherical degeneration: To deteriorate to a less than acceptable state on a **sphere**, such as Earth.

spherical: In reference to a sphere or heavenly body.

spiritual magnetical behavior: The behavior of the spirit within the **magnetic field**.

stagnation: stagnant: Ceasing to develop.

stagnetic value: The value of all the stages (of consciousness).

stanza: A verse or section in a poem.

starburst: Possibly referring to a nova or **supernova**.

static balance: A fixed, unchanging balance.

stave off: To put off, keep away by force or evasion.

strands: Cords.

stratosphere; stratospheric: Pertaining to the region of the upper atmosphere extending upward from the tropopause to about 30 miles above Earth.

strident: Possessing an irritating quality or character.

structural concepts: The organization of the component parts of a **concept**.

stupidicious; stupid: Completely lacking mental **astuteness**.

stupor: Diminishing mental acuity.

subatomic nanomatter: The minute physical matter that make up the **subatomic particles**, having the equivalence of "one billionth" in measurement.

subatomic particles: The smaller elements contained within the **atom**, such as **protons, neutrons** and **electrons**.

subatomic: The smaller elements contained within the **atom**, such as **protons, neutrons** and **electrons**.

subcutaneous osculation: A subsurface area where two curvatures come into close contact. A similar reference to an area between the layers under Earth's crust.

subcutaneous: The area just below the surface of the skin.

subduction: To subtract or remove.

subdural: A space within the brain between the dura mater and the arachnoid membrane.

subfracture: A break in the layer (under the energy line).

sub-impertinences: The underlying inappropriate or irrelevant (structural DNA).

subject: A person or thing (synapse) that undergoes some action (analysis of the universal event).

subjective: An individual's thoughts.

sublime: Elevated thoughts of grandeur.

subliminal: Occurring below the threshold of consciousness.

subscribed: To pledge to.

substance: The subject of discourse.

substantial: A considerable amount.

substantiate: To give considerable existence to; to give competent evidence.

subsurface: Below the surface.

sufferous; suffer: To feel pain or distress.

superfluous: In excess of what is required.

supernova: (Astron.) An explosion of a star, casting off its outer matter; its remaining **protons** and **electrons** collapsing into a strong gravitational field, forming either a **neutron** star or pulsar.

supersede: To replace and overrule a previous condition.

suppress: To put an end to the activities of another person. Withholding disclosure of truth.

suprecious: Of the highest level.

surmise: To assume without evidence.

surmount: To exceed in amount.

suropitous: "Wrapping about the **Self**-being."

surpass: To go beyond; exceed.

surplex: In addition to the dense network within the **neuronet**. "A concentration of energy within the network."

surreal; surrealious; surreality: Dream-like.

surrenderous atmosphere: A general mood of giving in to some influence or course.

survey; surveyance: To take a comprehensive view of a subject. To determine the exact boundaries of an area by the use of linear and angular measurements in the use of geometry and trigonometry.

swirling: Confusion or disorder.

synacious: Completely unified.

synapse; synaptic: The small area where nerve impulses (communication) are transmitted and received.

synergen: A combined interaction that produces an enhanced effect.

synopsis: A brief statement giving a general view of the subject matter.

synosis: A condition of togetherness, unity.

targnarius: "Targeted," as in a goal to be reached. A new species of animal.

tectonic plates: The structural plates within the earth's crust and/or the conditions that cause movement along the plate boundaries.

telepathic communication: The communication solely by means of the mind.

temperate: Moderate; not extreme.

template: A pattern or mold.

temporal; temporate; temporious: Pertaining to this world or period of time.

theology: The study of divinity and religious truths.

theoretical attributes: To hypothesize a particular cause for the result.

theoretical: A hypothetical explanation for something.

thesis: A stated or written formal discussion or thought put forward on a particular subject in which one has done the original research for.

third eye: The pineal gland and second chakra. See **pineal gland**.

Thoth: (Egyptian) The god of magic, learning and wisdom, depicted as the body of a man with the head of an ibis or a baboon.

thought being: A **conscious** thought.

thought entity: A conscious thought. "Thought throught **Light**."

thunderings: To go forth, strike or inflict with loud noise or violent action. Very great, extraordinary. Producing an effect like thunder.

time continuum: The continuous whole of time.

time-space continuum: A mathematical model that combines the three **dimensions** of space, height, width and depth, and the dimension of time to make a four-dimensional continuum. May also be referred to as space-time continuum.

time-watch: The time when the actual Earth changes occur at once, not the developing field.

tonial vibrations: Any sound with a particular quality, strength, pitch and source and its corresponding vibration.

tonial; tone: Any sound with a particular quality, strength, pitch and source.

torus: A doughnut-shaped surface, caused by the revolution of a circular formation around an exterior line, lying in its plane.

toxicological substances: The science encompassing toxic substances.

trance: A temporary state between sleep and wakefulness in which spiritual communication may be received.

transcontinental shift: Movement extending across a continent.

transecular: Moving across one age to the next.

transform; transformation; transformational: To change the appearance, character or nature of something into another form. (Physics) To change from one form of energy to another.

transitional: Movement from one position to another.

transmental: Through intellectual activity.

transpose: (Algebra) The movement of a term from one side of an equation to the other side of the equation, switching corresponding signs. (Music) To produce the same note on a different key by raising or lowering the pitch. To change position in relation to something else.

transposition: To change position in relation to something else, such as the planets moving in their **orbits**.

transverse: Extending across; to cross through.

traverse: To cross over or through. To examine, review, carefully consider, **survey**. To obstruct or counter.

triacular: Three-pronged in form. "Triacular integration of the pod; a stand-alone configuration."

triads: A grouping of three. Used in **meditation**, "feeds energy for **Self-understanding**".

triangular distallation: Positioned distally or out from the point of origin or point of attachment within a **triangulation**.

triangulation: The ability to find the distance or relative place between any two points from a third known side or length as measured from the ends.

tribulation: Severe suffering, distress, trouble.

triceptical: Awareness of three aspects.

triumphant: Success, victory, achievement.

trudence: Within truth. "True **Self**-identity."

tuning fork: A steel instrument with a handle splitting into two prongs, producing a monotone when struck, used to tune instruments and perform acoustic experiments.

tuning: To be in harmony with; **vibrational** harmony.

typeset: To set in type or text. This may be relative to genetics.

ulopic pattern: Scarred or destructive appearance.

una: (Spanish/Latin) One.

unbeholding: The inability to view or see.

underlings: Under the authority of another; placed in a lower rank.

underpinnings: The foundation or basis of.

unheeded: Not given attention.

uniform: Lacking variability; consistent understanding between universe and others.

unison: A state where all elements behave in the same way simultaneously.

unitarian aspects: A unified point of view.

unitarian concept: The combination of all parts into one **concept**.

unitarian process: A unified process.

universal consciousness or understanding: All that is known, understood and aware of within the universe of higher understanding.

universal equinox: A time of crossing of the universal equator, the plane that is equidistant between two universal poles.

Universal Law and Ordinance: **Parameters** of organization and regulations within the universe.

Universal Law of Existence: **Parameters** of organization relating to life within the universe.

universal law: **Parameters** of organization within the universe.

Universal Laws and Concepts: **Parameters** of organization within the universe and the associated **concepts** of understanding them.

universal life signatures: The distinctive set of characteristics for life forms within a given universe.

universality: A condition existing throughout or everywhere.

unperceptible: Not perceived.

unrealization: The inability to fully grasp or understand (the **Self**, as in the **higher self**).

unveil: To reveal as if by removing a **veil**.

upper self: The **higher self**.

uranium: A white, radioactive, shiny, metallic element, of which the 235 isotope is used as fuel in nuclear reactors and in making atomic and hydrogen bombs.

Utarus: According to these readings, the origin of the Hathors, another culture outside Earth within a section in the star system 251-01.

utterance: To speak, announce or write; to make known.

value: Having worth. (Math) The assigned symbol representing a quantity, **magnitude** or number.

variables; variance; variancial; variability; variation: Having the capacity to vary or change. (Math) Having a quantity or function that may be assigned any of a set of values. (Physics) The freedom of a system, measured in degrees.

veil: The vibrational veil that separates, hides, conceals or screens one world from another, such as the physical world from the spiritual world or one **dimension** from another.

verbatim: Repeated exactly word for word from the original **Source**.

verdiance: (ver dī'ans) Characterized by or serving in the capacity of truth. "Thirst for truth."

vibration; vibrational; vibratory: The particles of a mass that **oscillate** or move rhythmically back and forth. The generalized emotional or intuitive feeling one receives regarding another person, place or event. In this book, vibration also relates to levels of understanding.

vibrational aptitude: The natural or acquired ability to understand **vibration** associated with events and concepts.

vibrational attunement: To bring into **vibrational** harmony. "Vibrations are attuned to the magnificence of the human body; corrections are **attunements**."

vibrational awareness: The conscious understanding of a particular **vibration**.

vibrational distributional circumference: The area that encompasses the distribution of a **vibration**.

vibrational manipulation: Manipulation of thoughts of others through the use of **vibration**.

vibrational resonance: The prolonged resounding **vibration** or **reverberation**.

vibrational signature: The distinctive set of characteristics for a particular **vibration**.

vibrational surveillance: The comprehensive view of **vibrational** events occurring.

vibrational trudence: Within vibrational truth.

victition: The action of conquering.

virgocious: "A type of lineal progression within an **anti-matter** field."

virilacious: Vigorous, forceful strength.

virtue; virtuous: An effective power or potency. Conforming one's life to a moral code of conduct.

virulent: Extremely noxious, poisonous, infectious or deadly.

Voltarean region: The **cosmic** area encompassing one of two other galaxies that form a **triad** with the earth.

vortex; vortexical; vortices: The rapid and circular movement of cosmic matter, air, water (or energy) around a center.

wally: Strong; splendid.

wisdom of fortalis: "Equivalent to the wisdom of natural law."

wrapoflate: Expanded protection of.

youthful heredity: A period of time in an earlier existence held by our predecessors.

zenith: The culminating or highest point or state.

zero-point: An original starting point.

BIBLIOGRAPHY

Donald J. Borror, *Dictionary of Word Roots and Combining Forms*, 1960

(Renewed 1988 by Arthur C. Borror)

Random House, *Webster's unabridged dictionary*, Second Edition, 2001

Random House, *Webster's Universal College Dictionary*, 1997

ABOUT THE AUTHORS

Kent Miller, through a series of serendipitous events, learned that he had an innate ability to communicate with higher intellectual spiritual beings while in a trance. A two-time cancer survivor, he and wife Renee, a registered nurse and now scribe, receive conceptual lessons from these higher Source beings, transcribing and organizing the material for publication at the request of their mentors. Largely avoiding other author's works, so as not to comingle information, they have been entirely taught by these spiritual beings.

The true authors are the Ancients, ancient teachers and preceptors of our Creator. Other non-physical professors, appointed by the Ancients, have also contributed to this work.

The Augmentation of Man, A Study in Renaissance is the first book in what has now become *The Augmentation of Man* series. An introduction to the coming changes for Earth and humanity, *A Study in Renaissance* also teaches basic spiritual principles and corrects past misperceptions.

These messages are presented in their original dictation and, with permission from the Ancients, Kent and Renee have expanded upon the lessons in their own words. In order to assist the student in understanding these spiritual mysteries, they have added a YouTube channel, a blog and are now starting a podcast. The information is listed below:

Blog available on our website at verdiance.com
kent4838@inreach.com
YouTube channels: Renee and Kent Miller
                         The Augmentation of Man
Vimeo: Kent and Renee Miller
Podcast: The Augmentation of Man
Twitter: @verdiance

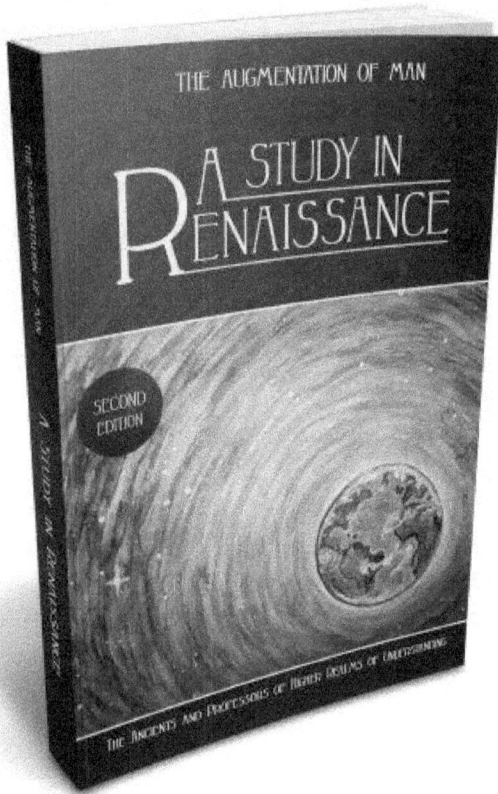

Addressing the great spiritual mysteries, *The Augmentation of Man: A Study in Renaissance* is dictated by ancient spiritual teachers, who bridge the gap between the purpose of life, science, math, spirituality, and astronomy, and open the true New Age of understanding for mankind.

Revealing the Creator's planned expansion of consciousness, including a new genetic upgrade, the messages bring forth a new paradigm in understanding our rebirth into a new cycle of expanded intellectual-spiritual awareness.

New to this second edition, Kent and Renee Miller have expanded the glossary and their interpretations of the lessons, enabling the reader to achieve profound spiritual growth in an accelerated learning process. A Study in Renaissance:

•Expands our understanding of the spiritual hierarchy.
•Discusses death, rebirth and karma.
•Teaches us the purpose of the soul and the higher self.
•Explains the Light mentioned in ancient texts.
•Introduces universal thought resonance.
•Describes a universal communication system of plasma cords.
•Delves into a universal network that supports expanding consciousness.
•Explains vortexes and triangulations.
•Clarifies chakras, the kundalini and spiritual communication.
•Explains understanding truth versus perception.
•Defines universal love.
•Introduces Universal Laws and Concepts.
•Teaches concepts relating to vibration and polarity.
•Explains the space-time continuum and time.
•Describes damage to Earth that man is not aware of.
•Defines a time of great Earth changes as she rebalances.
•Discusses the multiple influences to bring humanity to a new understanding.

The teachings introduce a new conceptual learning to humanity and clarify misunderstandings of the past, bringing new meaning to man's purpose and the evolving changes in our world, known as the transformation.
https://amzn.to/2G9czVe to order from Amazon.

www.ingramcontent.com/pod-product-compliance
Lightning Source LLC
Chambersburg PA
CBHW031041110426
42740CB00047B/766